For Jawis
with all best wishes,

Michael Wyschogrod

BODY OF FAITH

THE BODY OF FAITH

God
in the People Israel

Michael Wyschogrod

1817

Harper & Row, Publishers, San Francisco

New York, Grand Rapids, Philadelphia, St. Louis
London, Singapore, Sydney, Tokyo, Toronto

The author acknowledges the support of the Memorial Foundation for Jewish Culture in the preparation of this study.

FIRST HARPER & ROW PAPERBACK EDITION PUBLISHED IN 1989.

Library of Congress Cataloging-in-Publication Data

Wyschogrod, Michael,
    The body of faith : God in the people Israel / Michael Wyschogrod.
  —1st paperback ed.
     p.   cm.
  Includes bibliographical references.
  ISBN 0-06-069706-07
  1. Judaism—Essence, genius, nature. 2. Jews—Election. Doctrine of—History of doctrines. 3. God (Judaism) 4. Ethics, Jewish.
I. Title.
BM601.W955   1989
296.3—dc20   89-19922
                                             CIP

89 90 91 92 93 MAPLE 10 9 8 7 6 5 4 3 2 1

For Abigail, Daniel, and Tamar,
new cells in the body of faith.

Even though they [the Jews] are unclean,
the Divine Presence is among them.

Sifra on Lev. 16:16

CONTENTS

INTRODUCTION

The drive toward Jewish self-understanding has played a limited role in the history of Judaism. From time to time, individual Jews have stepped back from their immersion in Jewish existence and raised fundamental issues concerning the basic rationale of Judaism and its interpretation of such concepts as God, Israel, history, and redemption. The most famous of these was Maimonides, but others both preceded and followed him. Nevertheless, the main energy of Judaism has not gone into this enterprise. It is generally agreed that Judaism's main effort, at least since the beginning of the rabbinic period, has gone into the elaboration of the commandments of the Torah, which prescribe the conduct of the Jew in every conceivable aspect of his life. It is true that Torah never meant "law" in quite the sense that word is used today. The very fact that in the contemporary world law is considered a specialty properly studied by lawyers and judges but not the average person, while Torah was always considered *the* essential study of religious Jews, underlines the difference between the two. And because Torah was understood as the all-embracing teaching given as God's gift to Israel, it included the nonlegal, or agadic portions of the Torah. But even these texts do not generally raise theological and philosophical issues in a systematic and coherent way. It was the task of Jewish philosophers like Maimonides to weave the wealth of scriptural and rabbinic materials into systematic shape.

The essay that is before the reader is another attempt to think philosophically about Judaism. As such, it joins a relatively limited literature of uneven quality and influence on the development of Judaism. Most of these works were written in Hebrew and almost all were written by Jews deeply steeped in Torah learning. But in this century, thinkers such as Hermann Cohen and Franz Rosenzweig have made significant contributions. These were not Torah scholars with a secondary philosophic interest. They were primarily philosophers whose interest in Judaism grew out of their philosophic interests. That is not altogether the case with the author of this essay. Since Jewish education in a traditional home begins at an early age, my Jewish education preceded my interest in philosophy but not by much. Before my sixteenth birthday I had developed an interest in philosophy that has never left me. I therefore do not classify myself as an outsider who is discovering his roots but as as an insider whose Judaism has been deepened by his philosophy and whose philosophy has been enriched by his Judaism.

The basic orientation of the work is based on a number of convictions I have come to over the years, which the attentive reader will discover soon enough. But it may be helpful to state some of these beliefs immediately—if briefly—so that from the outset the reader understand both the presuppositions and aims of the argument.

1. My Judaism is biblical. It is biblical because the Judaism of the rabbis is biblical. It is, of course, supplemented by the oral Torah, which is considered to have been revealed by God to Moses alongside the written Torah. But the oral Torah is dependent on and is inconceivable without the written Torah. It is the written Torah that is the primary document of revelation. Only in the case of the written Torah is there an authorized text, which, when written as specified, brings into being a physical object—the Torah scroll—that is holy. It is therefore a distortion of Judaism to claim, as some have done, that the Judaism of the rabbis is discontinuous with biblical Judaism. While the rabbinic Judaism of Babylonia or eastern Europe does not follow deductively from Scripture, it is clearly continuous with it and no reader of the Bible would have any difficulty recognizing most rabbinic practices as biblically rooted.

2. Maimonides' demythologization of the concept of God is unbiblical and ultimately dangerous to Jewish faith. Jewish faith cannot survive if a personal relation between the Jew and God is not possible. But no personal relation is possible with an Aristotelian Unmoved Mover. The God who appears in the Bible is a very specific person with certain definite character traits. Because man is also

such a person, the drama of the Bible is the interaction of this God with a wide variety of persons and one specific people: Israel. The widely shared Jewish reluctance to come to grips with the real biblical God and the success that Maimonidean thinking has had in depersonalizing God are not unrelated to Christian Trinitarian developments. Because Christianity embraced a theology of incarnation in which a human being and God are alleged to be one, Judaism recoiled to the other extreme and made the absolute incorporeality of God essential. But the God of the Bible enters space by dwelling in the Tabernacle and the Temple in Jerusalem. Judaism must therefore avoid both making God too abstract and too concrete.

3. The election of the people of Israel as the people of God constitutes the sanctification of a natural family. God could have chosen a spiritual criterion: the election of all those who have faith or who obey God's commandments. The liberal mind would find such an election far more congenial. But God did not choose this path. He chose the seed of Abraham, Isaac, and Jacob. There are, of course, religious and ethical demands made of the elect. When they do not live up to those demands, they are punished. But the essential belonging to the people of election is derived from descent from the Patriarchs. The election of Israel is therefore a corporeal election. One result of this is that a Jew cannot resign his election. Were elections based on faith or ethics, a change in belief or conduct would terminate the election and the responsibilities connected with it. But because the election of Israel is of the flesh, a Jew remains in the service of God no matter what he believes or does. The Jewish body as well as the Jewish soul is therefore holy, a truth that was well understood by those enemies of God who knew that they had to murder the Jewish body along with the teachings of Israel.

4. The ethical plays a central role in Judaism. At almost every point of revelation found in the Bible, God makes very clear ethical demands of Israel. But the ethical is not autonomous in Judaism. It is rooted in the being and command of God, without which no obligation is conceivable. But because Israel is a holy people and remains holy even in its rebellion, many Jews who came to reject the divine aspect of Judaism transferred their religious energy to the ethical, and this led to various distortions that reduced Judaism to the ethical. In recent times, the reduction of Judaism to ethics has been accompanied by a denigration of the peoplehood of Israel. In its place, an unrooted international ethicism was substituted. At the root of this substitution is a spiritualizing heresy for which the body

of Israel is of very little significance. But the faith of Israel is a carnal faith. Judaism does not escape the real, material, and political world for a Gnostic heaven. Redemption must take place in the world in which men live, and if death is conquered, it is not conquered by the immortality of a Platonic soul freed of its material cover, but by the promise of resurrection into the materiality of human existence. Jewish ethics must maintain its relation to the heteronomy of God's command and the historical and existential soil of Jewish peoplehood.

5. Finally, Jewish thought since the emancipation has found itself drawn to philosophies of reason of the most universalistic sort. When Spinoza composed his *Ethics* in geometric form, he gave expression to the Jewish dream of a neutral and objective world ruled by ahistorical reason in which national and mythological forces are subdued and in which the Jew turns into the human and his exclusion from the Christian and national West ends forever. But the collective souls of the nations cannot be exorcised. The mythological national communities will not disappear because they, too, were created by God. A philosophy that wishes to remain in contact with human reality must examine not only geometry but also poetry, which is reflective of the particularity of the national consciousness and destiny. If Heidegger is the philosopher whose presence is most clearly felt in this work, it is because he is the philosopher of this century through whom the tradition speaks. That his name will forever be tainted with his association with Nazism is a commentary on the depth of the demonic forces unloosened by Nazism and the limitations of an autonomous philosophy. The need of the hour is for Judaism to struggle with the spiritual forces that are active in contemporary history.

Not a few Jewish philosophic works have, to a greater or lesser degree, engaged in dialogue with either Christianity or Islam or both. Sometimes this has been quite explicit, sometimes less so. In this work, there is an ongoing dialogue with Christianity. While the dialogue between Judaism and Christianity has been of interest to me for some years, it is not the primary focus of attention in these pages. Nevertheless, it is far from absent. Given the centrality of theology and the resulting high state of its development in Christianity, I have found it most helpful to compare the Jewish standpoint with that of Christianity at certain critical points in the discussion. At times, I was very conscious of doing this, at times, less so. In general, I have found such comparison most useful in formulating a Jewish view on various questions. The temptation here is to make the contrast as sharp as possible, thereby, at times, distorting Judaism. I have attempted to avoid this temptation. The incarnational direction of my thinking became possible for me only after I succeeded in freeing myself from the need to be as different from Christianity as possible. I am now convinced that a renewed, non-Maimonidean Judaism constitutes a return to origins in the deepest Jewish sense.

Chapter 1 ("A Partial Knowledge") deals with the role of reason in Judaism. Philosophy is a reaching for light, but the human condition is an interplay between light and darkness. This is particularly true of Jewish existence, which is tied to an as yet unfulfilled history and to the destiny of a national family. Jewish theology is therefore never more than a partial understanding of the Jewish situation.

Chapter 2 ("A Chosen Nation") explores the corporeality of Jewish election. God did not choose a community of faith or those who obey his commandments but the seed of Abraham. While commandments are imposed on this family—disobedience of which leads to calamity—the election as such is of the body of Israel. It is for this reason that philosophy, directed primarily at the realm of ideas, is not central to Judaism. This chapter also deals with the secular aspect of Jewish election.

Chapter 3 ("The Personality of God") focuses on the concreteness of the biblical God. The God of the Bible is a specific personality who stands in a specific relationship with the people of Israel. In spite of a tendency to depersonalize God in the spirit of Neoplatonism, the psychological concreteness of the biblical God has to be faced and incorporated into contemporary Judaism. The chapter concludes with a discussion of the mutual love between God and Israel.

Chapter 4 ("God and Deontology") explores the relationship between being and God. Is God a being among other beings? Is there a concept (being?) that embraces both God and the creation? Does being serve as a substitute for God in the philosophy of Heidegger? The chapter argues that nonbeing is the necessary corollary of being and that nonbeing, expressed in action, is violence. This chapter is somewhat more difficult than the others, though it should not be beyond the attentive, nontechnically trained reader.

Chapter 5 ("Ethics and Jewish Existence") discusses Jewish ethics in light of the interpretation of Jewish election previously developed. The tendency of philosophical ethics, especially in its Kantian form, is to construct universal laws. But human existence is concrete and historical, and ethical problems arise in discrete situations. Is God's will expressed in universal law or in particular command? The chapter attempts to reconcile the Jewish reentry into history with God's ethical law.

Chapter 6 ("The Unrealized") examines the messianic dimension of Judaism. The corporeality of Jewish election is connected to redemption in the earthly Jerusalem. The chapter concludes with a discussion of the danger inherent in a spiritualized messianism.

It is clear to me that Jewish life throughout the world is in the midst of a particularly stormy period. I can only hope that this work makes some contribution to Jewish self-understanding.

I am indebted to Esther Guttenberg for her patience in typing drafts of the manuscript and to Morris Wyszogrod for the design of the cover. My conversations with him have taught me much about the suffering and courage of the Jewish people.

Chapter 1

A PARTIAL KNOWLEDGE

I. LIGHT AND KNOWLEDGE

Man is a being who prefers light over darkness. The day is the normal time for human activity, the night for sleeping, for the suspension of consciousness. As the sun rises, man awakens and his consciousness is rekindled and remains illuminated until, once again, the light fades and the time for sleep returns. There are creatures whose cycle is the reverse of man's: they awaken at dusk and go to sleep at dawn. They cannot cope with light but are at home in the dark, which is better suited to their endowments. But human being is being in the light because vision, the primary human sense, functions only in the presence of light. There are other human senses that do not require the light. To some degree, the world reveals itself in smell and touch, hearing and tasting. But a dark world in which odors are smelled, surfaces touched, sounds heard, and flavors tasted but nothing is seen, remains a world that crowds man, that does not open itself but impinges upon him and turns man into a recipient of what the world wishes to deliver to him. Only the seen world, the illuminated world stretches off into the horizon. The daytime world releases man from its tight embrace and reveals to him vistas in all directions, toward which he can move and which he perceives long before he sets out toward them. Light is therefore the great liberator that bestows power because it transfers the inititative to man, whose gaze extends into the far distance, which is no longer protected from the power of man by its distance.

1

But light is not only an external illumination that surrounds man at certain times. In relation to the rest of creation, to inanimate matter and the animal kingdom, man is an illuminated being. Intelligence is illumination itself. A very "bright" person is experienced as enlightened. He understands while others are still in the dark, unable to penetrate the opacity around them. Animals also have eyes and they see, we think, and certainly in comparison with a rock, an illumination issues from them. For that matter, it does from all life, even the lowest. In a lifeless expanse when a living being suddenly appears, a certain transparency leaps toward us. Still, in comparison to man, the eyes of the animal issue forth from a darkness of consciousness that we, as human beings, will never understand. The illuminated cannot really understand the dark.

Human being has been an incredibly tenacious ascent to the light. There have been a number of different ascents made, each with its own successes and failures. One of the greatest is that of the Asian world, with its philosophy, religion, and art reflected in the aristocratic bearing of the Indian Brahmin or the civilized intelligence of the Chinese scholar. Another, and the one we know best, is that of Western civilization, with its roots in the Greek cosmologists, Socrates' life of virtue in which it is better to suffer injustice than to inflict it, and all the rest of Graeco-Roman civilization by whose fruits we, with our technological intelligence, rule the world. Each civilization has certain critical points at which particularly important breakthroughs to the light occurred. In Western civilization, one of these certainly took place when, in the Platonic dialogues, Socrates asked for definitions of concepts instead of accepting examples as definitions.[1] Compared to the clarity of definitions, examples remain in the dark. Something similar occurred when Socrates asked whether the holy is loved by the gods because it is holy, or whether it is holy because it is loved by the gods.[2] By asking this question, Socrates attempts to shed some light on the darkness that hides the likes and dislikes of the gods. Are these purely arbitrary or are they governed by some principle in virtue of which certain things are loved and others hated by the gods? If there are principles or characteristics that cause the gods to like what they like and to dislike what they dislike, then it is these principles or characteristics that make the holy holy and the unholy unholy and not the likes or dislikes of the gods. Once these questions have been raised, the darkness that formerly concealed the gods' choices has been rent and they are open to inspection and evaluation. And even if the reply is that the holy is holy because the gods love it and not because it has some independent quality in virtue of which it is loved by the gods, the arbitrariness of the gods' choices is exposed and the mystery has been dispelled. The light that is shed by such questions is a sharp, unshaded light that leaves little unexposed.

Man's meeting with God is in the realm of light. The divine has always been located in the heights, in the upper regions from which the lights that illuminate the earth shine. The association of God with illumination is ancient and phrases such as the "divine light" and the "inner light" remind us that in speaking about God we speak from the vantage point of those who dwell on the earth and who use its images—such as light and dark—to speak about the sacred. Viewed mundanely, the language of light when applied to the sacred is metaphorical language, applying an aspect of the material world to the divine domain. But after a while, we find ourselves less certain about our ability to distinguish the literal from the metaphorical. Does "seeing" literally refer to what we perceive with our eyes and only metaphorically to understanding or is it the other way around? Furthermore, seeing requires the opaque because without it there is nothing to reflect back the light, thus making something visible since light travels until it reaches that which it cannot penetrate and only then does it return to the observer, carrying the image of that which refused it passage. Illumination is therefore a dialectic with opacity, and because rationality is a form of illumination, the basic structure of rationality is thereby established. Reason thus requires the resistance of that which defeats it. Without meeting such opacity, reason would lose its contact with being and its light would become invisible.

2. BIBLICAL REASON

Reason as such is not an object of investigation for the biblical writers. It is true that Adam is assigned the task of naming the animals God has created,[3] and this has been seen as referring to the act of classification, which can be viewed as the foundation of reason. Whatever the significance that is properly assigned to Adam's task of naming the animals (that Adam names only the animals and not plants and nonliving things is itself interesting), this somewhat mysterious assignment can hardly be confused with a biblical doctrine of reason. The Bible is aware of man's uniqueness and of his special relationship with God. It further structures the whole of creation around man, making it amply clear that the whole of creation receives its significance only through its participation in the central events of human destiny, which have the world as their setting. The fact that nature is subordinated to man has recently come in for considerable criticism on the part of those who seek to integrate man into nature so that he take his place in it beside nature's other creatures instead of standing out as the favored acme of creation. Without attempting at this point to evaluate the validity of this criticism, it does draw attention to a fundamental biblical truth, the centrality of man. This centrality, however, was never defined by the Bible in terms of reason. To the extent that it was defined, it was in terms of the "image of God,"[4] which is uniquely assigned to man. Much of our understanding of human dignity is based on this characterization. Some have said that the "image of God" refers to man's possession of reason. The truth is that the definition of man in terms of reason is the contribution of Greek philosophy, perhaps its most significant contribution. But it is not the Bible's definition of the essence of man.

It is difficult to avoid asking why the Bible does not focus on reason as man's distinguishing characteristic, particularly when we realize that the Bible does stress the uniqueness of man. The Hebrew terms used are *tselem* and *dmus*, usually translated as "image" and "likeness." These are basically visual terms, and were it not for the long-standing resistance to anthropomorphism, we would interpret them in physical terms to refer to the kind of resemblance children have to their parents. It may therefore be the case that the Bible would find it difficult to focus on reason as the defining essence of man because reason is a mental capacity that does not take into account the physical uniqueness of man. For the Greeks, the material order was a lower or unreal one and there was consequently little difficulty in defining man without reference to his body. The Bible does not know of this dissociation and speaks of man as being created in the image or likeness of God without expecting that this will be taken automatically to refer to the nonvisual likeness of an endowment, such as reason. In addition, the whole framework of definition is foreign to the biblical mind, especially when applied to the being around whom creation revolves. The naming of the animals is possible because the animals are, after all, objects over whom man is given dominion. But man is not an object in the biblical narrative but the being to whom the events recorded happen. He is therefore, above all, subject, and to the extent that definition of this central subject is possible at all, it is only possible by relating him to the supreme Subject, God. Finally, and perhaps most important, the biblical view of man cannot focus on reason because reason is not the domain in which the fundamental task of man lies. Man's fundamental project is not understanding but obedience to the divine command. It is, of course, true that obedience is possible only for a creature who has understanding, but it is not in the domain of understanding that man's uniqueness is to be sought. Man is not a defined essence but an undertaking of possibilities who chooses himself as he constitutes his moral self. The focus on rationality is particularly incompatible with such a view because reason, particularly as understood by Plato and Aristotle, structures a world of necessity lacking the contingency of the historical. If the Bible is willing to assign essences to animals, this is so because animals do not participate in history. The essence of man, in contrast, remains open.

And yet, reason plays a very important role in the Bible. It is best, at this point, to stop talking about reason and to begin talking about intelligence. Reason is a philosophical construct with definite theoretical implications. Intelligence is a working endowment rather than a theory and can be active in the absence of a philosophical theory about the rationality of the universe and the structure of mind that enables it to grasp the rationality inherent in the world. Intelligence is a quality of brightness that enables all normal human beings to some extent and some to an extraordinary extent to grasp relations and implications in complex situations. There are various forms of intelligence, and an individual can excel in one and not in another, that is, in the verbal and not the mathematical or vice versa. In Judaism, intelligence has always played a rather prominent role. The intellectual complexity of the Talmud and the degree to which that work has been the central preoccupation of Jewish religiosity are both cause and effect of the phenomenon under discussion. The Jewish people, it is generally agreed, is an unusually intelligent people. Some explain this in terms of a very favorable "gene pool," while others would stress cultural factors, including the long-standing Jewish respect for learning and the necessity of a people living in a frequently hostile environment to bolster its intellectual resources, which were very often the only resources available to it to meet the challenges posed. In the Bible, personalities like Abraham, Moses, David, and others strike us as being very intelligent. It is difficult to explain very clearly the reason for this impression, but

it is one that is quite sharp. The status of Moses as the lawgiver probably has something to do with it. There is also a certain realism about
these people. The style of the Bible, which is economical and not
given to verbose descriptions, contributes to the impression we are
discussing by going to the heart of questions rather than circling
around them inconclusively. Biblical figures rarely misunderstand
issues, nor do they act foolishly very often. When they do, the fact
quickly comes to their attention and they usually repent instead of
avoiding the issue. Perhaps these are characteristics of epic literature
as such. Homer's characters display the same decisiveness and intelligence that we find in the biblical characters. In Judaism, the
presence and activity of intelligence does not end with the biblical
period but continues and possibly intensifies in the talmudic and
medieval periods. The charge of legalism and casuistry so often brought
against Judaism is reflective of the persistence of intelligence in the
development of the tradition as it is continually applied to new circumstances and situations. But this generates a conflict with the
purely religious.

There is a certain antithesis between the spirit and intelligence.
This comes out rather sharply when we contrast the Hebrew Bible
to the New Testament. Our purpose may be served by a quick comparison of the persons of Moses and Jesus as they emerge from their
respective narrations. The personality of Jesus is spiritually powerful. His demands are uncompromising and eschatological, calling on
his followers to pay little heed to the kingdom that is of this world.
He does not have much respect for the wisdom of this world, but
he does think highly of the innocence of little children, whom men
must come to resemble if they are to have a place in the heavenly
kingdom. While it would be foolish to overlook the intelligence of
Jesus, it is important to understand that it is intelligence totally conquered by the spirit, by the overwhelming expectation of apocalyptic
events which must undermine the stable order that reveals itself in
the present to human reason. While here and there Jesus does
reason legally in accordance with the rabbinic tradition, his fundamental thrust is toward a cutting through the careful, methodical
distinctions of legal reasoning to a spiritual vision, a law of love that
stands to the involuted caution of the law as the hurricane to a house
of cards, which simply disintegrates before the might of the storm.
For Moses, too, the spirit is very real. But the difference is that God
speaks to Moses about both great and little things, loving one's
neighbor and the details of building the Temple and specifying the

sexual liaisons permitted and those forbidden. The spirit that speaks in and through Jesus aims to lift man out of the finite and partial into the absolute, whereas intelligence is responsive to complexity and relations and therefore to distinctions and to the inherent ambiguity of the human situation. Intelligence therefore has a skeptical dimension because it is so deeply rooted in human existence and its limitations. When the spirit and intelligence meet, the human dialectic begins.

3. A Dark Reason

Human intelligence is powerless before the power of God. This is the basic truth that becomes apparent in the meeting of spirit and intelligence. The great elaborations of reason in the histories of the major religions occurred after the initial spiritual upheavals that brought these religions into being had run their course and the time for consolidation had come. In its direct encounter with the holy, intelligence is calmed, brought up against its limits, and at least temporarily silenced. It is not destroyed, as man is not destroyed. But it is endangered, as man is endangered. Here we approach the heart of the matter. Intelligence is the virtue of man. It is excellence in human functioning, both in body and mind because intelligence is a skillfulness of the whole man, and very intelligent persons generally are also more adept with their hands and the rest of their bodies. But when man comes up against the divine, the puniness of his excellence is revealed and then two options are left to him. He can put God, that which threatens his integrity and the joy of his power, out of his mind and continue as if nothing had happened. This requires constant effort because the awareness of what he has come up against does not easily disappear but continues to lurk in the background of human consciousness. Or man can yield totally to the power of God and lose confidence in himself, both in the worst and the best in him because both are as nothing before the might that he has met. Both of these options are destructive of the integrity of human existence. Superficially, the humanistic option appears to honor the human because it affirms the power of man and refuses to anchor human existence in a transcendent source. But it is a pose of bravado, a putting on of a face of confidence in the presence of great fear, with the bravado increasing in proportion to the fear. When, on the other hand, man finds it impossible to assert the human claim in the presence of God, when he stands in utter terror before his creator without a shred of equality in the relationship, the religious seems to have triumphed. But the question is whether this is the being whom God created in his image and with whom he has entered into relationship or whether this loss of nerve deprives God of the partner whose existence and integrity he desires. Hegel's master-slave dialectic comes to mind,[5] particularly Hegel's understanding that mastery is real only if the slave is a human consciousness whose conquest is worthwhile. A slave who is totally enslaved is an inanimate object, the control of which does not bestow mastery. God's lordship therefore requires the humanity of man rather than the collapse of man before God.

How does this apply to man's reason? We have already said that reason, more than anything else, represents the humanity of man. It cannot be and is not God's will that human intelligence do violence to itself, that man slay this endowment and bring it as his Isaac to God. But God also does not desire that man be so pleased with what God has bestowed on him that he forget the source of the gift and use it to establish his sovereignty, as philosophy, by and large, has done. The human reason that God approves is reason within rules or bounds that are beyond reason. It is the reason that we find in chess, that supremely rational of games. Chess offers the greatest possible scope for calculation, for the exploration of consequences and the weighing of alternatives, the tasks at which reason excels. But all this takes place in accordance with a set of rules that determine which moves are permitted and which are not and how the pieces are set up. The rules themselves are the limits of reason in chess. They are not questioned nor need they be justified because the rationality of chess begins after the rules have been set down and the game made possible. This is Jewish intelligence as reflected in talmudic rationality. The rabbis of the Talmud, too, could have asked whether something was good because God commanded it or whether God commanded it because it was good. They did not ask this question because obedient intelligence has a sense of limit, of the vanity involved in hurling questions at the limits, the very limits that make the asking of questions possible. Jewish intelligence therefore applies itself to delineating concrete moral and ritual issues using biblical legislation as its point of departure. What is negligence? What kind of work is prohibited on the Sabbath? When must lost objects be returned? The best of postbiblical Jewish intelligence has been invested in such questions, which the philosopher finds difficult to understand because he is straining to get to the basic questions, the fundamental issues, which seem never to be raised in rabbinic thought. Rabbinic thought speaks to these questions by not raising them. As the complexity of its reasoning inside the bounds it sets for itself increases, its silence about questions directed at the bounds becomes ever louder and a witness to the sovereignty of Israel's dialogue partner, who is the author of the premises upon which talmudic reasoning is based. And the same is true of the midrashic method. Here the rabbis stay within the biblical narrative, to which they add or fill in details. Very often we sense philosophic questions in the background, which are answered, or at least dealt with, by the midrashic elaboration. But the questions are not raised directly and there is no sharp confrontation between the drift of the stories and the philosophic questions we are eager to raise. Israel does not arrogate to itself the right to hail the Bible before the tribunal of reason, but it also does not abrogate the human right to ask questions, without which man abdicates his humanity.

The reason of Israel is therefore a dark reason, a reason that remains entangled in the dark soil in which the roots of reason must remain implanted if it is not to drift off into the atmosphere. The tendency of the spirit is to rise away from the earth toward a more ethereal environment. And the higher it wishes to rise, the more ballast it must shed in its ascent. The result is that many religions are affairs of the spirit with little regard for the everyday world in which men are entrapped. This is true of much oriental religion but it is also true of Christianity. Jesus' relative lack of interest in the political order, his absolutist and uncompromising ethical demands, the absence of law (which embeds the moral vision into the soil of the created order) in the New Testament are among the symptoms of Christianity's liberation from the darker side of reality. Christianity therefore shuns the darkness, from which it attempts to escape into the light of redemption and sinlessness. Judaism, on the contrary, does not shun the darkness. It, too, has been illuminated with a great light that has transformed its existence into a standing before God. But Judaism will not be unfaithful to the darkness of human existence, which remains cut off from the light but which is not therefore beyond the perimeter of divine concern. There is no question but that God could dispel the darkness and permit it to be vanquished by a light that nothing could withstand. But the very existence of man is at stake here. A world in which the divine light penetrates and fills all is a world in which there is nothing but God. In such a world no finitude and therefore no human existence is possible. Human existence is possible only in the shade of the divine light as that light comes up against its limit and the solidity of matter. The creation of man involves the necessity for God's protection of man from the power of God's being. This protection involves a certain divine withdrawal, the *tsimtsum* of the kabbalist,[6] who were also puzzled by how things other than God could exist in the light of the absolute being of God. To answer this question they invoked the notion of *tsimtsum*, by which they meant that the absolute God, whose being fills all being, withdraws from a certain region, which is thus left with the divine being thinned out in it, and in this thinned-out region man exists. We see it in terms of a darkness that is required by human existence which Judaism preserves in its very fabric.

And therefore Jewish theology arises out of the *existence* of the Jewish people. The divine presence in the created order had to become embodied in a people of flesh and blood. In a universe of pure light, the divine would have appeared in totally illuminated and illuminating form. It would have been spirit and idea, speaking to the highest in man but having nothing to say to the lowest in him. In such a universe, the dark would not have been sanctified but destroyed, as the body is destroyed by Augustine when he teaches that in the resurrection we will receive a noncorruptible body,[7] a form of body that seems indistinguishable from spirit. But God did not want to destroy man and his world. His desire was to make human existence in the created order of finitude possible and, even more amazing, was his decision to enter the finite world so that the men who reside in it have a relationship with their creator. Were God to have entered this world in the fullness of his being, he would have destroyed it because the thinning out or the darkening we have spoken of would disappear and with it the possibility of human existence. He therefore entered that world through a people whom he chose as his habitation. There thus came about a visible presence of God in the universe, first in the person of Abraham and later his descendants, as the people of Israel.

This people is, on the one hand, like any other people in the world. It has its history, its ups and downs, its villains and heroes. On the other hand, it is unlike any other people in the world. From the human point of view, the dissimilarity is puzzling. Above all, it seems to be an indestructible people. While all the peoples of the ancient world have long disappeared, the Jewish people continues to live and has lived for two thousand years without a homeland, dispersed over most of the globe. These are some of the puzzles that an external observer notices when he looks at the Jewish people. They add up, from the biblical perspective, to the conclusion that God is with this people in some special way, that they are peculiarly his property and that the fate of God in the human universe seems to be tied to this people. The matter of God's name is of no small importance here. The God of Israel has chosen to hyphenate his name with the people of Israel. He is identified as the God of Abraham, Isaac, and Jacob. After all, what other name could he go by? The Tetragrammaton is ineffable, beyond human comprehension, and surrounded in Israel by an awe that reflects the secrecy of God, his hiddenness from the world of man. The name of God that is given to Pharaoh by Moses,[8] usually translated by "I am who I am" but that should be translated "I will be who I will be," is a mysterious name intended more to confound Pharaoh than to serve as an appropriate name for God. The only viable name is the "God of Abraham, Isaac, and Jacob," tying God's identity to the people of Israel. It is as the God of this people that he becomes known by all the people of the earth. To such an extent does God permit his identity to be intertwined with that of the people of Israel.

4. THE INDWELLING OF GOD

How are we to characterize the relationship of Israel to God? Is he incarnated in Israel? No, that would be going too far. The notion of incarnation makes best sense in an Aristotelian or Platonic context, where we are dealing with substances on various levels, one of which can enter the other, as the mind is in the body for Descartes. But God certainly dwells in the midst of his people in some special way. Perhaps it would be best to say that he does not dwell *in* the people of Israel but among or alongside them. In making such a distinction, we are thinking spatially, and in spite of the instinctive horror this arouses among many Jews whom Maimonides has thoroughly trained to shun anthropomorphisms, we cannot refrain from speaking about God in the language of the Bible. Living *in* a city does not involve fusing with its walls but residing in it, now here and later there, but all the time being an inhabitant of the city, dwelling in it. There is no distinction between living *in* a people or *among* a people; it is linguistic usage that dictates the use of one rather than the other word. Musicians are *in* an orchestra, while employees are *with* a firm, proving that *in*, *with*, *among*, and similar terms are very often interchangeable. Difficulty arises only when spatial *in*-being is considered paradigmatic and all other uses of *in* somehow metaphoric and ultimately reducible to spatial *in*-being.[9] Spatial *in*-being, however, is only one and probably not the most fundamental kind of *in*-being. In the light of this, we may be able to say that God is *in* the people of Israel with just a bit less fear than otherwise. He is not in the people of Israel the way a book is in a briefcase. Even the soul is not in the body the way the book is in the briefcase. God is in and with the people of Israel and that is all that matters.

God is with and in Israel because God loves Israel. Love is a drawing to another, a wanting to be near the beloved. Love also requires distance, so that what is loved does not become a part of the self, turning love into self-love. Without forgetting this significant caution, we can also not deny that love is a seeking of communion and merger, of oneness and unity. Israel is a favorite child of God's. It knows that it is loved, and it is this awareness that has enabled it to survive thousands of years of persecution without internalizing the anti-Semite's view of the Jew. Self-hatred is not absent from Jewish consciousness. No group can totally avoid some degree of internalization when it is hated for so long and so profoundly. But Jews suffer from this much less than other persecuted groups, with the degree of self-hatred of Jews being often proportional to the degree of alienation from the Jewish tradition. In spite of all the persecution to which Jews have been subject, the deepest layers of Jewish consciousness have been self-affirming because of the deep sense of love with which the people of Israel has felt itself loved by its God. And this sense of being loved has not left the people even when it interpreted its misfortunes as punishment coming from God. Punishment of the magnitude meted out to Israel can destroy a people's very will to live unless the foundation of love is so strong that it can even carry the most severe punishment without destroying the underlying experience of being loved and therefore being worthy of love.

In speaking of God's love for Israel, one finds oneself alternating between the language of man-woman love and parent-child love. God's frenzy when he detects affection on the part of Israel for other gods, the deep sense of hurt God shows when Israel is not faithful, are typical of romantic love. The tenderness for the people, the nurturing and caring for it, are characteristic of a parent's love for a child. At first glance, the parent-child aspect is far more palatable than the other. The love of parent for child is *agape*, while the love of man for woman is *eros*, far more difficult to ascribe to God than *agape*. If both are present in God's love for Israel – and both are – then we must reexamine our frame of reference, which makes *agape* a more acceptable kind of love for God to feel. If ascribing *eros* to God is a scandal, then this only emphasizes that ascribing any kind of love or any other emotion to him is the fundamental scandal. We are either permitted or not permitted to do such things. If we are not, we avoid such difficulty, but we also deny that God has entered the world of man and made himself accessible to man, who can therefore live in relationship with him. This is the fundamental scandal, and if we can accept this, even *eros* becomes possible because it is a more human love, since it is not totally selfless but makes demands on the other, who must also give and not only receive. The *eros* element in God's love for Israel is therefore the element that maintains the separateness of the people of Israel from God, without which God's love would simply absorb into his being that which he loves. If this is not to happen, then the divine *tsimtsum* makes it appropriate (if not necessary) that the God who enters the world that has been made possible by *tsimtsum* be a God whose glory is a self-imposed humanization,[10] which preserves the independence of the world and of Israel. It is this that enables Israel to retain its being and not simply be absorbed into God, and it is this very same humanization of God that introduces into his love for Israel a need for Israel's response and leaves God deeply hurt when this response is not forthcoming. It is this divine vulnerability that makes real the relationship between God and man.

We have been led to a discussion of God's love and presence in Israel by our claim that Jewish theology arises out of the existence of the Jewish people. The existence of this people is the medium by means of which God enters the universe. Jewish theology must therefore be a theology of this created order and not of God himself, as he is independent of creation and prior to the coming into being of a world that is not God. A theology of the fullness of God's being independently of creation would be a fully rational theology. It would be a theology of light without darkness in which the transparency of reason would be total and history not possible. But such a theology is not human theology. The God whom man knows is the God who has humbled himself by making place for the world. The rationality of human theology is an embodied rationality. This means that reason is circumscribed by a domain that it cannot completely penetrate. In the act of knowing, reason knows not only its object but also itself, so that the object is known as it is subsumed under the categories of reason. There is therefore a content that is closed to reason, whose presence reason can surmise but not absorb into the act of knowing. The created order is found to be a world of facticity, which is neither completely opaque nor completely transparent to reason. Were it completely opaque to man, he would then be living in total darkness, which would be incompatible with his having been created in the image of God. Were reason able to penetrate all, were there no aspect of reality that hides from the light and becomes visible only in full or partial darkness, then man would not be man but something more. As it is, man is rendered helpless by total darkness or total light, neither of which is compatible with the human condition.

5. FAILURE

The human condition is thus a mixture of light and darkness. Judaism thinks of man as the inhabitant of an unredeemed world in which Israel clings to the promise that it has received, but it is also aware that there is something that remains outstanding that has not yet occurred but has been promised and will therefore occur. To disregard the darkness of the human condition would be to ignore human suffering, while to forget the light that illuminates the human path would be to overlook signals of hope along this path. Judaism steers a midcourse between these two alternatives. It believes the promise, but it can also accept failure. In failure, reason comes up against the hardness of reality, its indifference not only to the aspirations and loyalties of man but also to his knowledge, which is always partial and never penetrates any but the uppermost layers of his ignorance. Failure is possible because man is suspended between darkness and light, so that there is enough light to hope but often not enough to succeed. In failure, darkness temporarily triumphs, or so it seems, particularly when the vision of redemption has been so vivid and apparently so close to realization. When failure occurs, it can be accepted or rejected. Rejection of failure can take two forms. One is total nihilism. Nihilism pretends to be an acceptance of and coming to terms with failure but is, in reality, a rejection of it because failure is what it is only in the context of the possibility of success. If the game were rigged so that no one could win, there would be no losing either. The other form that rejection of failure takes is the unilateral declaration that the war has been won when it is still in progress or perhaps even already lost. The temptation of this strategy is great, particularly for the man of faith who hears God's promise and is unable to distinguish it from the fulfillment precisely because the promise is God's. When dealing with humans, there is indeed a great distance between promise and fulfillment. A man may be unable or unwilling to fulfill a promise. But the promise of God is, after all, like money in the bank, and what reason is there then to postpone the celebration until the check has cleared? The error here consists of a refusal to meet the God of humiliation. The God whom man encounters is a God who exposes himself to failure. To rule out that possibility, except in the most ultimate sense, is to deny the act of creation, which is an act of withdrawal, of the limitation by God of his power and presence so that there is brought into being a realm where failure and death are possible and cannot simply be declared unreal. Those who cannot accept failure are afraid of themselves, afraid that if they were to admit that the promise has not yet been fulfilled, they might cease to believe altogether. To avoid such a collapse of faith, the very possibility of which cannot be admitted, failure must be proclaimed success and the unredeemed world must be proclaimed redeemed.

Israel knows how to accept failure without plunging either into nihilism or the fantasy of success. It can do this because it feels itself so loved. Because it is loved, it does not doubt that it will be redeemed, that God will master his anger and be reconciled with his people. Because it feels itself loved, it does not interpret its suffering, the failure that it has endured for two thousand years, as success. Such fantasy is the last resort of those who cannot tolerate failure. But Israel coexists in failure with its God. When Rabbi Akiba said,[11] "Happy are you Israel! Who is it before whom you become clean? And who is it who makes you clean? Your father which is in heaven," he was speaking, after A.D. 70, as a Day of Atonement approached but there was no Temple, and no sacrifices could be offered that would bring about God's forgiveness of the people. Judaism could have responded to this in a number of ways. In spite of the long tradition of opposition to sacrifices elsewhere than Jerusalem, it could have decided that with the destruction of the Temple this prohibition no longer held and the sacrifices of the Day of Atonement were to be brought by each Jewish community, wherever it might be. This was not done. Not only were no sacrifices permitted after the Temple was destroyed, but no cultic act was substituted for the sacrifices. The Christian mass is the sort of sacrament that could have made its appearance in Judaism and should have appeared when we take into account the importance that Judaism before A.D. 70 attached to the service of the Temple. Instead, rabbinic Judaism developed a totally nonsacramental substitute for the sacrifices. It may be that this can be accounted for by the persistent criticism in prophetic literature of the sacrificial order and the reliance on it instead of justice and repentance. There is little question that such criticism is a major theme of some prophets. But it must also be remembered that the prophets criticize reliance on sacrifices when such reliance is accompanied by absence of compassion and disregard of the commandments. It is to this combination that the prophets object, but not to sacrifices as such. If any further proof is needed that the reason for not substituting sacraments for the sacrifices was not due to reservations the rabbis had toward the sacrificial system as such, we need only remember that the system of prayer that was instituted after the destruction of the Temple had a very close relationship to the order of sacrifices. Various portions of the prayer service correspond very consciously to the sacrifices in the Temple, so that, for example, on the Sabbath when an additional (Musaf) sacrifice was brought in the Temple, the prayer service had an additional portion (Musaf), corresponding to the additional sacrifice offered on the Sabbath in the Temple. Lack of respect for the sacrifices could therefore not have been the reason that Judaism felt no necessity for retaining them in sacramental form.

The true reason is Judaism's ability to face up to defeat. The Temple in Jerusalem was, for ancient Judaism, the holiest place on earth, the place that had been chosen by God for his abode on earth. In the Temple the Jew stood in the presence of the possibility of forgiveness not available anywhere else. The Temple in Jerusalem, in short, was the center of Judaism. And now it had been destroyed. The place of the Holy of Holies was being trodden by pagan feet and the Temple Mount had become a rubbish heap. In the light of this there were two possibilities. The nation's will to live could have expired or it could have denied the magnitude of the catastrophe by the sacramental substitution mentioned. Judaism chose neither. It did not lose its will to live, nor did it deny what had happened to it. That it did not lose its will to live is clear enough. Had it done so, there would be no Jews and no Judaism today. But it also did not deny the truth of what had happened, nor did it attempt to ameliorate what had happened by producing a substitute sacrament for the remission of sins. It accepted what had happened, realizing that the primary channel for the remission of Israel's sins had been abolished. And instead of plunging into despair because there were now no means of cleansing the people's sins, it turned to its father in heaven and remembered that it is he who forgives sins and he can do so with or without the Temple.

But we must guard against a profound misunderstanding. There are those for whom prayer and repentance as the basis for forgiveness of sin is a great advance over reliance on bloody sacrifices. Those who hold this view—it is not our purpose now to examine it on its merits—cannot possibly understand what was involved in Judaism's shifting to prayer and repentance as the center of its religious existence. The shift from cult to prayer is so difficult as to seem almost impossible. Cult is concrete and incarnated. In it, the holy appears with predictability and there is therefore a security in God's dwelling with Israel in the Temple. That Jews who survived the destruction of the Temple could be made to believe that on the Day of Atonement their sins would be forgiven even though there was no Temple and no sacrifices, borders on the miraculous. It was possible not because the prophets long ago had taught that sacrifices were not important (which is not what they taught), but because the ancient Jew felt God's love for him and could therefore come to believe that his sins would be forgiven without the Temple and its sacrifices.

6. SACRIFICES

Rabbinic Judaism shaped a nonsacramental religion arranged around a complex of ideas, of which the commandment (*mitzvah*) and Torah were central. These cannot be called a *kerygma* because they are essentially a set of demands rather than a message of redemption and the forgiveness of sin. From the rabbinic point of view, especially in retrospect, the Temple sacrifices were incorporated into the system of commandments and, as they saw it, the bringing of sacrifices was one set of commandments among the many others found in the Torah. In one sense, this is undoubtedly true, since the sacrificial system must have been understood as the carrying out of what God desired and commanded. Nevertheless, it would be a mistake to overlook the discontinuity between the sacrificial system and the Torah-*mitzvoth* Judaism of the rabbis. The commandments of the Torah are demands that surround the existence of the Jew more or less continuously. There is no sharp discontinuity within that system between obedience and disobedience because the commandments are often obeyed in part and disobeyed in part. There is no Jew who disobeys none of them, nor is there one who obeys all of them. Everybody is a mixture of obedience and disobedience, sometimes more of one, sometimes the other. Furthermore, the Judaism of the commandments is a movement toward individual responsibility. Each Jew carries with him his own account of credits and debits in accordance with his deeds. The sacrificial order is different. It is not as much a matter of degree as the commandments. The obligatory sacrifices of the day either have or have not been brought. Further, the sacrifices are brought for the nation as a whole, so that not each Israelite stands alone before God on the Day of Atonement or on any other day to be forgiven or not to be forgiven. While there are individual sacrifices that are obligatory for the individual, the central sacrifices as well as the system as a whole is a national rather than an individual one. Above all, sacrifice is not idea but an act. Prayer and repentance are ideas. They are contemplative actions, of the heart rather than the body. For this reason, rationalists of all times have been delighted by the termination of the sacrifices. For them, the "service of the heart" is self-evidently more appropriate for communication between rational men and their rational God than the bloodbaths of a Temple-slaughterhouse, whose atmosphere must have been quite different from that of the seminar room, or the "house of study" of rabbinic Judaism. Rabbinic, non-Temple Judaism was therefore, however unintentionally, an early form of rationalized Judaism.

And yet, the darkness of the sacrificial order must not be ignored. In sacrifice, man alleviates the darkness of his situation. A dumb animal is to be slaughtered. Does it understand the fate that awaits it? Does it realize that at this spot thousands upon thousands like him have perished? The priestly slaughterer approaches the animal with the lethally sharp knife in his hand, yet the animal does not emit a sound of terror because it does not understand the significance of the instrument. It is then swiftly cut, the blood gushes forth, the bruiting begins as the struggle with death begins, as the animal's eyes lose their living sheen. The blood is sprinkled on the altar, the animal dismembered, portions of it burned, and portions eaten by the priests who minister before God in the holiness of the Temple. This horror is brought into the house of God. What is the bridge that leads from this slaughter to the holy?

Sacrificial Judaism brings the truth of human existence into the Temple. It does not leave it outside its portals. It does not reserve sacred ground only for silent worship. Instead, the bruiting, bleeding, dying animal is brought and shown to God. This is what our fate is. It is not so much, as it is usually said, that we deserved the fate of the dying animal and that we have been permitted to escape this fate by transferring it to the animal. It is rather that our fate and the animal's are the same because its end awaits us, since our eyes, too, will soon gaze as blindly as his and be fixated in deathly attention on what only the dead seem to see and never the living. In the Temple, therefore, it is man who stands before God, not man as he would like to be or as he hopes he will be, but as he truly is now, in the realization that he is the object that is his body and that his blood will soon enough flow from his body as well. The subject thus sees himself as dying object. Enlightened religion recoils with horror from the thought of sacrifice, preferring a spotless house of worship filled with organ music and exquisitely polite behavior. The price paid for such decorum is that the worshiper must leave the most problematic part of his self outside the temple, to reclaim it when the service is over and to live with it unencumbered by sanctification. Religion ought not to demand such a dismemberment of man.

In light of the centrality of sacrifice in classical Judaism, the route taken by rabbinic Judaism requires clarification. Why was the sacramental ignored and the word chosen to replace it? We have referred to the prophetic critique of sacrifice and the temptation to interpret the rabbinic attitude as a carrying out of the prophetic thrust by taking advantage of the destruction of the Temple to bring to an end a mode of worship that the religious sensibility of the day had already outgrown. While we have earlier argued that the prophetic critique was directed not against sacrifice as such but against sacrifice without the internal equivalent—repentance—and that the prophets demanded not the abandonment of one or the other of these but their fusing into one act of obedience, we must now look at this question again so as to be sure that we understand its ramifications.

In the context of the messianic future, the prophets speak of a circumcision of the heart that will complete the circumcision of the flesh,[12] which seems to have left the heart insufficiently transformed. Israel has remained hardhearted; the word of God has not entered into its spirit but only its flesh, and this does not please God. It is difficult not to connect this with the prophetic attitude to sacrifice.

There, too, we are dealing with a service of flesh, which the prophets seem not overly impressed with. They point to the inner man and his actions toward his fellow man as the primary focus of God's interest. Circumcision is, after all, the vestigial remains of human sacrifice in Judaism. The knife that cuts into the flesh of the animal in sacrifice cuts into the flesh of man in circumcision. And the prophets have little good to say about either. And yet, circumcision has remained holy to the Jewish people. And the rabbis structured the prayer service around the sacrifices, so that it took the Reform Judaism of the nineteenth century to cleanse the prayer book of its supplications for the return of sacrifices. As heirs of the prophets, the rabbis share some of the prophets' ambivalence to sacrifice. The prophets had limited all sacrifice to Jerusalem, with the constant recurrence of violation of this prohibition by the bringing of sacrifice outside of Jerusalem and the prophetic castigation of that practice.[13] The usual explanation given for the prohibition against sacrifice outside of Jerusalem is a political one. It is interpreted as a measure against the breaking up of national unity, which was often tenuous at best, given the tribal structure of the nation. While it is difficult to deny some validity to this point, the difficulty with it is that it attempts to explain a religious prohibition in purely political terms, and while politics and religion are intertwined in Judaism, the religious must still be understood in its own terms even if there is also a political dimension. There seems to be some connection between animal sacrifice and circumcision and the prohibition against sacrifice outside of Jerusalem. We must remember that it is this prohibition that largely explains the noncontinuation in any form of the sacrificial service after the destruction of the Temple.

The original sacrifice to which all subsequent sacrifice points is the sacrifice of man before God. More specifically, it is the sacrifice of Isaac, who is Abraham's promised son of his old age, the son through whom his seed will become a great nation. At this point of the origin of God's love for Abraham, the love from which all later love for the Jewish people is derived, the principle is laid down that to be loved by God requires the willingness to accept death at the hand of God. The choice of Abraham to carry out this deed roots it in Israel's deepest experience of fatherhood. The hand of the father stretched out to take the life of the son is thus deeply engraved in Israel's consciousness. There are those who maintain that the significant feature of the Isaac sacrifice narrative is God's intervention, which made the carrying out of the sacrifices unnecessary and thus abolished human sacrifice for all time. But this is a rationalistic misunderstanding of the worst kind. The essence of the story consists of the praise that is heaped on Abraham for his willingness to carry out the divine command. The divine intervention that saves Isaac is presented as an undeserved act of divine grace neither Abraham nor Isaac had any right to expect and from which it can clearly not be inferred that God in any way lacked the right to demand the sacrifice he did. Jewish consciousness did not infer from this episode that the ethical in some way rules independently and therefore serves to check God's arbitrary demands, but rather it deduced a model of human behavior definable as obedience. But it is a very special kind of obedience that is here to be found. Both Abraham and Isaac are obedient, one to the command of God and the other to that of his earthly father. Just as Abraham obeys God, so does Isaac obey his father. And both trust him whom they obey. The obedience is not based on terror but on love. It is as if both knew that they are loved by him who demands and that therefore nothing bad can come of it. It is worth noting that while the narrative heaps great praise on Abraham, no admiration is expressed for Isaac, who let himself be bound and almost slaughtered, all without the slightest resistance or protest. Isaac is so certain of his father's commitment to him that nothing can shake this certainty, even the outstretched arm holding the sharp knife. Isaac's merit is therefore one-sided: he needs only trust his father and the horror of the incident dissolves. But Abraham is caught in a double bind. He, too, trusts God, as Isaac trusts him. But he is also trusted by another, and it is against this trust that he is commanded to act. It seems that the trust required to inflict harm is greater than that required to permit harm to be inflicted on oneself. That is why Abraham's merit is the greater.

7. ISRAEL AS SACRIFICE

Without some insight into the uniqueness of the relationship between Jewish father and son, Abraham's sacrifice of Isaac makes little sense. This incident takes place in a world in which human sacrifice, including the sacrifice of children by parents, is a commonplace. The incident takes place in the context of a literature that condemns such human sacrifice. How, then, can such an attempted human sacrifice be permitted and transformed into the patriarch's greatest virtue, the incident to which Israel will refer when it is in special need of God's compassion? The answer must be based on the uniqueness of the relationship between Abraham and Isaac. In what does that uniqueness consist? One is tempted to turn to God's promise to Abraham that his seed will become a great nation. Because such a promise has been made, the relationship to the child through whom the promise must be fulfilled is transformed and becomes radically different from the relationship of any other father to any other son. Whatever validity there may be in this insight, it must itself be seen as the result rather than the cause of the unique relationship between Abraham and his son. It is this relationship that makes possible the divine promise that his descendants will become a great nation. Who, prior to this, gave much thought to his descendants? Ancestors have been thought about. They have existed and shaped the person who is what he is because of what he has received from them. Looking back is therefore a source of strength that establishes identity against the uncertainties of the future. But who has, prior to Abraham, looked ahead to his descendants: nonexisting persons over whom one has no control and at whose mercy one will be? The dead are delivered into the hands of the living, in whose power it is to give meaning to the lives of those who came before them or to deprive them of all meaning by the choices the living make. The promise made by God to Abraham concerning his descendants presupposes a relationship of trust and identification with those to come that is the crux of the Jewish parent-child relationship. It is only because of this that the promise means so much to Abraham and is ample recompense for his faithfulness to God. It is no exaggeration to say that the promise under discussion takes the place of immortality in the Bible. Biblical religion, unlike Egyptian and Near Eastern religion in general, is not obsessed with the problem of death and does not offer elaborate assurances of immortality. The most probable reason for this is that the continuation of the Jewish people takes the terror out of death for the Jew. Abraham's love for Isaac is so great that a divine promise of something good for him is of far greater interest to Abraham than his own welfare or even immortality.

It is for this reason that Abraham's sacrifice of Isaac must be understood above all as self-sacrifice or, more accurately, sacrifice of what is even more precious than the self. Two themes therefore coalesce in the election of Abraham. On the one hand, to be elected by God is to be reassured by the power of God and to participate in that power as God vows a secure future for the people of promise. On the other hand, to be near God is to become a friend of death because of the terrible danger that surrounds all human intimacy with God. On the ontological level, this is expressed by the nihilating power of the Absolute, against which the finite invites destruction. And this is the ambivalence of the stance of Israel. It is a stance that is partly drawn from the affirming power of God and the self-affirming self-confidence that this produces for the people of Israel. But it is also a self-lacerating stand, which is visible not only in the suffering of Israel but in its disobedience, which accompanies its election from the very beginning. The love that Israel receives from God cries out for a return, for the giving by Israel to God of its substance, as God gives of his. And this giving is self-sacrifice, in some form. Israel's acceptance of the law is such a sacrifice of the uncurbed biological appetites that are at the service of the species' life-force. The law cuts into all the human modes of exercising the life-force: eating, drinking, appropriating property, etc. All of these are circumcised in Judaism, which means that they are not rendered inoperative but curbed, permitted to exert themselves in some ways but not in others. In each case, the life-giving and the life-taking aspect of man's relationship with God is reflected. Never is the prohibition so overwhelming that the life-focus is totally negated, that the circumcision becomes full sacrifice. But never is the affirmation of life uncurbed and left without limits. There is little doubt that ultimately the promise and therefore affirmation of Israel's assurance wins out over its opposite. But there is no cheap grace. There is no declaration of redemption in the midst of an unredeemed world. And there is no theology of full self-understanding. Instead, there is darkness in which there are occasional clearings but much of which the sun never penetrates.

This is the paradox of Jewish existence. It is a people intelligent beyond all measure but at the same time not philosophic. It devotes its intelligence to the realities, to the applications of the apocalyptic demands for justice to the infinite ambiguities of concrete situations that remain after the prophets have delivered themselves of their fiery orations. Here the concrete instances of clashing rights demanding qualification, discussion, and patience will not go away. And in this darker realm the full light of justice is rarely seen. Here, too, there are clearings that have more light than the thick underbrush, but even in these clearings it is light only in comparison with the greater darkness. Israel is a people of great spirituality, but it is also a people of flesh, which was well known to the prophets who lamented the seductive tinkle of the ornaments that bedecked the daughters of Israel.[14] Because Jewish existence is an existence in promise and because that promise is of children and children's children and of the multiplication of the holy tribe, there is a celebration of sexuality that is of the flesh, of the gait of Jewish women. It is true that Jewish sexuality is in the service of the promise, and therefore sanctified, co-opted into the service of Jewish survival and therefore into redemption history. But there is no requirement that this insight serve to spiritualize the sexual, as Christian mystics and some Jewish mystics have done. Israel does not leave the flesh. The daughters of Israel do not fully understand the function of their beauty, the role in the divine plan played by their charm. These qualities are in the service of God anyway, even when the nation does not understand its mission. As would be expected, the degree of theological understanding among Jews varies greatly. Some possess considerable clarity with respect to Jewish existence, while others are very much in the dark about it. Nevertheless, the people of election is not only the self-conscious minority that always exists but is almost always a minority. It is the whole people, including those who constitute the corporeality of the people: its flesh, sexuality, commerce, and all those concerns that motivate the majority of any people. The election of a biological people rather than, as in Christianity, of a community of faith, puts into the service of the redemptive plan both the soul and the body of the elect people, which are two aspects of one reality, the people of Israel.

It is in this light that Jewish sacrifice must be seen. The Jewish people must be and is prepared to be sacrificed for the sanctification of God's name. This is a dreadful truth to realize, and it is not at all certain that it is a truth Israel should know. Undialectically understood, such a realization is possible only for a people that seeks death, that hates itself because it sees itself unloved and therefore is prepared to join in its destruction. The desire for such self-punishment is rooted in a horrible self-perception, a deep realization of one's total repulsiveness. But this is not the self-perception of the Jewish people. There is no nation with a greater feeling of self-worth than the Jews. It feels itself loved as no other people. This gives it its will to live under the most adverse circumstances. Suicide is as foreign to it as anything can be. And yet it "knows" that its existence is an invitation to aggression and that by raising Jewish children it is raising the sacrifices of the future and that the dreadful future will come, no matter how long the peaceful intervals may be. It is almost as if the world of the Jerusalem Temple, with its animal sacrifices, were an unreal suspension of the sacrifice of Israel. In the Temple, the people are forgiven and protected. There, the death that everywhere else hovers over them is diverted to animals, so that while the animals die, the people is strengthened by its proximity to God. But everywhere else, this diversion is not permitted. Everywhere else, and particularly when there is no Temple, the people is the sacrifice, as Jewish history has shown so many times. The rabbinic attitude toward sacrifice may not be unconnected with this point. We asked why, upon destruction of the Temple, the rabbis permitted the service of prayer to take the place of the sacrifices. We speculated that perhaps the rabbis had absorbed the prophetic critique of sacrifices and had therefore taken the occasion of the destruction of the Temple as an opportunity to let an institution that had outlived its usefulness die rather than having it perpetuated, at least in part, by a sacramental substitute. The implausibility of this hypothesis depends on various indications, among which are the elaborateness with which rabbinic literature continues to treat the laws of sacrifice as well as the fact that the service of prayer is structured by the rabbis around the order of sacrifices. In the light of what we have said, is it not possible that the rabbis understood that the destruction of the Temple and the cessation of its sacrifices, rather than signaling the termination of sacrifices as such, restored the people of Israel to its role as the sacrifice whose blood is to be shed in the Diaspora when the holy service in Jerusalem is suspended? If there is no need for sacrament in Judaism, it is because the people of Israel in whose flesh the presence of God makes itself felt in the world becomes the sacrament.

Israel cannot and perhaps must not understand this fully. Man never understands his body. On the one hand, I am my body. When my head or foot hurts, I am in pain. And yet my body is also foreign to me. It has its own laws, which I do not understand or control. I know only the surface of my body. Its interior is hidden to me and yet I know that processes are taking place that have the most vital bearing on my well-being, including my consciousness, which I cannot identify with my body but which is clearly dependent on events in my body. Human consciousness is therefore always an upsurge from the darkness of a body not fully understood by the consciousness that resides in the body. And the same is true of the other. While the body of the other is the first presence behind which I seek his consciousness, I soon reach a presence that transcends his body. Perhaps the word *presence* is better than *consciousness* in view of the dualistic implications of the latter. Nevertheless, the body of the other never disappears from the totality of his presence. When I think of my friend, I think of a presence in which the physiognomy of his face, his gait and bearing, his posture and the intonation of his voice play a decisive role. My knowledge of my friend includes his body, and just as my body is largely hidden from me, so is his. Consciousness therefore arises out of the body of the subject, and this same consciousness encounters another body as it seeks the fellow with whom it coexists and to whom it speaks. Consciousness is therefore embodied consciousness, and this is not merely an external coupling that leaves both body and consciousness as separate and discrete systems with a merely correlative relationship. Embodied consciousness is human consciousness. It is consciousness surrounded by darkness, and not only with respect to its object but also in terms of its own being. The darkness of the body, the fact that it is the dwelling place of consciousness but never fully illuminated by it, confers on human consciousness its uniqueness. It counterbalances and corrects the thrust of consciousness toward autonomy, toward self-transparency of the Husserlian variety. If the apodictic phenomenology of the early Husserl gave way to the phenomenology of the life world, it was because phenomenology—and this is its genius— had to discover the situation of the subject as a human being rather than a disembodied consciousness.

The being of Israel is embodied being. Jewish theology can therefore never become pure self-consciousness. Here and there, as in its saints and mystics, Jewish being breaks through to the light, to an understanding of its constitution and destiny. But these occasional illuminations never become the totality or even the essence of the Jewish people. Only the Jewish people in its totality is the essence of the Jewish people, and that includes not only its understanding segments but also the mute and heavy masses who have suffered for the covenant with a minimum of understanding and who have sinned because they responded to the craving of their flesh and the tiredness of the exile, whose significance they understood very little. It is customary to treat with derision the phenomenon of "delicatessen Judaism." There are those for whom their Jewishness means gefilte fish, bagels with lox and cream cheese, or the smell of chicken simmering in broth. Those who think of such things with derision do not understand Jewish existence as embodied existence. Just as the gait and face of a person is that person, at least in part, so the physiognomy of the Jewish people is, at least in part, the people. It is of no small significance that those who hate the people of Israel hate the particular physique of the Jewish people, whose characteristic features they caricature. It is generally fashionable to deny the reality of the Jewish face as an invention of anti-Semites. But there is a typically Jewish face that is the result of the absence of significant outbreeding over many centuries and therefore gives the Jewish people its characteristic family resemblance. There exists also a typically Jewish cuisine, which varies among the different cultures to which Jews have adjusted but retains something specifically Jewish in relation to its gentile counterpart. The physical can thus also be Jewish.

For the philosophers of Judaism these are embarrassing topics. They would much prefer discussion of the ideas of Judaism, its theory of man and God and particularly its ethics, for which they have the highest respect. But for the body of Israel these things are not primary. Jews for whom Judaism is an idea do not coalesce with their bodies. They do not particularly love Jewish idiosyncracies, the particular intonation of Jewish speech and the way Jews carry their bodies. In fact, the degree of revulsion against these qualities must not be underestimated. While we have emphasized the love that the Jewish people has for itself, reflecting its sense of being loved by God, we must not overlook the opposite phenomenon. A people that has endured the suffering that the Jewish people has endured could hardly have escaped unscathed from it. It is true that Jewish self-esteem has suffered far less than could have been expected, and we have already attempted to account for this. But it would be foolish to believe that there is not a certain amount of self-hatred detectable among some Jews. And because the body is such an important component of the self, the Jewish body has attracted a considerable proportion of the self-loathing under discussion. The Jewish body is perceived as puny and weak, while the gentile's is seen as athletic and strong. Because Jews for so long have been victims whose pride was in intelligence and learning rather than physical prowess, the Jew is often seen by both Jews and non-Jews as a weakling and a coward. It is only in the context of this that the psychic meaning of Israel for Jews can be understood. Israel produced the image of the fighting Jew who is not puny and weak but strong and proud. Nevertheless, a certain degree of self-loathing continues and expresses itself often in a sexual context, as, for instance, in Philip Roth's *Portnoy's Complaint*. In the fantasy life of the male there is often a focus on unbridled libidinal satisfaction. Such an individual has also interiorized certain "moral" standards that cause him to despise himself for having these fantasies, and the result is self-loathing. When this occurs with a Jew, the moral standards that seem to stand in the way of the realization of the fantasies are identified with Judaism. The parents, as those who have transmitted the Judaism, become the focus of the anger and when this is combined with the usual tension between son and father, a psychologically combustible mixture results. The loathing of the Jewish body is frequently expressed, as with Portnoy, in yearning for the non-Jewish girl, whose body is experienced as liberating the Jew from his fate of incarnation in a Jewish body.

All this is, of course, caricature and pathology. But caricature often points to otherwise unperceived truths and pathology is often rooted in reality, which pathology distorts but also reflects. The truth we seek is the theology of the Jewish body. We are entitled to speak of such a theology because the divine covenant is with a biological people, the seed of Abraham, Isaac, and Jacob. The biological being of this people therefore comes first. Whatever truth arises out of the covenant between God and Israel, it is never a disembodied truth. It is never a truth valid for all except in the most indirect and complicated sense. It is never a truth beyond history, subsisting in any kind of Platonic heaven. Neither is it a universal morality, as so many modern Jews have thought. Judaism can be presented as a system of thought or an ethical philosophy. This is proven by the fact that it has been so presented very frequently. But Judaism is nothing without the Jewish people. Only this people can bring this truth off, almost like a joke that a particular performer can bring to life but when told by others falls flat. Jews have known this from ancient times and they therefore generally thought of the Torah as binding only, for them but not for others. The Torah was the record of their relationship with God, and its teachings therefore could not be transferred to other peoples precisely because it was not a Platonic truth. Gradually the thought crystallized that there was a covenant for the gentiles and that this covenant included a number of moral commandments that were binding on non-Jews. It is interesting that the moral life of the gentiles was also tied to historical reality. Just as the Torah was the record of the covenant God concluded with Israel after he had brought it out of the land of Egypt, so the Noachide commandments were the record of a covenant God had made with Noah after he had saved him and his kin from the flood that destroyed all the rest of humanity. Covenant, as moral demand, does not arise in a vacuum. It arises in the context of man's gratitude to God when God has mercifully saved him from some great danger. Receptivity to the command is therefore rooted in gratitude for salvation, for bringing into being (Adam), and for saving from nonbeing (Noah) and bondage (children of Israel).

8. PERMITTED KNOWLEDGE

How much is Israel instructed to know about its situation? This is by no means a frivolous question. It goes to the heart of the relation between philosophy and revelation. If there is one axiom that is sacred to philosophy it is the self-justification of knowledge. Aristotle distinguishes between instrumental and terminal goods,[15] the former encompassing those esteemed not for their own sake but for their consequences, and the latter, goods appreciated for what they are and not for the results they bring to pass. While knowledge is sometimes an instrumental good in that it can help satisfy needs, as those for food and shelter, for Aristotle knowledge is to be pursued primarily for its own sake. The reason for this is that the pursuit of knowledge is the activity that preeminently can make man happy. This is so because happiness is related to the ability of an organism to function effectively in accordance with its nature. Since it is the nature of birds to fly and fish to swim, the happy bird or fish is the one who is able to fly or swim without hindrance. While the flying and swimming also have instrumental value in relation to food gathering and other such needs, a healthy animal engages in the activity appropriate to its nature not only to obtain its needs but also and perhaps mainly for its own sake, for the sheer pleasure it obtains from flying, swimming, or whatever else it does well. Since reason is the unique gift of man, which distinguishes him from all other creatures, human happiness, in Aristotle's view, consists in the rational or contemplative life pursued for its own sake as the pure search for truth. And even in modern times when the interest in the application of scientific ideas to technological goals became a dominant motif, the loyalty to pure research, to the search for truth for its own sake, was not suspended. The great scientists continue to see themselves as pure researchers, and there remains more than a touch of arrogance in the attitude of the pure researchers toward the engineers and their practical concerns. This attitude has contributed heavily to the political neutrality of science, which serves social orders of the most diverse kind just because it is not interested in applications but only in truth itself.

Out of these ideas has arisen the Western university, which was created to enshrine science, the great invention of the Western mind. And if there is one conviction that science holds with a minimum of critical reflection, it is the belief that knowledge is good and ignorance bad and that it is therefore always better to have knowledge than to remain ignorant. Because this belief is so fundamental to the Western philosophic and scientific mind, it is apt to be held without much realization of the problems connected with it. If it is justified on pragmatic grounds (i.e., that pure research, in the long run, yields very useful results), then the whole enterprise becomes practical and the purity of science is lost. Furthermore, there is considerable need for distinguishing between those truths worthy of pursuit and those not so worthy. It was Kierkegaard who pointed out that any individual who devoted his life to knowledge that is not needed (e.g., the average weight of all persons with surnames commencing with a given letter or the number of windows in a particular city) was a madman.[16] Truth comes in many forms dealing with many subjects, and if all truth is of equal value, the compilers of the telephone book must be taken as seriously as those who give us insight into an ancient civilization or determine the structure of the atom. The point, is of course, that not all knowledge is of equal value though all of it may be true. And once this is recognized, it is understood that the search for truth cannot be absolutized in its own right—as if it were not related to the human enterprise as a whole.

Before examining this question from the point of view of Jewish faith, it must be conceded that there is a difficulty in extricating oneself from the sovereignty of the search for knowledge. In raising this very question, it can be maintained that a search for knowledge is in progress simply because all thought is a search for knowledge. We encounter here the circularity of certain concepts such as truth, which must be presupposed even in being questioned. What is not as clearly understood is that a very similar circularity obtains for the question, what shall I do? Since in asking this question I have determined that it is this that I ought to do, namely, inquire what I ought to do. Such circularity is a reflection of the truth that man is not his own ontological foundation, that he finds himself in a situation not of his making, and that all inquiry is after the fact and without the total distance that is theoretically required but never possible for man. And it is for this reason that the search for theological knowledge, knowledge about God, must be conducted in obedience to the divine command. We should only know what God wants us to know and that may not be as much as man wants to know.

Secrecy is a theme often encountered in the religious domain. There is a pervasive feeling that there exists knowledge about God not meant for the common man. Such knowledge is reserved for the initiates who demonstrate special virtues, on account of which the knowledge in question may safely be entrusted to them. Made available to the common run of men, the same knowledge can harm them because they are not able to cope with it spiritually. Underlying the division of mankind into two segments, the initiates and the noninitiates, is the insight that extreme proximity to God is dangerous and that knowledge of certain mysteries constitutes such proximity. That there are initiates to whom such knowledge may safely be entrusted ought not to obscure the inherently perilous character of the knowledge. Much of religion can be thought of as the technology required to cope with the divine so that it benefit rather than harm man. And yet, the interesting thing is that the Bible pays relatively little attention to secrecy. It has been pointed out, for example, that the elaborate descriptions and measurements of the Tabernacle are reported in great detail in the Pentateuch in order to strip Temple worship of its mysteries. There seems to be a desire to demystify this knowledge, to inform the Jewish masses of its details so that it become the common heritage of the Jewish people rather than the reserved domain of a professional priestly class. While the actual practice of the cult was to remain the exclusive domain of the descendants of Aaron, it would not be only the priests who would be the sole possessors of the required knowledge. And the same is true, generally speaking, of the rest of the Bible. It is expressed most clearly in Deuteronomy 30:11–14:

> For this commandment which I command thee this day, it is not too hard for thee, neither is it far off. It is not in heaven, that thou shouldest say: "Who shall go up for us to heaven, and bring it unto us, and make us to hear it, that we may do it?" Neither is it beyond the sea, that thou shouldest say: "Who shall go over the sea for us, and bring it unto us, and make us to hear it, that we may do it?" But the word is very nigh unto thee, in thy mouth, and in thy heart, that thou mayest do it.

The teaching of the Torah is not complicated and intended only for an elite, nor is it so mysterious that it can be entrusted only to the initiated. Instead, it is the open and common heritage of the Jewish people. Unlike the Greek oracles, noted for their cryptic messages, the prophets of Israel delivered crystal-clear messages calling the people to repentance and predicting catastrophe if it was not forthcoming. The great acts of revelation on which Judaism is based, such as the parting of the Red Sea and the covenant at Sinai, were acts performed before multitudes, a fact of which the Bible seems particularly proud.

It must be conceded that the secrecy theme is not absent in kabalistic literature. To the extent that this is so, kabalistic thought is nonbiblical and therefore problematic. The Talmud was well aware of the dangers of immersion in kabalistic thinking when it remarked that of four great masters who entered into this domain only one emerged unscathed.[17] There is in the Talmud an almost conscious looking away from God. It has often been noted that the Mishnah does not often directly mention God. Its concern is the duty of man in this life rather than knowledge of the nature of God. And while God does not go unmentioned in the Bible, here too there is no knowledge given of God as such, as he is in himself, apart from his activity as creator of the universe and guardian of man. It is a fact of great significance that the Bible starts with the creating God, the God who makes heaven and earth. There is no discussion of God before the creation, of the deliberations, if any, that took place before the creation. Neither is there any discussion of the creation of the heavenly hosts, the angels who serve God in heaven. The Bible wants man to know only about the God who turns to man and engages him. It does not seem to want man to know about the privacy of God, when he is turned inward into his own being. Knowledge about God in his true nature, as he is in himself and apart from his relation to man, is inevitably objective knowledge. Objective knowledge is made possible by a stepping back in order to discover the contours of what is known, of its place in the whole and its relation to other things. The Bible does not approve of such knowledge of God. God is encountered in command and command is an experience of the subjectivity of God, of his commanding and observing man rather than of man observing him. Objective knowledge of God would give man power over God because it is inherent in objective knowledge to relativize its object and to gain power over it. The Bible is therefore not a theological work if by *theology* we mean a reflective analysis of the nature and purpose of God. In the New Testament the Gospels are also not theological works to any significant extent because they are primarily the telling of a story rather than the drawing of more or less systematic conclusions. It is in the Pauline epistles that we get rather sustained theologizing, and it is very significant that Paul tells almost nothing of the story of Jesus, so that it has often been pointed out that if our total knowledge of Jesus of Nazareth were derived from the writings of Paul, we would know very little about his life and the circumstances of his death. As a theologian, Paul is not so much interested in the biographical details of his master's life and teaching as he is in the cosmic significance of life, death, and resurrection for a humanity heavily laden with sin and hoping to escape the wrath of God. The inclusion of such a theological writer in the Scripture of Christianity foreshadows the centrality of theology in the Christianity of the future.

Theology does not enjoy a comparable centrality in Judaism. We can now draw together some of the reasons for this. There is first the element of Jewish incarnation. The election of Israel is an election that does not exclude the flesh of this people. No theory can therefore encompass such an election, since theory can deal with a faith that consists of teachings but not one that reaches into the existence of a people. Existence can be expressed in narrative form and it can also be thought about, but such thought is always tentative, partial, incomplete, subject to correction by life processes that no theory can forecast but only follow. Related to this is the second factor that must be taken into account in explaining the smaller role theology plays in Judaism: the incompleteness of Jewish destiny, which awaits its completion and which therefore does not have a whole to view, as Christianity does. It must be remembered that while Christianity speaks of a second coming, to which considerable significance has been attached from time to time, the central redemptive event in human history has already taken place and whatever unfinished agenda remains does not erase the completeness that makes Christian theology possible. Finally, there is the directness of the biblical relation between God and man, which resists objectivization. When the period of such direct encounter between God and man came to an end with the close of the biblical period, Jewish religiosity did not devote itself to a philosophical survey of the biblical material but rather to a survey of the commands in the biblical material. While this involves to some extent an act of objectivization, it is applied not to God but to his commandments. It is worth noting that rabbinic activity in the more theological realm escapes the danger of objectivization by means of the midrashic form, which, as elaboration of the biblical story, remains much more closely tied to the story form of the Bible than the legal systematization of the Mishnah, which breaks radically with the biblical format and substitutes a topical order totally missing in the Bible. The fact that the rabbis felt free to depart from the biblical order in legal matters but not in nonlegal matters in which they carefully followed the biblical order and thus produced only midrashim but never Mishnah-like systematization is evidence of the greatly increased fear of objectification in the theological as compared to the legal realm. The law, after all, is directed to the world of man. While is comes from God as his will, it nevertheless deals with man and his world rather than the being of God. It could therefore be systematized rationally because of the probable correlation between the rational universe created by God and his will as it pertains to man's conduct in that world. But this is not so of the very being and personality of God, which is not revealed to man as a philosophical first principle but as a living and interacting father concerned about the well-being of his children. Even in the biblical account, in spite of its nonmystifying posture, there is a profound privacy reserved to God, so that he cannot be outflanked by man and cannot be understood as the Greek gods were by the Greeks.

9. POSTBIBLICAL OPTIONS

There is therefore a looking away from God in rabbinic literature, which is a fact that had the greatest possible effect on the development of Judaism. Here is the origin of the strain of secularism that is so powerful today in Jewish life. Jews were, it is safe to conclude, the chief religious victims of the Enlightenment. No faith has suffered as much from the modern world as has Judaism. There are clearly social reasons for this. Jews had much to gain by the vision of the Enlightenment, since it promised more to Jews than to anyone simply because Jews were the one tolerated foreign body in a Christian world. As such, the promise of a nondenominational world ruled only by science and purged of the Christian influence on the West that made Jews feel excluded seemed like a long-held dream come true by its promise of a neutral, humanistic world. Without in any way overlooking this important social consideration in explaining the extensive secularization of Jews in modern times, it is also necessary to look into the Jewish tradition for those aspects of it that made this development possible. There are those, such as Sartre, who are quite satisfied to explain the very existence of Jews as a result of the existence of anti-Semites. We cannot place the key to Jewish existence in the hands of others, least of all anti-Semites. Jewish existence as well as the forms taken by it follow an inner dynamic that is not only a reaction to external events. Jewish secularization is therefore, in the first instance, an inner Jewish choice. The Jewish people, in the course of time, has come to realize the cost of its election. It has been a very high and bloody cost. Tired of paying this cost, Jews have sought a normalization of their existence, with secularization seen as the path to normalization. Even though suffering has been the destiny of Jewish existence, Jewish consciousness has never raised suffering to normative status. The suffering Jesus on the cross has been the symbol of Christianity, but Judaism starts out with an Abraham whose obedience is rewarded by material wealth, as is that of the other Patriarchs. At its source, the election of Israel is an act of divine favor to the man Abraham, and because Abraham is a man, God's favor reflects itself not only in spiritual but also in material gifts. This remains operative in much of subsequent formative history. The liberation from Egypt and the destruction of Pharaoh and his hosts, the conquest of Canaan, culminating in the throne of David, and the extension of the kingdom under Solomon continue a tradition that equates divine election with worldly prosperity. It is for this reason that the subsequent history of suffering that proved to be Israel's fate was never accepted as normal. It was perceived as an aberration, as a derailing of the destiny intended for Israel, which could therefore only be temporary. The Jewish people was therefore never comfortable with its suffering and grasped the first opportunity that presented itself for terminating two thousand years of pariah existence. When the opportunity presented itself after the Enlightenment, the exodus from the covenant that occurred in modern times was the result.

We have tried to show that this exodus is partly related to the inability of the tradition to accept suffering as normative for Jews. While external events (e.g., the Enlightenment) play a role in Jewish developments, it is also necessary to look into Jewish tradition if we are to understand how Jews and Judaism appropriated these events. Events by themselves mean very little, since they can be interpreted in many ways and how they are interpreted is a function of the inner dynamics of a culture responding to its environment. Jewish secularization is a response to the Enlightenment, but it is also connected with the conviction in the deepest layers of Jewish consciousness that suffering is not normal for Israel. But there is more than even this to Jewish secularization. It is foreshadowed in the tradition: the tradition turns away from the directness of the biblical encounter with God to the study of God's law in the rabbinic framework. Here a certain human autonomy seems to prevail. The favorite text quoted in this connection deals with the rabbis who reject the divine voice that intervenes to settle a dispute about the law on the ground that once the Torah was given to man, it became his property to interpret in accordance with human rules of interpretation.[18] But even apart from this specific text that has probably been made to carry a heavier burden than was intended, there is little doubt that in rabbinic literature, particularly in its halachic (legal) portions, there is a reduction of God-talk, to put it in the current idiom. The law seems to have a life of its own, as does the world, once it has been created. Just as there is a natural order with its own laws and procedures, so the Torah seems to enjoy an analogous autonomy. In the biblical world, the presence of God is far more direct. Alongside events that even in the Bible follow the natural order (the fact that miracles are noticed as a departure from that order presupposes that there is a normal order), there is the word of God, which interprets the events from God's point of view. When the word of God comes to an end, Judaism comes to a decisive turning point. It could have redoubled its focus on God. This would have been understandable in a culture that clearly took the presence of God for granted, difficult as that may be to understand for twentieth-century man. Judaism could have substituted elaborate philosophic or mystical teachings for the biblical immediacy of God, and to a certain extent it did so in kabalistic literature. But fundamentally it took none of these options. It chose halachah (rabbinic development of the legal portions of the Pentateuch), agadah (rabbinic development of the non-legal portions of Scripture), and kabalah (Jewish mysticism).

Of the three, halachah predominates. It is the common denominator that has united all the various manifestations of Judaism for at least two thousand years. It has not, of course, existed in a vacuum. It has not been, contrary to what is sometimes thought today, an abstract, rational geometry that has been applied by human syllogism machines. It has always been rooted in the realities of Jewish life and the quality of Jewish religiosity. The halachah is not excessively intimate with God. It senses that it lives in a time when God is remote from Israel, so that it is not God directly that Jewish faith confronts but what he has left behind to guide the people in his absence. And because God is somewhat absent from the halachah, in it reason comes into its own, which it cannot do when it stands before the direct word of God. Jewish halachic rationality recognizes that in the absence of direct presence, man lives by reason, but this is not an autonomous reason but rather a reason shaped by the memory of the direct presence of God and therefore a reason chastened. The exercise of halachic rationality has therefore confirmed the self-confidence of Jewish existence as a human enterprise and, at the same time, preserved the self-understanding of the people as the people of election ruled only by God. Within the "four cubits of the law" a complete Jewish life was lived by many Jews. And what is even more important, halachic Judaism kept biblical Judaism alive. It could have been otherwise. The Bible and the rabbis could have clashed more sharply. Because the biblical mind is not syllogistic but historical, it could have, and to an extent was, experienced as threatening to rabbinic maturity and patience. The rabbinic world is a far more grown-up world than the biblical. The rabbinic mentality does not thrive on risk; instead, it avoids it for the sake of safety and in the name of caution. The biblical is a far more dramatic and far less cautious environment. The natural instinct of the rabbis was therefore to contain the biblical, with its visions and risks, expressed from time to time by messianic outbreaks that did grave injury to the people and that the rabbis therefore could have undertaken to eradicate by its roots. But the halachah did not choose to do that. It chose to live with the caged tiger that was the biblical, knowing full well that it could not forever contain it but also knowing that its task was to calm the atmosphere without extinguishing the fire whose time would come because God had so promised. Had rabbinic Judaism erred in one direction, it would have witnessed conflagration after conflagration, with the early demise of the Jewish people assured. Had it erred in the other direction, it would have presided in safety over a lifeless people destined never to rise again. It attempted to avoid both extremes by, above all, preparing the rebirth that had to come.

Unlike halachah, agadah positions itself within the story universe of the Bible. It adds to the biblical narrative by filling in many details and incidents lacking in the biblical account. Since the further details of a story cannot be deduced syllogistically, the agadah must present itself as tradition, as coming from the same source from which the original story was obtained. It therefore lacks the potential for infinite development that halachah possesses. Once the narratives that

were orally revealed have been exhausted, the agadah cannot gener-
ate new material unless it shades into the writing of creative fiction,
and that is a mode of consciousness totally foreign to the agadic. It
is for this reason that midrashim did not continue to be produced
after the close of the talmudic period (c. 500 AD). There is no agadic
literature comparable to the continuation of halachic writing after the
close of the talmudic period. There are no agadic responses and
there is even a paucity of midrashic commentary. Above all, there
are no agadic codes, which would have been theological or philosophical works, had they come into being. Instead, the philosophic
production of the Middle Ages did not mainly draw its inspiration
from the midrash but from biblical and talmudic sources. The midrash is not as reserved about the presence of God as the halachah
is. It does not hesitate to recount story after story in which God is
a central figure and in which he speaks and acts very much as in the
Bible. Still, there is a lighter quality to these tales as compared with
the biblical. Because the midrashic story is controlled by the biblical,
which determines the outline of the narrative, and because the midrash can only fill in the details that are missing in the biblical story,
the midrashic storyteller finds himself acting as commentator on the
original story even though his medium is also a story. But a story is
particularly unequipped to act as commentary on another story. The
midrashic storyteller compensates for his inability to carry out the
demands of his own story by seeking voids in the story that he can
fill and then filling them as emphatically as possible, giving to the
midrash a quality of exaggeration and fancy. Here and there, profound and genuinely religious flashes can be observed, but that level
is not sustained evenly. The overall impression is one of less than
full seriousness and the tradition has responded to this by its casual
attitude to midrash.

There is finally the kabalistic option. Modern Jewish scholarship
ignored it for a long time because it clashed with the Enlightenment
ideology that gave birth to that scholarship. This has changed in recent years, largely due to the work of Gershom Scholem, who demonstrated that "mysticism" can be studied within the framework of
historical scholarship without having to abandon the "scientific"
presuppositions of the historical method. Much of kabalistic literature is consequently available even to the non-Hebrew reading student. The world that this reveals is a highly God-centered one. The
absence of God that we noted in halachic literature does not apply
here. Kabalah has relatively little reluctance to delve into the God-

head with great energy. Like the midrash, it supplies much information lacking in the Bible, but the information it supplies is of a different sort than that supplied by the midrash. It does not deal with filling in the details lacking in the text, but with the metaphysical nature of God and especially with the mystery of God's relation with the created universe as well as the rationale for the creation that brought the universe into being. Central to the kabalah's explanatory schemes are the sefiroth, the realms of emanation that mediate between the totally transcendent and unthinkable En-Sof ("Without End") and the observable universe. The emanation metaphysics expressed in the theory of the *sefiroth* is rooted in Neoplatonic thinking. This is very far removed from the God of the Bible, who stands in direct relation to man and who is not an impersonal metaphysical construction but a deeply passionate creator. Attempts to combine biblical categories with Greek philosophic ones are not, in themselves, rare. But usually such synthesizing attempts occur in the philosophic realm where the Greek presence, as in Philo and Maimonides, is very obvious. The kabalah appears to be a purely Jewish enterprise carefully guarded from gentile and even unworthy Jewish eyes. It understands itself as the very inner sanctum of Jewish existence, as the holiest aspect of Torah scholarship precisely because it deals with the inner mysteries of the Godhead, which the other branches of Jewish learning avoid. The kabalists were men to whom God was obviously, in one sense, very close. And yet, the intellectual categories of the kabalah ruled out genuine, personal intimacy in true relation. The mystery is that Jewish religiosity overcame the constraints of the system. Without ever realizing the incompatibility between the biblical God and its theosophic speculations, the kabalah kept alive a God consciousness that is not discontinuous with the biblical. It was not equal to the biblical because it could not be, because God had withdrawn from the immediacy of his presence in the biblical period to a more indirect and remote relationship. And because kabalistic thought was to a large extent an exercise in knowledge rather than obedience, it was possible for it to flourish in a dehistoricized Judaism that sought the traces of God's presence not in the events of history but in nature and the cyclical Jewish calendar, the ever-recurring cycle of Sabbaths and festivals that was Jewish existence in exile.

Chapter 2

A CHOSEN NATION

1. JEWISH PHILOSOPHY

The Jewish presence has not been a decisive one in the history of Western philosophy. Had there been no Jewish presence at all, it would have been explained without much difficulty on the basis of two considerations: philosophy is a legacy of the Greek spirit, and biblical and rabbinic Judaism are not a philosophy but a way of life and a mode of national-religious existence. There is, however, a Jewish presence in Western philosophy, though not a decisive one. Philo in the Greek world, Maimonides in the medieval, and Spinoza in the modern are examples of such a presence. Philo and Maimonides are relatively straightforward attempts to harmonize the Jewish world view with the Greek. Spinoza is more problematic in that some would question his credentials as a Jewish philosopher. Curiously enough, it is Spinoza, of the three mentioned, whose place in Western philosophy is most secure. Philo and Maimonides play a role in Jewish thought but a much smaller role in the history of philosophy. They are pioneers in that Philo is the first to attempt a reconciliation of Plato and the Bible and Maimonides does the same for the Aristotelian tradition, thereby setting the stage for scholasticism. Their role is therefore historically interesting but not philosophically central. They do not introduce new categories of thought into Western philosophy. They are reconcilers of two worlds. Within Judaism, Maimonides plays a central role, but more for his legal than his philosophic writings. Philo, on the other hand, had no significant impact on Judaism. Perhaps because he wrote in Greek, he seemed a remote and somewhat foreign figure to most Jews. This is not so in the case of Maimonides though he, too, wrote his major philosophic work in Arabic rather than Hebrew. Arabic has never seemed as foreign to Jews as Greek, and then Maimonides was first and foremost a great Talmudist, which secured his place in Judaism. Viewed from the philosophic as well as the Jewish standpoint, Jewish philosophy has a somewhat tangential quality to it.

The great philosophers of the modern period such as Descartes, Leibniz, Kant, Hegel, and so on were not Jews. Spinoza was the only possible exception. He certainly played a central role in the rationalism of the seventeenth century. Was he, however, a Jewish philosopher? Is there anything in Spinoza's philosophy that is Jewish? These are the questions that are naturally raised by Spinoza, and they, in turn, raise the question of Jewish philosophy itself. Is there or can there be a discipline such as Jewish philosophy or is that notion as absurd as Jewish mathematics or chemistry would be? These questions deserve thought both for their own sake and for the light they throw on a proper understanding of philosophy as well as Judaism.

The case against the possibility of a Jewish philosophy is easy to state. Philosophy, it can be argued, seeks to answer certain problems by the use of reason. Reason is the same everywhere and pertains to man as a rational being. Irrespective of his national identity, there exists a commonwealth of reason that unites all men and rejects loyalties along ethnic and national lines as irrelevant. In the cases of chemistry and mathematics there is widespread agreement that national boundaries have no meaning, an attitude that is put in doubt very occasionally by such lunatic notions as "Aryan science" of the Nazi period, a notion that deservedly received the unanimous derision of the civilized world. But is philosophy quite the same as the natural sciences? We do, after all, speak of Oriental philosophy, of Greek philosophy, of French philosophy. Are these merely geographic or historic categories—such as philosophy written during the seventeenth century which need not have any real but only an external unity—in this case, its having been written in the seventeenth century? On the other hand, the fact is that historians of philosophy do speak of a century not as an accidental conglomeration of ideas but as an ongoing developmental system, so that centuries have dominant themes and viewpoints that constitute a pattern. The same is true for concepts such as French or German philosophy.

French philosophy is not merely a linguistic but a philosophical notion, so that it would make sense to say of someone that, though he writes in French, he is not a French philosopher in any but a linguistic sense. Philosophy is a cultural enterprise, in many ways more akin to music and painting than to physics and chemistry. The internationalism of the natural sciences cannot therefore be applied automatically to philosophy. Jewish philosophy thus becomes a somewhat more viable possibility.

We have already alluded to the ambiguity that attaches to Jewish philosophy. There are those Jewish philosophers for whom the faith of Israel is an important aspect of their world view. For them, the notion of Jewish philosophy is quite comparable to Christian philosophy, which is Christian because of its allegiance to Christian faith. But there are also Jewish philosophers, such as Spinoza and Husserl, who are not ideologically Jewish. They were born Jews but they are not committed to Jewish faith, and common sense would demand that the sense in which they are Jewish philosophers be distinguished from the Jewish philosophy of Maimonides or Saadia b. Joseph, who are Jewish not simply by accident of birth but by conviction. That there is considerable validity in this distinction cannot be denied. There is an obvious difference between a philosopher who struggles with basic Jewish ideas that he attempts to incorporate into his philosophy and one who was born Jewish and then proceeds to philosophize without any apparent reference to his origins. To modern sensibilities it may even be objectionable to refer to such a person as a Jew and particularly as a Jewish philosopher because the modern mind grants to each human being the right of defining himself ideologicallly in accordance with his convictions. And yet the fact remains that Marx and Freud are considered Jews irrespective of their opinions. This would not be so of someone born Christian who declared himself an atheist. It would not occur to anyone to refer to such a person as a Christian philosopher. It would therefore seem that being Jewish is significantly different than being Christian. Christianity is a set of beliefs as reflected in conduct. No one can be a Christian and explicitly deny the basic tenets of Christianity. There are those who would argue that more important than beliefs is conduct, so that anyone professing to be a Christian who does not act accordingly would not truly be one. Those who adhere to this view agree with Descartes that to learn a person's beliefs it is more useful to observe his conduct than to listen to his declarations.[1] Conduct is thus the more reliable indicator of belief and whether verified verbally or by conduct, being a Christian is incompatible with the holding of some beliefs. A Jew whose conduct violates the teachings of Judaism or one who verbally denies fundamental Jewish beliefs remains a Jew, though not a very good one. This is so both according to the classical teachings of Judaism and the common opinion of mankind, as evidenced, for example, by the fact that Marx and Freud are commonly considered Jews.

The simplest and most direct explanation of this discrepancy is that, unlike Christianity, Judaism is not only a religion, if by religion we mean a set of ideas reflected in conduct. It is also a nationality, though perhaps a somewhat unusual one. The unusual aspect is that for a very long time Jews had no national territory or common language, features possessed by most nationalities. If we can think of Judaism as a national identity in spite of these differences, we might be able to explain rather easily why persons who have severed their bonds with Judaism intellectually are still referred to as Jews by others. The Jewishness of Marx and Freud, it therefore follows, does not consist of any commonality of intellectual orientation but refers to an unusual kind of national identity possessed by them. But we have already said that even national philosophic groupings are not totally without intellectual interest. To some degree, British, French, and German philosophy reflect the history and national character of these peoples. It is unlikely that the absence of a rationalist tradition in British philosophy and its prominent presence in French and German philosophy are purely accidental and not connected with traits in the cultures of these countries. It is undoubtedly true that there is a process of mutual reinforcement of philosophy and national character. Philosophies play a part in shaping the national character and traditions of a people, and the national character also shapes the philosophy that emerges. If we view Judaism as a national identity, what characteristics pertain to this identity as it expresses itself in philosophy?

2. MARRANO PHILOSOPHERS

Even if Judaism is a kind of nationality, it is, as we have pointed out, a rather unusual kind of nationality. For the last two thousand years, it is a nationality that has always been combined with another national identity simply because Jews have lived in many countries and have assimilated in varying degrees the national cultures of their countries. This is true in some degree of all Jews, even the least assimilated, but is particularly true of philosophers such as Spinoza and Husserl who thought of themselves in the context of the European culture of their day rather than in any Jewish context. Nevertheless, they were aware of being Jews. Behind them, as Jews, was a long history of exclusion from European civilization. Once Europe had been Christianized, the Jews were the only non-Christians tolerated in the Christian world. The attitude toward them was ambivalent. Having perfidiously rejected the savior, Jews had to be punished for their obduracy. But because the second coming of the Christian savior was somehow thought to be connected with the conversion of the Jews, Christendom generally also thought it necessary not to eradicate the Jewish presence completely but to tolerate it, though in an inferior position. Added to this, we must consider the Marrano experience, which is especially relevant in the case of Spinoza. The Marranos were Jews who had embraced the Christian faith. The records of the Inquisition contain tens of thousands of cases of such converted Jews accused of continuing to practice Judaism in secret. Many of these cases are replete with elaborate and detailed confessions in which such Marrano Jews, some of whom had become priests and monks, recount their secret loyalty to Judaism in spite of their external Christianity. A minority of historians believe such secret practice of Judaism by converted Jews to have been far less common than the records of the Inquisition would tend to suggest. These historians proceed from the probably sound assumption that the Inquisition had ways of making almost anyone confess anything and they therefore caution against simply accepting such confessions at face value. From their point of view, we are dealing here with converted Jews who were not at all interested in continuing to practice their old faith but who, quite to the contrary, were eager to be accepted as genuine Christians. The charges of the secret practice of Judaism are interpreted as politically and economically motivated slanders designed to ruin a social class that, if admitted into Christian society on an equal footing, would have constituted serious competition for the older Christians. Interpreted in this light, we are dealing with the rejection of Jews who were willing to convert and abandon their Jewish faith. It must be emphasized that this is a minority point of view and that by far the majority of historians think of the Marrano experience in terms of Jews who were not steadfast enough to resist conversion and the resulting economic ruin but who nevertheless were loyal Jews and who therefore went to extraordinary lengths to continue practicing their ancestral faith in secret. The Amsterdam of Spinoza was full of such Marrano Jews who reverted to the practice of Judaism openly once they arrived in Holland and were beyond the reach of the Inquisition.

Whether interpreted in terms of false charges lodged against former Jews who wished only to be accepted as Christians or in terms of Jews who secretly practiced their faith while pretending to be Christians, the Marrano experience must have reinforced the sense of exclusion that was the fate of Jews in Christian Europe. It probably contained, furthermore, an element of double alienation: both from the Marrano's identity as a Jew and a Christian. The Marrano had, after all, converted and rejected his Jewish faith, whether with or without the intention of continuing to practice it secretly. He was also clearly alienated from his Christian identity, which he proceeded to shed as soon as he entered a jurisdiction where he could safely afford to do so. It is understandable if, in the minds of such people, there germinated the dream of a neutral society in which human beings would not be separated on the basis of irrational religious identities but in which all men would have an equal identity as rational beings. Understood in this light, Spinoza's biblical criticism in the *Tractatus* is the opening assault on the book that fixes the identities of Jews and Christians and that must be relativized if the emancipation of Jews is to become a possibility. The self-interest of the assimilationist Jew dictates an assault on the mythic component of European consciousness and the substitution for it of internationalist structures. The new science, with its proclivity for the mathematical and the quantifiable, is the ideal vehicle for the emancipation from the mythic. In the case of Spinoza, this is reflected by the choice of Latin as a universal language and of the use of the geometric form in a work entitled the *Ethics*. Of all seventeenth-century rationalists it is Spinoza, the Jew of Marrano background, who finds it necessary to apply a quasi-geometric reason to the domain of ethics. It is interesting that Descartes, the other great rationalist figure of the century, is almost totally innocent of any ethical interest. It is natural that in a period when the first intoxication with the power of the mathematical as a philosophic tool begins to appear, the focus of the new mathematics-related philosophy is on metaphysics and logic, the branches of philosophy most naturally akin to mathematics. Descartes concentrates his attention on precisely those issues, and while he does deal with proofs for the existence of God, his interest in this question arises only in connection with his attempt to justify belief in the reality of the external, material universe, toward which the proof for the existence of God is a step. Ethics, which is deeply enmeshed in religious and historical aspects of civilizations, seems the least promising domain for mathematical philosophizing. Nevertheless, Spinoza's attention is devoted to ethics in a primary way. His *Ethics* is also devoted to metaphysics, which receives considerable attention in the work. But it is *Ethics* that is the title of the work. Spinoza's interest in the ethical, an interest that is rather untypical of the rationalism of the period, may well be connected with a realization that only by recasting Europe's ethical consciousness into a nonmythic mode would the emancipation of Jews become possible. It is more than likely that Spinoza was, at most, only dimly aware of the hidden agenda in his work. It nevertheless played an important role in his thought.

Marx is another fascinating figure among the secularized Jews of modern thought. His anti-Semitic writings are well known in spite of attempts to conceal them or explain them away.[2] For Marx, the Jew is the symbol of capitalism because he identifies Jews with money. In so doing, Marx reflects the typical medieval image of the Jew as the moneylender. To a certain extent, this image is rooted in reality inasmuch as the medieval church prohibited moneylending at interest, a prohibition that did not apply to Jews. But we must also understand that to Jews money represented portable wealth in a society in which land was the most common source of wealth. The Jew experienced himself as being in exile, inhabiting a given location only temporarily, always prepared to move at short notice. It was therefore essential for him to concentrate his wealth in the form of precious metals, jewels, and money, which he could easily carry with him. All this presupposes and results in an alienation from the culture of the soil, which tends to be mythic. It fosters an internationalism, a critical and comparative attitude, because wandering inevitably results in comparisons and limits the more natural rootedness of homogeneous populations. The Jewish attitude therefore becomes one of translatability, a notion that is worth further thought.

Time and again, Marx vilifies the capitalist on the ground that nothing is holy for him, that everything has a price, on the basis of which he is willing to do business. One Bible, complains Marx,[3] can be sold for six loaves of bread because everything has monetary value, making exchange possible. The assumption is that we start with concrete, noncomparable entities. A loaf of bread has an essence and so does a hat, and these two essences retain their identities as discrete natures. Implicit in this first stage is a very limited horizon that encompasses a community with deep roots and the almost total absence of comparability. Fluidity and transmutation are missing in this setting, which is most favorable for the preservation of traditional social forms and the growth of land-based and therefore mythic civilizations. The first note of translatability enters with the invention of barter. Here, there is a shaking of the absoluteness of identity, which is the foundation of the previous stage and its metaphysics. An object is compared to another object and soon the notion of quantification enters because it is determined that one fish is worth three potatoes. We must understand this discovery to be a new way of thinking, a way that looks away from the natures involved and constructs a framework by means of which comparison becomes possible and things can be exchanged for each other by means of trade. The broader ramifications of this are profound. A new fluidity is introduced into reality that will soon be reflected not only in social relations but in the very development of reason, whose formal aspects (as in Aristotelian logic) are made possible by the looking away from unique essences toward a more mutable universe. This development reaches its high point with the invention of money. At the barter stage, translatability operates on an *ad hoc* basis, with each identity having to be compared with every other identity and a unique ratio of translation determined. The money system brings into play a permanent system of translation that monitors relations continuously and, what is more important, makes it unnecessary to confront individual essences but enables the monetary system to perform the translation without an encounter between individual objects being necessary. When it is determined that a fish is worth three units of gold and a potato one unit, the interaction between the fish and the potato is almost eliminated because both are absorbed into a system of quantification that permits value comparison of the most disparate entities. At first, the abstract system is based on precious metals, which lend themselves to this use because of their uniformity and repeatability. Because each weight unit of gold or silver is like any other weight unit of it, the weight unit becomes an abstract measure of value into which the value of everything else can be translated. The invention of paper money merely pushes the process of abstraction one step further by substituting something that has no inherent value for the actual units of precious metals. The quantification of value has thereby been completed.

It is difficult to overlook the conceptual relation between the process we have been describing and the method of modern science. Both have a tendency to minimize the ultimacy of qualities in favor of quantitative relations. A good example of this is the physics of color, which interested Goethe, whose battle on behalf of a qualitative science of color is not often remembered today. Contemporary physics expresses color in terms of the wavelength of light subject to numerical measurement, much different from the phenomenology of color in the everyday world. The parallel between the money system, which coordinates the values of all possible things, and the wavelength theory of light, which coordinates all possible colors, is striking, making it difficult to believe that the emergence of a money economy was not related to the appearance of those modes of thought that became modern science. The parallel is not, of course, restricted to the physics of color. Wherever possible, science seeks the quantifiable regularities behind the confusing qualitative world, to which only subjective significance is attached. The fact that colors were recognized by human beings long before anyone conceived of the wave theory of light is not denied by the modern physicist, but neither is he prepared to draw any particularly significant conclusion from this fact. When the criticism is advanced that the measurement of the wavelengths of light in no way does justice to the reality of color as perceived, the physicist is usually forced to concede that his work leaves that which cannot be quantified out of consideration. And Marx's criticism of capitalism has very much the same ring. He is appalled by a system that is able to assign a monetary value to anything, no matter how unique, noble, or precious. His experience resembles that of the homeowner who attends an auction at which the objects with which he has been living all his life are on the block. He is pained as each object is auctioned off and a number is called out for which it is sold. He learns that the objects that are an extension of him have a market value and are perceived by the bidders in the light of the impersonal market, which tears away his precious belongings and hurls them into a public world in which he, along with his belongings, becomes an object alienated from himself because perceived through the eyes of others. While Marx, like Spinoza, dreamt of a science of history and of an international proletariat liberated from national loyalties, he did not fail to see and to some degree to lament the quantification of reality introduced by capitalism. Instead of opposing the process, he went much further in its application than anything done previously. Such contradictions are not infrequent when new ideas emerge whose implications are not fully understood.

We are contending that a large portion of modern Jewish consciousness is devoted toward advancing a less qualitative, history-oriented, and national consciousness in favor of an international, quantitative, and nonmythological universe. It is not our contention that only Jews hold this point of view. The Enlightenment is not a Jewish phenomenon, and it would be folly to overlook the fact that powerful non-Jewish forces must be reckoned with if we are to understand the birth of modern consciousness. But we are investigating the Jewish aspect of this development, and while it would be a mistake to overemphasize the Jewish contribution to modernism, it would be no less a mistake to overlook the Jewish contribution to it. For the last two hundred years, Jews have played a role in shaping modern consciousness much beyond their proportion in the population. From the inner Jewish point of view, these tendencies have dominated the Jewish intellectual community in western Europe and the United States and continue to do so. Marx, whom we have been discussing, is an outstanding example of this. He is an antinationalist internationalist who prides himself on being a scientific socialist whose interest, he pretends, is not moral preaching but scientific analysis. We have shown that the seeds of a critique of modern science can be discovered in Marx and that his theory of money implies a critique of the consciousness of quantification. But all this is presented under the rubric of science. The moral passion, the messianic imagination so active in Marx, is repressed, thereby turning him into a paradigmatic example of Jewish alienation. He must objectify his concerned advocacy, which is moral in nature, and pass it off as a force of nature, a law that operates in society as the laws of nature do in the realm of the natural. Another way of expressing this is to think of Marx as an alienated Hegel. The Hegelian dialectics of Spirit is turned into a dialectic of the material, which, for Hegel, is Spirit alienated from itself. Marx destroys the primacy of the idea, which is the core of Hegel, but the idea reappears in the material dialectic, which is applied to a matter bearing little resemblance to matter as usually understood. We interpret this as an expression of Jewish alienation. The prophetic role is externalized by converting it into science, perceived by the assimilated Jew as the vehicle of Jewish liberation.

With Freud we are dealing with another expression of the same syndrome. Science is once again central but this time it is applied to the behavior of the individual rather than society. The prophetic dimension of Freud revolves around his image of himself, more prominent in the earlier writings, as the liberator of man from dark and irrational forces, largely identified with the Church, which conspire to repress man's instinctual satisfactions. In Jewish consciousness, the Church is the symbol of Jewish exclusion from European society. The Church is also the symbol of sexual repression as exemplified in its teachings and in the celibacy of its clergy. In the mind of Freud, these two roles coalesce most conveniently, so that he can become the liberator of man from the repression of the Church but also, covertly and as part of the hidden (unconscious?) agenda, the liberator of Jews from Christian bondage. Freud's identification with Moses,[4] the liberator of Jews from Egyptian bondage, completes the picture that emerges. Here again we observe the alienation found in Marx. The enterprise is carried out under the cover of objective science, the fundamental vehicle of Jewish liberation. Since scientific analysis must take the form of a particular science, it takes the form of economics in Marx and psychology in Freud. Both of these are neutral sciences, which obscure the Jewish agenda satisfactorily. But here a difference sets in. The sexual repression that Freud battles is soon realized by him not to be the invention of the Church but the legacy of Judaism to the Church. The symbol of repression is Moses, the author or messenger of the most fateful "Thou shall nots" of Western civilization, who then becomes Freud's real dialogue partner. But the battle now also becomes much more ambivalent. The Church could simply be set up for destruction because it was only the enemy, having very little hold on Freud. Moses and Judaism are different because they are a part of Freud's own identity, the rejection of which is a rejection of his own self. Gradually there emerges a more sympathetic view of repression, reinterpreted as sublimation and appreciated as the necessary prerequisite of all civilization. Freud's attempt to turn Moses into an Egyptian is the final attempt to throw off the yoke of the law without damaging his own being excessively. If Moses was not a Jew, then rejection of his law is not a self-laceration because the lawgiver is not of the house of Israel, the ultimate source of Freud's identity.

Before leaving Freud we must diagnose another of his contributions: the creation of psychological man. We are referring to the appearance in the last half century of the person whose motivation is primarily psychological. Part of this syndrome is an attitude of self-analysis, as if the person involved were always asking himself, "Now why did I do that?" Psychological man is distinguished from others in that he does not look to his society and its institutions as his sources of justification. Nonpsychological man has a much clearer conviction of what is right. It is to this right that he looks for guidance in his conduct, and because this right comes to him from outside of himself, from his religion as transmitted by the society, he is not constantly searching himself for the sources of his conduct. The creation of psychological man is thus a symptom of the decay of the outer authorities in motivating conduct. What is the relation of the Jew to psychological man?

Jews have played a leading role in this process. Psychoanalysis was invented by a Jew and its practitioners have been Jews in unusual proportion. Jews have also flocked to psychoanalysis as patients in disproportionate numbers. Psychoanalysis has also gained its greatest acceptance in the United States, whose ethos is more influenced by Jews than that of any other country. The Jewish affinity to the psychological vision of man is not very difficult to fathom. For many centuries, Jews have viewed the authority of non-Jewish society around them with great skepticism. It was seen as a world hostile to Jews and therefore morally compromised. As long as the inner Jewish controls were operative, and they almost always were, there was no problem. The lack of authority of the outside world was amply compensated for by the powerful authority of the Jewish tradition, which acted as a totally socializing agent. The Enlightenment and emancipation undermined this inner Jewish authority. The emancipated Jew, however, could not overnight invest the outer authorities previously held in contempt with instant legitimacy. The skepticism toward the moral legitimacy of gentile society continued, except that this was no longer balanced by the powerful legitimacy of Jewish authority as transmitted by the tradition. This brought into being the modern Jewish intellectual, whose contribution to European culture was significant because he was sufficiently alienated and unimpressed by the established order that he found it easy to distance himself from it and discover its flaws, which, of course, were not few. The critical role that he thus performed was not without value. Yet, if we can see beyond juvenile iconoclasm and if we refuse to become permanently arrested adolescents—an occupational hazard of professors —we will have to concede that the critical role that has proven so natural for the modern Jewish intellectual is hardly a role worthy of the people of the covenant. It is not a culture-creating role. It is fundamentally derivative because it lives off the creation of others, which it undermines, since this is easier than to create. That is not to say that this is true of all secular Jewish intellectuals. In some cases the role played has been a very constructive one in spite of everything. But more often it has been destructive and ultimately self-destructive because alienation from gentile society when not compensated for by the strength of Jewish identity results in a spiritual homelessness that must be destructive, for others as well as oneself. The fact that those with ill will have used these insights for their anti-Semitic purposes must not blind us to whatever truth there is in them, for the Jewish people knows that the anti-Semites' goal is the destruction of the people irrespective of the truth or falsity of any specific charges. In the light of this, a calm and honest spirit of self-criticism can only serve the cause of truth and strengthen a people whose destiny requires all possible strength.

3. JEWISH AND CHRISTIAN PHILOSOPHY

We have been discussing three Jewish thinkers—Spinoza, Marx, and Freud—who rather specifically repudiated their Judaism, if by Judaism we refer to the complex of ideas and institutions developed by the Jewish people during its history. We have tried to show that even for them their being Jewish was by no means irrelevant to their projects and that even they were "Jewish" in more than a purely external or accidental sense. But admittedly these are not Jewish philosophers in the most direct and primary sense of the word. That honor must be reserved for Jewish philosophers such as Judah Halevi, Saadia b. Joseph, and Maimonides, who are deeply commited Jews thinking philosophically about their faith. We must now attempt to understand how Jewish philosophy relates to the phenomenon that is Judaism and the Jewish people. Classical Jewish philosophy has fallen into the hands of the historical scholars. The result is that we probably know more about it and enjoy it less than any comparable body of literature. It is a remarkable fact that contemporary Jewish philosophers such as Rosenzweig, Buber, and others rarely make reference to the classical Jewish philosophers. Nowhere in Judaism has anything like neo-Thomism occurred. Whatever limitations that chapter in Christian thought may have had, it does represent an attempt to think Saint Thomas in a living way and it has produced philosophers (e.g., Étienne Gilson, Jacques Maritain, Gabriel Marcel) who must be reckoned with. Nothing even remotely comparable to this has happened in Judaism. To the extent that there has been modern Jewish philosophy, it has been totally discontinuous with classical Jewish philosophy in the historical sense. The only possible exception to this is Judah Halevi, whose historically oriented approach has found echoes in Rosenzweig and perhaps in one or two others. Judaism stands midway between Christianity and Islam in this respect. As far as I can determine, Islam has just not entered the modern world, and this in spite of an illustrious medieval philosophical tradition. One simply does not hear of modern Islamic thinkers comparable to the Christian and Jewish names just mentioned. This fact is not without significance not only for Islam but for Judaism and Christianity also because these three religions have a deeply intertwined intellectual history, which is discovered by anyone who reads Maimonides and Saint Thomas. To some extent, Judaism shares with Islam the latter's silence about the modern world. In spite of some attempts, beginning with Moses Mendelssohn and continuing to our day, there has also been on the part of Judaism in modern times a noticeable lack of will to take the offensive, to develop Jewish self-understanding in living terms. Judaism has been deeply impressed and influenced by historical scholarship, which, in the Jewish camp, came to be known as *Wissenschaft des Judentums* and which has certainly increased our knowledge of many facets of Jewish history, including intellectual history. But it has done so in a nonliving way. It has exuded an atmosphere of the museum, of the study of dead civilizations destined never again to rise. Its models have been the scholarship of ancient Egypt and Greece, in the image of which it fashioned itself. And it did all this at a time when the need for Jewish revival was greater than ever.

To understand the peripheral role played by medieval Jewish philosophy in contemporary Jewish thought, it is first necessary to look at the relatively peripheral role played by Jewish philosophy within Judaism as a whole. It has often been pointed out that philosophy has played a much smaller role in the shaping of Judaism than of Christianity. At this stage we need not distinguish between philosophy and theology because both have been considerably less central in Judaism than in Christianity. Philosophy and theology have in common a certain systematic frame of mind with a tendency to ask fundamental questions. We must remember that at the center of both Judaism and Christianity stands a document, the Bible, which is above all a story. The philosophic-theological mind cannot be satisfied with the story and insists on raising questions of the sort that can only be answered by abandoning the story medium and transposing its "content" or its "teaching" into the medium of discourse. The drive behind the abandonment of the story medium is the search for a higher measure of rationality. There are those who distinguish philosophy from theology on the basis of faith: philosophy does not demand faith, while theology does. While there is some truth in this, there is a danger in overlooking their similarity. The focus of attention is then shifted to the question of truth: What are the rational grounds on which this assertion is made? If this question is made preeminent, the distinction between philosophy and theology does become very sharp and we can then appreciate why the *Summa Theologica* of Saint Thomas is at least partly philosophical, while Calvin's *Institutes* is almost completely a work of theology. Yet both are expositions of the Christian faith and both make use of reason. It is true that in Saint Thomas's work will be found proofs for the existence of God that are absent in that of Calvin. But Calvin, as a preacher, finds it necessary, on the basis of Scripture, to proclaim the Christian faith in at least somewhat systematic fashion. Calvin's problem, for example, concerns human freedom. Given what Scripture tells about God and man, does it seem that man chooses obedience or does God choose whether man will obey? A question of this sort arises only in a framework that is beyond the reality of the story alone. It is exactly the kind of question that we can and often do ask about a story that we observe happening. We can be intimately involved with and knowledgeable about an occurrence and still be very uncertain about questions of this sort, if they are raised. It would therefore seem useful to draw the distinction not as it pertains to philosophy and theology but to the story and the standpoint that is outside the story.

We must first note the obvious. Christianity is born into a world in which the philosophic-theological standpoint, the standpoint that stands outside the story medium and raises questions about it, is very much alive. While Jesus and his disciples were probably not very conversant with Greek philosophy, Greek ideas were in the air of Palestine and certainly in the minds of the writers of the Gospels, whose language was Greek and whose knowledge of Greek thought could not have been negligible. And this is certainly true of Paul, who neglects to tell the story of Jesus almost completely. It has been pointed out that if the Pauline epistles, which are generally dated earlier than the Gospels, were our only source of information about the life and doing of Jesus, we would know almost nothing about the subject. Paul is so eager to inform his readers of the significance of the life, death, and resurrection of Jesus that he devotes almost no effort to telling the story. Instead, he is interested in explaining the meaning of what happened. The point then is that philosophic consciousness is present in the very origins of Christianity mainly because Christianity is born at a time when the philosophic consciousness is already developed. This is not true of Judaism. Judaism comes into a world in which the story still reigns supreme. Rabbinic energy devotes itself primarily to elaborating the biblical story by adding details not found in the text. The midrashim work in the same medium in which the biblical text does, the story. Where the biblical story tells only the highlights, expressing itself generally very concisely, the rabbinic texts fill in the details, telling us what Abraham said to Isaac on the way to the sacrifice and on the way from the sacrifice and so on. Quite frequently, we can detect in the rabbinic elaboration the presence of some questions that could also be posed in the philosophic framework. But it is posed in the story form so that it is we, if we are philosophically minded, who must infer what questions are behind the rabbinic elaborations. Nothing could be further from Paul's mind then the midrashic method of story elaboration. Paul is a theologian, the only theologian in the Old and New Testaments. His epistles do not consist of and hardly concern themselves with the story that is at the basis of his message. They are concerned with the effects of the story, the changes brought about in the human condition as a result of the saving event that is the center of his faith. It is worth noting that with some very few exceptions, Christianity developed no midrash on the Gospels. There are no works that fill in the many details that the Gospels omitted. There is no body of literature consisting of further incidents in the life of Jesus, beyond those recounted in the Gospels. The reason for this is that the world in which the Gospels were born was a world that, to a large extent, had moved beyond the story stage, so that elaboration took the form of philosophic-theological formulation rather than the elaboration of the story as such.

The first reason, then, for the more organic relation of philosophy to Christianity is the fact that Christianity came into being in a world in which the philosophic consciousness was highly developed, while Judaism, being much older, is born into a prephilosophic world. But there is another consideration: until now we have argued that there is an organic relationship between philosophy and Christianity, which is not true of Judaism. But we have not claimed that Christianity *is* a philosophy. The truth is that Christianity cannot be interpreted to be a philosophy, in the sense in which Epicureanism or Stoicism were. Christianity is based on a saving event that took place in history at a specific time in a specific place. It is therefore tied to contingent historical knowledge in a way that no philosophy can be. But it is also true that Christianity is much closer to being a philosophy than Judaism is. To become a Christian involves believing certain ideas. It is true that in believing these ideas faith plays a crucial part, though Christian theologians disagree on the exact function to assign to faith. Belief in a philosophic system, presumably, cannot be based on faith, though even this distinction may not be as sharp once these terms are more carefully analyzed. Apart from the element of faith, philosophy and Christianity both consist of a body of beliefs each affirms. It is for this reason that Christianity thinks of itself as the bearer of a *kerygma*, a message that it wishes to proclaim to the whole world. Becoming a Christian involves coming to believe the message proclaimed by Christianity. No one is born a Christian. One becomes a Christian in baptism, a ceremony that leaves no physical mark because it is a symbol of an inner spiritual and mental metamorphosis. It is true that infant baptism is incompatible with this understanding, since the infant cannot be said to have adopted a new set of beliefs at the time of baptism. But the institution of infant baptism must not mislead us concerning the essential nature of baptism. Infant baptism has always had its determined critics who have seen its incompatibility with Christianity's basic self-understanding. We can understand infant baptism as a solution emanating from the faithful who believe that only Christians are saved or that Christians are more readily saved than others and who do not wish to deprive their newborn young of salvation. It is not particularly strange that simple people do not realize the full meaning of baptism and come to believe that anyone, irrespective of mental competence, becomes a Christian as long as the ceremony is properly performed. In spite of infant baptism, true Christian baptism cannot be divorced from an inner mental and spiritual transformation. The affinity of Christianity to philosophy is therefore the affinity of one ideological system to another.

All this is much different for Judaism. Judaism is not a set of beliefs, however broadly that term be interpreted. A full definition of Judaism does, of course, involve a whole complex of ideas, beliefs, values, and obligations posed by Judaism. The whole of the immense literary output of Judaism consists of the elaboration of just these ideas. But however crucial these are, they are, in a sense, superstructure rather than foundation. The foundation of Judaism is the family identity of the Jewish people as the descendants of Abraham, Isaac, and Jacob. Whatever else is added to this must be seen as growing out of and related to the basic identity of the Jewish people as the seed of Abraham elected by God through descent from Abraham. This is the crux of the mystery of Israel's election. Seen through the eyes of man, a divine election of a group defined by some ideological criterion would seem far more plausible. It would have been far more understandable had God elected all those who feed the hungry and clothe the naked or, if our sensibilities are more contemplative than active, all those who have grasped the Absolute or achieved Nirvana. These are accomplishments of individuals and reflect unusual endowment or effort or both. But being born into a particular family is hardly an achievement for which anyone deserves either credit or blame unless perhaps in those cases where individuals overcome specific handicaps associated with particular environments, and even there the credit is earned by the achievement in spite of the handicap rather than by the family membership itself. And yet, in spite of all this, God chose Abraham as his favorite and promised to make his descendants into a great nation. The God of Abraham chose this people as his vehicle in history, so that his identity is irrevocably attached to this people because he made himself known to man as the God of Abraham, Isaac, and Jacob, thereby conferring on this people a defining function in regard to this God. There is thus created a relationship of great intimacy between a people constituted by its divine election and a God who chooses to appear in history as the God of this people. The relation between God and this people is not a symmetrical one. While God remains absolute, as the God of history made known to man in revelation, he has made himself a partner in the fate of the Jewish people, whose vicissitudes do not leave him unaffected. Jewish theology can therefore be God-centered, but it must also be Israel-centered because if God is thought about in isolation from the people of Israel, the grave risk arises that the God so conceived is not the true God, namely, the God of Abraham, Isaac, and Jacob. When Pascal distinguished between the God of the philosophers and the God of Abraham, he realized that only by invoking the name of

Abraham could God cease being an abstract universal and become a concrete individual identifiable by man. It is for this reason that Judaism, and even God, cannot be defined except in reference to the people of Israel, a fact whose implications must be examined.

4. Love and Election

Why does God proceed by means of election, the choosing of one people among the nations as his people? Why is he not the father of all nations, calling them to his obedience and offering his love to man, whom he created in his image? More fundamentally, why must the concept of nation intrude itself into the relation between God and man? Does not God address each individual human being as he stands alone before God? Because those questions are so fundamental, we must answer them with caution.

We must avoid an answer that does too much. Any answer that would demonstrate that what God did was the only thing he could have done or that it was the right thing to do would be too much of an answer. God must not be subject to necessity or to a good not of his own making. He is sovereign and his own master, and must not be judged by standards external to him. Much of religious apology misunderstands this fundamental point and therefore defeats itself just as it succeeds because it limits God's sovereignty as it proves that he could not have done anything other than what he did or, more usually, that what he did measures up to the highest standards of morality. Having thus succeeded in providing the best possible reasons for God's actions, the apologist does not realize that he has subjected God to judgment by criteria other than his free and sovereign will and that, however much he has justified God's actions, he has infringed his sovereignty and is therefore no longer talking of the biblical God. We must avoid this sort of justification at all cost and therefore begin our answer to the questions posed by noting that God chose the route of election, and of the election of a biological instead of an ideological people, because this was his free choice. He could have acted otherwise. He could have dispensed completely with election or he could have constituted the elected group in some other way, and had he done so, we would have praised those choices as we now praise these. Rarely has any theology come to grips with the contingency that follows from God's freedom. Christian theology has rarely conceded that God could have decided to save all men without the need for an incarnation, crucifixion, and resurrection. The vast preponderance of Christian thought makes it seem that given man's fall, only the sacrifice of God's only begotten son could have served as atonement for man's sin. The Christian faith ought to contend that the way of the incarnation was the way chosen by God, though he could have chosen another. Correspondingly, we will assert the same of the election of Israel, dispensing with all claims of necessity or that this was the best possible course for God to take.

Having said this much, we must also permit the praise of God. There is hardly any literary activity more prevalent in the Bible than the praise of God. The Bible is first and foremost the word of God, in which man is told what God wants him to know. But the Bible is also the word of man as man responds to the word of God. This response takes a number of forms. There is the direct response of those, like Abraham, Moses, and others, whom the Bible reports as being addressed by God and whose responses are reported as part of the dialogue. There is the biblical Wisdom literature most prominent in Proverbs, which, in a sense, is the form that most closely resembles philosophy because it seems to consist of the insights of human experience distilled over the centuries. There is also the praise of God that we find in Psalms as well as many other places in the Bible. The human encounter with God that is expressed in praise is the one response most difficult for modern man, and particularly for the contemporary Jew, to understand. For post-Auschwitz Jewry it is the voice of Abraham contesting the justice of the divine decree against the corrupt cities of man that speaks most recognizably of the human condition. There has crept into our consciousness a profound anger at God, and this anger is shared by all Jews, even those who will not permit this anger to become conscious. Yet we must recognize that there was a time when men in general and Jews in particular were overwhelmed by a deep emotion of gratitude for the wonderful favors bestowed by God. In Psalms this is rooted in David's unshakable faith in his election and the divine protection that insured triumph over those wishing God's anointed ill. Praise of God is thus rooted in gratitude and wonder at the complexities and beauty of creation. Most important for our purpose is the recognition that praise does not involve measuring God's creation and conduct by external standards and declaring them good because they live up to those standards. Praise is an act of gratitude that is totally focused on God to whom we are grateful. Gratitude rises in the human soul when an act of love is bestowed that is felt not to be deserved. It is difficult to be grateful for what is owed one. When, however, man is dealt with kindly without deserving it, it is natural for him to be grateful. In gratitude there is a feeling of loving dependence on the other because gratitude makes it necessary for man to feel his vulnerability, in the absence of which he would not need the favor that has been bestowed on him. Israel must therefore praise God. This will not justify God's election of Israel, but it will enable us to express our wonder and gratitude for the election of Israel.

All this has been preliminary to our discussion of election, which we will not justify but which we might come to understand somewhat from the standpoint of praise. The question we asked was, Why does God proceed by election rather than by being the impartial father of all peoples? Behind these questions lurks the pain of exclusion. If God elects one individual or group, there is someone else whom he does not elect and that other is left to suffer his exclusion. With exclusion comes envy of the one elected and anger, perhaps even hatred, of the one who has done the exclusion. David's love for God reaches great peaks because he is so deeply grateful for his election, but the modern reader finds it difficult not to have some sympathy for his enemies, whose downfall is so certain because they have not been chosen and have dared to conspire against the elect of God. We begin to feel the pain of exclusion and ask why it was necessary for pain to be caused by love. Would it not have been better for God not to have favored Israel, so as not to hurt the other peoples of the world?

This leads us to think about the wonder of love. Western man has, as we have seen, distinguished between *eros* and *agape*. *Eros* is sensual love, the love of man for woman, where jealousy is a possibility. In *eros* the other is a means toward the pleasure of the self, so that *eros* is really self-love. *Agape* is the love of parent for child. Sometimes this love is distorted where children are made into appendages of the parents and used for self-gratification. True *agape* demands nothing in return because it is a love truly directed to the other, to his welfare and prosperity, to what is good for him rather than the pleasure of the one who loves. *Agape* is thus charity in the purest sense but without condescension and any sense of superiority. The love of the Greek world, it has further been said, is *eros*, while that of the Judeo-Christian, *agape*. The question we have posed is thus a question about *agape*. God's love for man is surely *agape* rather than *eros*. How, then, can it exclude? Does a parent who loves one child exclude another? Is not equal love of all children the essence of parental love?

There is something wrong about the distinction between *eros* and *agape*. It resembles the distinction between body and soul. *Eros* seems to be a bodily love and *agape* love of and by the soul. Such a distinction would be valid if the distinction between body and soul were. But in the biblical view, body and soul are aspects of the one being that God created in his image. Human love, correspondingly, must not be bifurcated into the *agape-eros* mold or any similar scheme. There is no doubt that there are imperfect examples of human love, as there are imperfect human beings. But it is simply not true that love as charity applies equally to all and makes no distinctions as to person. This would be conceivable if charitable love were primarily an emotion within the person who loves, with the recipient of the love being a dim image at the periphery of consciousness serving as an occasion for the activation of love. If this were the case, we would be dealing with an I-It relationship in Buber's sense, hardly the model of true love in charity. Love that is in the realm of the I-Thou is directed toward the other who is encountered in his being and on whom we do not impose our preconceptions. Undifferentiated love, love that is dispensed equally to all must be love that does not meet the individual in his individuality but sees him as a member of a species, whether that species be the working class, the poor, those created in the image of God, or what not. History abounds with example, such fantastic loves directed at abstract creations of the imagination. In the names of these abstractions men have committed the most heinous crime against real, concrete, existing human beings who were not encountered in their reality but seen as members of a demonic species to be destroyed. Both the object of love and that of hate were abstract and unreal, restricted to the imagination of the lonely dreamer who would not turn to the concretely real persons all around him. Unlike such fantasies, the divine love is concrete. It is a genuine encounter with man in his individuality and must therefore be exclusive. Any real love encounter, if it is more than an example of the love of a class or collectivity, is exclusive because it is genuinely directed to the uniqueness of the other and it therefore follows that each such relationship is different from all others. But difference is exclusivity because each relationship is different, and I am not included in the relationship of others.

And it also follows that there must be a primacy of relationship.

The authentic person is open to all. When he is with a particular individual, he devotes himself to that person completely, listening with all of his being to the presence of the other. Such listening cannot be a technique that succeeds equally in all cases at all times. The counterfeit of such listening could presumably be standardized and applied with regularity to person after person. But it would then clearly not be a real encounter but a clever imitation of real relationship. In any true I-Thou encounter, nothing can be controlled, no certainty of result can be preordained. It is for this reason that those who live with the possibility of meeting find that it happens with some and not with others. Instead of lamenting this fact, they pray for the continuing possibility of meeting, while recognizing the inherent exclusivity of those meetings that have happened. There is no denying a dimension of guilt in the knowledge that the primacy of relationship with a few cannot be repeated with many others who thus remain strangers. Even among the small circle of persons with whom there is an ongoing relationship, some are loved more than others because each is who he is and because I am who I am. The only alternative is a remote, inhuman love, directed at universals and abstractions rather than real persons.

Our praise of God expresses our gratitude that he loves man in a human way, directing his love to each one of us individually, and that by so loving he has chosen to share the human fate such love involves. The election of Israel is thus a sign of the humanity of God. Had he so willed it, he could have played a more godly role, refusing favorites and loving all his creatures impartially. His love would then have been a far less vulnerable one because impartiality signifies a certain remoteness, the absence of that consuming passion that is a sign of need of the other. Herein resides the inhumanity of *agape* and the humanity of *eros*. *Agape* demands nothing in return. It asks only to give, never to receive. However noble this sounds at first hearing, it must quickly be realized that it also implies an incredible position of strength. To be able only to give, never to need, never to ask for anything in return for what we give, is a position that truly befits a God. And to need something from the other, to need the body of the other for my satisfaction, is the misery of human being. Human being is need, the state of incompleteness within myself and therefore the longing for what the other can give. The *eros* of Don Juan is therefore a more human condition than the *agape* of the saint who needs nothing and no one and distributes his gifts from the height of his Olympian self-sufficiency. The truth is that human love is neither *eros* nor *agape*.

Both are caricatures because reality is a combination of the two, which are not different kinds of love but aspects of human love with a constantly changing composition of elements. No human love is totally indifferent to the reaction of the other. If the relationship is a human one, if the person loved is not perceived as an object to which things are done but a person to whom one speaks and whose answer one awaits, then the response received must be an important element in the direction of the developing relationship. This does not mean that a rebuff necessarily results in the termination of concern or even love. It is possible to love—and here is the truth of *agape*—in spite of rebuff or absence of response. But such absence is never a matter of indifference and plays an important role in the relationship because response is always sought, needed, and hoped for. Similarly, there is no erotic relationship without an element of concern. The sexual, even in its most exploiting and objectifying form, reveals a glimmer of gratitude and affection. If totalitarian states find it necessary to repress the sexual, it is because they are dimly aware that the person to whom the sexual is a reality is a person whose humanity has not been totally deposited with the state and who is therefore untrustworthy for the purposes of a system whose presupposition is dehumanization. All this is not to deny that there are loves in which *agape* predominates and those in which *eros* does. But none is exclusively one or the other because man is created in the image of God as a being constituted by need who gives and also asks to be given in return.

The love with which God has chosen to love man is a love understandable to man. It is therefore a love very much aware of human response. God has thereby made himself vulnerable: he asks for man's response and is hurt when it is not forthcoming. For the same reason, God's love is not undifferentiated, having the same quality toward all his children. God's love is directed toward who we are. We are confirmed as who we are in our relationship to God. And because God is so deeply directed toward us, because his love is not self-love (in spite of Plato, Neoplatonism, and the tradition flowing from these) but true meeting of the other (and there is an other for God; this is the mystery of creation), there are those whom God loves especially, with whom he has fallen in love, as with Abraham. There is no other way of expressing this mystery except in these terms. God's relationship to Abraham is truly a falling in love. The biblical text tells us this when it fails to explain the reason for the election of Abraham. The rabbis, of course, were aware of this omission and perplexed by it. They supplied reasons, making of Abraham the first natural philosopher who saw through the foolishness of the idol worship of his time and reasoned his way to the one God. In the Bible, it is not Abraham who moves toward God but God who turns to Abraham with an election that is not explained because it is an act of love that requires no explanation. If God continues to love the people of Israel—and it is the faith of Israel that he does—it is because he sees the face of his beloved Abraham in each and every one of his children as a man sees the face of his beloved in the children of his union with his beloved. God's anger when Israel is disobedient is the anger of a rejected lover. It is above all jealousy, the jealousy of one deeply in love who is consumed with torment at the knowledge that his beloved seeks the affection of others. To much of philosophical theology, such talk has been an embarrassment in urgent need of demythologization. But theologians must not be more protective of God's dignity than he is of his own because God's true dignity is the sovereignty of his choice for genuine relation with man.

What, now, of those not elected? Those not elected cannot be expected not to be hurt by not being of the seed of Abraham, whom God loves above all others. The Bible depicts clearly the suffering of Esau. The Bible is, after all, the history of Israel and could therefore be expected to be partial to the Jewish cause. And yet, in recounting the blessing of Jacob and the exclusion of Esau, no careful reader can fail to notice that the sympathy shown Esau is greater than that for Jacob. God shows Esau compassion even if Jacob does not. The consolation of the gentiles is the knowledge that God also stands in relationship with them in the recognition and affirmation of their uniqueness. The choice, after all, is between a lofty divine love equally distributed to all without recognition of uniqueness and real encounter, which necessarily involves favorites but in which each is unique and addressed as such. If Abraham was especially loved by God, it is because God is a father who does not stand in a legal relationship to his children, which by its nature requires impartiality and objectivity. As a father, God loves his children and knows each one as who he is with his strengths and weaknesses, his virtues and vices. Because a father is not an impartial judge but a loving parent and because a human father is a human being with his own personality, it is inevitable that he will find himself more compatible with some of his children than others and, to speak very plainly, that he love some more than others. There is usually great reluctance on the part of parents to admit this, but it is a truth that must not be avoided. And it is also true that a father loves all his children, so that they all know of and feel the love they receive, recognizing that to substitute an impartial judge for a loving father would eliminate the preference for the specially favored but would also deprive all of them of a father. The mystery of Israel's election thus turns out to be the guarantee of the fatherhood of God toward all peoples, elect and nonelect, Jew and gentile. We must, at the same time, reiterate that none of this amounts to some sort of demonstration of the "necessity" of election in any sense. It can be understood only from the point of view of man's gratitude for the fatherhood of God, since only the invocation of the category of "father" and the divine permission we have to apply this category to God enable us to begin to fathom the mystery of election. When we grasp that the election of Israel flows from the fatherhood that extends to all created in God's image, we find ourselves tied to all men in brotherhood, as Joseph, favored by his human father, ultimately found himself tied to his brothers. And when man contemplates this mystery, that the Eternal One, the creator of heaven and earth, chose to become the father of his creatures instead of remaining self-sufficient unto himself, as is the Absolute of the philosophers, there wells up in man that praise that has become so rare yet remains so natural.

5. National Election

There still remains the problem of the national election of Israel. Even if we see the election of Abraham as flowing from the fatherhood of God, we can still remain in the darkest of puzzlement in regard to the election of a whole people, the seed of Abraham, unto all eternity. What is the meaning behind the spontaneous emergence of the nation at the moment God enters into romance with Abraham? What is the "great beast" of national existence (to use Simone Weil's phrase) doing in the inner sanctum of man's relationship with God? Is this not properly the domain of the "single one," the man who stands alone before God and is able to hear God only because he has escaped the power of the crowd, which drowns out the voice from above? Finally, and perhaps above all, why a covenant with the carnal instead of the spiritual seed of Abraham?

Is it physical relationship that is essential? Are there not those who are Abraham's children in the spirit who are more dear to God than a crass, perhaps unbelieving, Jew who is related to Abraham in the flesh but whose spiritual illumination is quite dim? Are not the real elect the aristocrats of the spirit, who derive from all peoples, cultures, and races? These are the questions that are hurled at Israel. Most often, they are not real questions because no answer is expected, since none is thought possible. The faith of Israel is dismissed as prespiritual, a carnal and early phase of human consciousness destined to be outgrown in the maturation of the race. Christianity's self-understanding as the new Israel of the spirit expresses this conviction and so does, though proceeding from sharply different premises, modern historical scholarship, which is determined to find early and late stages in everything, with the early always inferior to the later. Against all of these, Israel reaffirms its election in its physical descent from Abraham, a physical bond every Jew who is not totally alienated from his being experiences every day of his life as he moves among men, all of whom are his brothers—in whom he perceives the image of God—but all of whom are not Jews—in whom he perceives a family kinship unique to Jews. It is this that we must try to understand.

The nature of God is spiritual. This is the almost unanimous, and not untrue, wisdom of most religions, East and West. As spirit, God's natural kinship is with the spiritual man, with his soul and mind, which is uniquely capable of grasping the reality of the spiritual God. Man's relationship with God therefore comes to be centered in the spiritual and, more particularly, in the ethical, which is spiritualized by the elimination of law and the substitution of love as the dominant theme. The difficulty with this spiritualization of the God-man relationship is that it is untrue to man's nature, which is largely carnal. The division of man into the spiritual and the material is itself an act of abstraction that has a limited validity but that must not obscure the basic unity of human existence. This unity must not be conceived as a coupling of the spiritual and the material because any coupling presupposes an original separation, which is simply not warranted. Man is not a coupling of the spiritual and material but a creature who thinks and runs, grieves and cries, is amused and laughs. He is, in short, what he is: a being with an identity and a world in which he lives. Here, again, God could have played a godly role, interested in certain features of human existence, the spiritual, but not in others, the material. He could even have assigned man the task of wrenching himself out of the material so as to assume his spiritual identity, which is just what so many religions believe he did.[5] Instead, the God of Israel confirms man as he created him to live in the material cosmos. There is therefore no possibility of a divine requirement for the discarding of a part of human existence. Instead, there is a requirement for the sancification of human existence in all of its aspects. Israel's symbol of the covenant is circumcision, a searing of the covenant into the flesh of Israel and not only, or perhaps not even primarily, into its spirit. And that is why God's election is of a carnal people. By electing the seed of Abraham, God creates a people that is in his service in the totality of its human being and not just in its moral and spiritual existence. The domain of the family, the most fundamental and intimate human association, is thereby sanctified, so that obedience to God does not require hate of father and mother.[6] It is also true that simple, undialectical attachment to the natural can be incompatible with a hearing of the divine command. Abraham is commanded to leave his land, birthplace, and father's house and follow God to a place that he will show him. The man who hears God's word is therefore wrenched away from his natural setting, from the bonds that tie him to his parents, brothers, sisters, and the whole world into which he was born and that gives man his natural security. If the divine command went no further, if it merely instructed him to leave his birthplace and then preach a moral vision or religious discovery, then the natural would have been slain once and for all and Kierkegaard would be right in saying that a real relation with God excludes real relations with human beings.[7] But the divine command does not stop there. After commanding Abraham to leave his father's house, it promises to make a great nation of his seed. The natural is now reinstated, projected into the future instead of rooted primarily in the past, and, above all, sanctified as a natural community. The divine does not, therefore, destroy the natural but confirms it by placing it in its service.

And very much the same is true of the national order. Simone Weil is far from wrong in speaking of society and the nation as the "great beast" to which men sacrifice their individuality,[8] so that they never dream it possible to become a "single one" before God. No one who has read the prophets of Israel can be unaware of the extent to which Israel's faith fears the arrogance of the collective. But the question is, What to do? Shall the domain of the state be written off as the domain of the Devil, beyond the hope of sanctification, or shall it be seen as the most difficult challenge of all, which must be won for the holy precisely because of its remoteness from it? Israel attempts to sanctify national existence in obedience to the divine election, which is a national election. And it is a national election precisely because the nation is most remote from God and is therefore commanded to be the most proximate. To believe that the individual can be lifted out of his nation and brought into relation with God is as illusory as to believe that man's soul can be saved and his body discarded. Just as man is body and soul, so man is an individual and member of a nation. To save him as an individual and to leave the national social order unredeemed is to truncate man and then to believe that this remnant of a human being is the object of salvation. The national election of Israel is therefore again a sign of God's understanding of the human predicament and the confirmation of and love for that humanity. By sanctifying the nationhood of Israel, God confirms the national order of all peoples and expresses his love for the individual in his national setting and for the nations in their corporate personalities. In the case of Israel, the relationship that started with Abraham, the individual, soon becomes a relationship with a nation that becomes the elect nation. The promise of salvation is thus not held out to man as an individual but as a member of his nation. It is held out to the complete man and therefore to all nations, without which we have a part rather than all of man. In addition, by taking the national order seriously, redemption of the historical order becomes a possibility. History pertains to nations and if only the individual is real, history is not real. Purely spiritual religions, those that do not hesitate to address only the spiritual in man, do not take history seriously. This tendency is pronounced in early Christianity, which distanced itself from the political order because its citizenship was in the heavenly city that was not of this world. The salvation that Israel awaits must occur in the historical order, and it therefore is forced to continue to wait as long as that order is unredeemed. Israel cannot believe that in the midst of an unredeemed world there is an island of redemption, the Church, to which men can flee from the sorrows of the world. But this tenacity in its hold on reality flows from God's confirmation of that reality in refusing to exclude from the promise of redemption those structures that the spiritual religions have no hesitation in discarding but that, because they are real, defeat their purely spiritual visions.

We were led into an exploration of Jewish existence as a national family from our discovery that philosophy has played a less central role in Judaism than in Christianity. Judaism, we said, was not first a set of ideas but an existing people on whom commands are imposed and from whom ideas are generated but whose own being is the existential soil from which everything else emerges. Before we can explore this relationship between soil, or ground, and idea, we must allude to another fundamental reason for the different roles played by philosophy in Judaism and Christianity. Christianity sees before it a completed salvation history. Creation to resurrection constitutes a totality of promise and fulfillment that is available to viewing and therefore to thought. Israel's story is incomplete. It is replete with great peaks and deep disappointments, but it is, above all, incomplete. The redemption implicit in the very first promise to Abraham is still in abeyance. The Exodus, Sinai, the Temple are all peaks and previews of what is in store for Israel and humanity in the fulfillment. But that fulfillment has not yet occurred, and we are therefore dealing with an uncompleted tale whose outcome we know because of our trust in the source of the promise. Nevertheless, however great our trust, we must not confuse promise with fulfillment, especially for man, who lives in time and for whom the future is shrouded in darkness.

Because this is so, the philosophical cannot now be central for Judaism. Philosophy demands a revealed and therefore knowable object that it can investigate. It requires stable categories by means of which it can grasp its object. Philosophy, as a form of knowledge, is therefore most comfortable with the past and least secure with the future, about which it knows little. Because Judaism—though this is often forgotten—is so much a venture into the future, the mode of knowledge will never be as natural to it as to a faith that is fulfilled. It is by no means a coincidence that Maimonides, the greatest Jewish philosopher, is also the man who had the most profound problems with the resurrection and the messianic idea as a whole. In regard to the resurrection, it is the materiality of it that causes him difficulty. With the Messiah, it is the apocalyptic dimension that must be toned down, so that the future not be made too dissimilar to the past. All these are expressions of the incompatibility of the philosophic standpoint with a genuinely transformed future whose dissimilarity to the past is a premise of prophetic thinking. A Judaism that remains true to its messianic faith can only place provisional trust in categories of thought derived from an unredeemed world destined to pass away. If the future is decisive, reason must be prepared to see itself transcended by developments that cannot yet be dreamt of. But no reason worthy of itself can be that modest, since it would then be untrue to its essence, which consists in confidence in the power of its illumination. In its own way, reason participates in the illusion of redemption for which Judaism is prepared to hope but the reality of which it is not prepared to proclaim. Because it is therefore still on the way, Judaism cannot easily express itself in the philosophical idiom, much of which is rooted in a metaphysics of completion.

6. TWO TRADITIONS

We have now dealt with the Jewish role in Western philosophy and contrasted the more organic ties of Christianity to philosophy with the more reserved relationship between Judaism and philosophy. The groundwork has thus been laid for a deeper understanding of the issues that arise between Judaism and philosophy. Historically speaking, "Judaism" and "philosophy" appear on the stage with sharply delineated historical identities. Judaism refers to a body of history and literature stretching from Genesis to the Holocaust and Zionism, while philosophy points to Plato and Aristotle, Descartes and Kant, a specific intellectual tradition within Western civilization. The relation between Judaism and philosophy turns then on the contacts between these two traditions. Such contacts have occurred and are usually discussed under the heading of "Jewish philosophy." The names that leap to mind in this connection are well known, Maimonides being the best known among them. When viewed in this light, the conclusion is inescapable that we are dealing with the interaction of two seperate traditions in the history of spirit. Biblical, rabbinic, and medieval Judaism represent cultures quite different from Graeco-Roman culture, which is the intellectual home of the philosophic tradition. Christian civilization is heir to both of these traditions, which together constitute Western Christian civilization. But this is not true of Judaism. While it also came into contact with the Graeco-Roman world in ancient times and with the Christian heir to that civilization after the Christianization of Europe, Judaism never made Graeco-Roman civilization part of its own being. The dialogue with it and therefore with philosophy was always a dialogue with an outsider, with something essentially different from what it was. Jewish philosophers, such as Maimonides, had a dual identity: they were Jews, usually that more than anything else, but they were also philosophers, which was understood as allegiance to

Plato, Aristotle, and, for later Jewish philosophers, Kant, Hegel, and other figures in Western philosophy. The Jewish philosopher had a double identity, which he sought to harmonize, and this attempt at harmonization came to be known as Jewish philosophy. The enterprise of harmonization has a long and honorable tradition among Jews going back at least as far as Philo. But the fact remains that Jewish philosophy was not exclusively or perhaps even essentially an inner Jewish development but a function of the double identity that so many Jews possessed but that never really fused into a single identity. One could usually tell when a Jewish philosopher was speaking as a Jew and when out of gentile sources. And the two were not the same.

It is interesting to compare the situation obtaining in Jewish philosophy with the state of affairs in kabalah, which often appeared as the rival and sometimes almost the antithesis of Jewish philosophy. Kabalah also had its intellectual debts to Neoplatonism and other non-Jewish sources, such as, for example, Gnosticism. Nevertheless, kabalah homogenized these foreign elements much more successfully than Jewish philosophy ever did. In the case of kabalah, foreign influences must be inferred, and while this is not very difficult for anyone conversant with the non-Jewish literature from which kabalah borrowed, it must nevertheless be noted that kabalah took care to obliterate obvious traces of such foreign influence, so that no kabalistic work would dream of quoting or referring to a non-Jewish source. Jewish philosophers, on the other hand, show very little reluctance to refer to and quote from non-Jewish philosophers. Maimonides, as is well known, speaks of Aristotle with the greatest possible deference. The reason for this difference in attitude between Jewish philosophy and kabalah is not very difficult to imagine. Jewish philosophers saw their enterprise as the work of reason. Reason was the common heritage of all men and no monopoly of Jews. The kabalists, on the other hand, understood themselves to be transmitting a secret doctrine revealed by God to Moses. As such, non-Jewish influences could not legitimately have played a role in either the transmission or discovery of the most sacred teachings of the Torah, which were hidden beneath its exoteric exterior. Kabalah therefore had to appear as an exclusively Jewish enterprise free of any foreign admixture. The more open attitude of Jewish philosophy in respect to its intellectual sources is an altogether admirable act of recognition by a culture that was frequently not well disposed to the possibility of foreign influence. It must be understood that such openness to pagan influence comes much more easily to Christianity than to Judaism. While Christianity always viewed itself as heir to the Jewish tradition and to the Hebrew Bible, which became part of the Christian canon, the fact remains that most Christians were former pagans who had converted to Christianity. Pagan culture was therefore part of their tradition and identity, whereas Jews, in spite of Alexandrian Judaism and the person of Philo, saw themselves as engaged in a long-standing battle with the culture of the Graeco-Roman world, which was seen as a threat to Jewish existence. In spite of this, many Jewish philosophers found no difficulty in acknowledging their intellectual obligation to Greek philosophy, an act that played no small role in stimulating the antiphilosophical forces that never disappeared completely within Judaism and were particularly active in the anti-Maimonidean controversy after the death of the most famous of Jewish philosophers.

If by philosophy we therefore mean the tradition that began with the pre-Socratics and continued with Plato and Aristotle, Descartes, Kant, Hegel, and so on, it will simply be necessary to recognize that it is a tradition that will continue to remain foreign to Judaism. That does not mean that Jewish dialogue with philosophy will not continue to prove interesting and helpful both to Judaism and philosophy. But we must reconcile ourselves to dialogue rather than the emergence of a fusion of the two. There is no work of Jewish philosophy in existence, including Maimonides' *Guide for the Perplexed*, in which the duality of Judaism and philosophy is not clear and which is not therefore a work of dialogue in which Judaism and philosophy, each with its own identity and universe of discourse, talk to each other in full consciousness of their difference. This tension is not unique to Judaism; it can be found in many Christian authors. Augustine is a good example because he has his allegiance to Scripture and is also profoundly Platonic. Nevertheless, while it would be false to claim that a perfect fusion is achieved in Augustine, we come much closer to it than in any Jewish philosopher not only because Augustine lacks the inner distance that any Jew experiences toward Greek philosophy as a gentile enterprise but because he thinks of Christianity as a set of beliefs that he is trying to define. The Jewish philosopher, even when he finds it necessary to formulate the beliefs of Judaism, cannot avoid being aware of the relative noncentrality of his enterprise because his basic identity as a Jew is derived from his belonging to a people and his obeying the commands of the Torah rather than from his assent to any creed, even if the formulation of a Jewish creed were possible. Augustine, on the other hand, sees himself as the cutting edge of Christianity, engaged in a philosophic enterprise that is at the very heart of his faith. It is for this reason that theologians play a far more indispensable role in Christianity than they do in Judaism.

Up to this point we have spoken of philosophy and its relation to both Judaism and Christianity, but we have not spoken of theology, the term most commonly used in Christian literature to describe the enterprise of men such as Augustine and Aquinas. If, as we have maintained, philosophy is destined forever to remain outside the bounds of Judaism, is the same true of theology? Can Jewish theology be an integral part of Judaism or is theology an essentially Christian enterprise, just as philosophy was Greek? What are the differences between philosophy and theology and how are they related? Or is the enterprise of thinking about Jewish existence expressed by neither of these terms?

Augustine invokes the word *theology* in Book VIII of the *City of God* after he has dealt with the mythic account of the gods in Graeco-Roman mythology. Having disposed rather easily of the humanly motivated gods as not being worthy of man's worship, Augustine is ready in Book VIII to tackle the philosophers and their views. While these are also far from the truth, it is nevertheless quite clear that Augustine takes them far more seriously than the childish tales he has just disposed of. Still, the views of the philosophers must also be refuted and it is in this connection that he writes: "For I have not in this work undertaken to refute all the vain opinions of the philosophers, but only such as pertain to theology, which Greek word we understand to mean an account or explanation of the divine nature."[9] It is clear that for Augustine theology is that branch of philosophy that is concerned with the nature of God. The term *natural theology* is therefore a redundancy, since all theology is natural in the sense of being a form of natural or rational knowledge. Augustine, in fact, means by the term *natural theology* the views of the philosophers concerning the gods. Earlier he had, quoting Varro, distinguished natural from fabulous and civil theology,[10] with fabulous theology referring to doctrines concerning the gods taught by the poets (who write fables) and civil theology referring to the established religion of the state as taught and administered by the priests. Augustine has outright contempt for fabulous and civil theology but considerable respect for natual theology especially in its Platonic form, to the extent that he expresses the opinion that Plato probably read and profited from the Hebrew Scriptures. Here the foundation is laid for that intimate bond between the Christian faith and Greek philosophy of which we have spoken. It would, of course, be quite untrue to maintain that theology as understood by Augustine was nothing but Platonic philosophy. Augustine has a deep reverence for Scripture and understands the importance of faith. Being a Christian is therefore not identical with being a Platonic philosopher, however close Platonic philosophy is to the Christian faith.

Lest we forget the degree of proximity of Platonism and Christianity in the mind of Augustine, it behooves us to remember that while Augustine rejects the view that Plato met Jeremiah—inasmuch as Plato, as Augustine calculates it, was born about a hundred years after Jeremiah prophesied—he seriously entertains the possibility that Plato somehow read or learned the content of the Hebrew Scriptures. He is led to this speculation by the affinity of the doctrines he finds in these two sources. In spite of this, as was pointed out, it would be a distortion to maintain that for Augustine Christianity and philosophy were one and the same thing. But it would not be a distortion to conclude that whatever differences Augustine saw between the two, he did not sharply delineate philosophy from theology. As a writer whose purpose it was to convince as many as possible of the plausibility of the Christian faith, Augustine is constantly arguing for the truth of his claims on all possible grounds, ranging from religious experience and the logic of the heart to rational demonstrations of all sorts. Convinced of the truth of his beliefs, moving in a world in which philosophic justification is respected and demanded, Augustine is quite willing to pass philosophic muster and to demonstrate the superiority of the Christian faith to pagan philosophy not as antithetical enterprises but as collaborations, with the Christian faith depicted as philosophy perfected, shorn of its irrationalities and idolatries and emerging as the most plausible of all doctrines.

While philosophical Christianity of the Augustinian and Thomistic variety is the dominant strain in the medieval period, it is by no means the only one, and there is always an undercurrent that insists on a far greater separation between philosophy and theology than found in the dominant tradition. This tendency expresses itself in a number of ways, among which we might mention only the "double truth" doctrine, which assigns to philosophy and theology different and sometimes conflicting truths. There is reason to believe that some of those who taught this doctrine were more interested in protecting their nonbelieving philosophical conclusions from theological criticism than in protecting the legitimacy of philosophically unfounded theological conclusions. But this was certainly not true of all the adherents of the double-truth doctrine, many of whom believed in the autonomy of theology from philosophy.

But it is not until the Reformation and the work of Luther and Calvin that the gulf between philosophy and the Bible is perceived. It is important to note immediately that the gulf perceived by the Reformation was between philosophy and the Bible and not between philosophy and theology. In fact, theology achieves its identity separate from philosophy only when the Bible is made the foundation of theology. The difference between philosophy and theology is then seen to revolve around the Bible: philosophy looks to reason for its foundation, whereas theology is rooted in the biblical text, to which alone it is responsible. Defined in these terms, the "–ology" element of theology becomes somewhat problematic, inasmuch as it introduces the Logos orientation, which is foreign to the biblical frame of reference. Disciplines with the "–ology" ending (some, such as physics, lack the ending but are conceptually identical) aim for theoretical elegance complete with rationally certain first principles in the Aristotelian mold. A genuinely biblical orientation is not easily cast into such a framework, with the result that either the word *theology* is dropped or its etymological root is ignored. The thought of the Reformation is theological only if we use that term in a nonphilosophical sense. It is the kind of thinking to which we must now turn.

7. Reformation Thought and Judaism

The major twentieth-century voice of the Reformation is Karl Barth, whose monumental multivolume work is entitled *Church Dogmatics*. It is worthy of note that the term *theology* does not occur in the title of the work. Barth begins his work with the following statement: "As a theological discipline, dogmatics is the scientific test to which the Christian Church puts herself regarding the language about God which is peculiar to her."[11] As that statement stands, it might be thought that for Barth dogmatics is one of the branches of theology. If this were so, one would naturally ask what the branches of theology other than dogmatics were or just how dogmatics were to be defined in relation to theology. A careful reading of Barth makes clear that there is no genus-species relation-ship between theology and dogmatics. Barth seems to use the two interchangeably, except that the word *theology* disappears very quickly and *dogmatics* remains the operating term for the remaining thirteen volumes. While Barth never explains the dropping of the term *theology*, there is reason to believe that he dislikes it because of its philosophic overtones. He therefore substitutes the term *dogmatics*, which has more clearly Christian associations referring generally to the teachings of the Church. To understand dogmatics properly we must therefore understand it in the context of the ex-istence of the Church, of which it is an activity.

For Barth the Church is the community of those elected in grace for testimony to their faith. This testimony takes three forms: the testimony of the life led both by individuals and the community, the testimony of the public worship of the Church, and the testimony of the Church's proclamation. The root of all three forms of testimony is the very concept of testimony itself. Having elected the Church as the people of God, God expects the Church to devote itself to the dissemination of the fundamental message that in Christ man's sins are forgiven and that he is reconciled to God. This dissemination is an act of witnessing the truth. A witness is someone who has a per-sonal experience that he is willing, if not eager, to divulge to others. In the case of the Church, this divulging can be done in a number of ways. It is done first in the life lived. This is perhaps the most fun-damental form of witness, since wisdom has long taught that in determining belief, observing behavior is a more reliable indicator than listening to verbal assertions. Public worship is another form of testimony, since in worship the believing community gathers together to make petition for its needs but, more important, to praise God publicly. There is a problematic element in the testimony aspect of worship in that prayer is addressed to God and yet uttered so as to be overheard by an audience to whom it can be experienced as addressed.

Nevertheless, for Barth, the element of testimony is present in worship. There is finally the proclamation of the faith of the Church, which is dogmatics. Barth insists on speaking of dogmatics as "the scientific test to which the Christian Church puts herself regarding the language about God which is peculiar to her" to distinguish it from simple testimonies of faith (which presumably would not fill fourteen volumes) and in order not to abandon science to its own heathen self-understanding. Dogmatics is thus an act of proclamation by means of which the Church remains faithful to its trust from its founder. Dogmatics is therefore not an intellectual discipline that merely seeks to establish the truth. As a search for truth for its own sake, only a phenomenology of religion or perhaps even of Christianity is possible. Such a phenomenology would take the events and documents of faith as past history but not as living reality. Whether such a detached attitude is best even in the service of objective truth is debatable. In any case, that is not the standpoint of dogmatics, which is rooted in and depends on the existence of the Church. That is the reason that Barth refers to his work as "Church Dogmatics" rather than just "Dogmatics" or even "Christian Dogmatics." The witness to God's reconciliation with man is not dogmatics but the existence of the Church. Even a mute Church could be such a witness as long as it was obedient to the demand for its witnessing in other possible ways. This is not to minimize at all the centrality of dogmatics as the most self-conscious and clearly formulated proclamation of the Church's essence. But Barth's point is that only because there is a Church is such a proclamation possible and that is why dogmatics depends on and is derived from the existence of the Church.

Having established the roots of dogmatics in the existence of the Church, we must focus on the concept of proclamation before we can attempt to raise these questions from a Jewish point of view. In the Protestant context, proclamation is closely related to preaching. The emergence of preaching at the center of Protestant worship is undoubtedly related to the change in the understanding of the Eucharist that came with the Reformation. Before the Reformation, the center of Christian worship was the miraculous transformation by the priest of the wine and the wafer into the blood and body of Christ. The believer thus witnessed not so much a reenactment but rather a reoccurrence of the original sacrifice of Golgotha. The power of this event was such as to take the matter out of the realm of language into that event. Because only a priest could make this miraculous event happen, the Church was more and more identified with the clergy, who were the channel through which redemptive grace flowed to the faithful. While mass could be accompanied by the preaching of a sermon, no such preaching was necessary and was therefore often omitted. The Reformation broke with this interpretation of the priesthood. Neither Luther nor Calvin set out to reinterpret fundamentally the meaning of the mass, but such reinterpretation was probably inevitable once the notion of the priesthood of all believers supplanted the older doctrine of a special priesthood deriving its status from an unbroken line of succession going back to the apostles. The evolution of the understanding of the Eucharist in Protestantism makes a fascinating history, which cannot be repeated here. Suffice it to say that with the decline of the ontological interpretation of the Eucharist, the preaching of the word moves to the forefront as the central act of worship. There is a parallel to this in the history of Judaism at the time of the destruction of the Temple. Prayer develops as a central religious category only after the end of the sacrificial cult. There seems to be a tendency for the word to come to the forefront only when the sacrificial act ceases to be possible. In any case, preaching did become central in Protestantism and this gave birth to Protestant theology, or dogmatics, the term preferred by Barth.

Preaching occurs in church. The setting is important because it gives it its tone, its modulation. Preaching a sermon does not require entering into discussion, listening to objections, and replying to them. The preacher, because he is preaching in a church, more or less presupposes that his listeners are believers. He does not therefore feel bound to start from the standpoint of unbelief and reason his way to belief. Instead, he conceives his task to be the exposition of the faith, and he therefore naturally turns to Scripture as his authority because Scripture is the most authoritative source of the Church's teaching. Once he turns to Scripture, he faces a problem. He cannot simply read a passage from Scripture and let it speak for itself, since this would be a reading and not a sermon. A sermon is an interpretation of Scripture, an attempt to distill from the many voices and occasions that speak in Scripture a teaching that is faithful to Scripture in its totality. Preaching therefore involves balancing various texts against each other, correcting one by the light of the other and vice versa. Preaching is therefore a thinking about and from Scripture in the context of worship. Good preaching reflects something of the prophetic tone, which is authoritative because it delivers a message not of its own making but entrusted to it by him who sends the prophet. It therefore has a theatrical or dramatic quality to it that no philosophic rhetoric has or that only philosophic rhetoric pretending to be prophetic (e.g., Nietzsche in *Thus Spake Zarathustra*) can have. In fact, the characteristics of preaching just enumerated describe the content and style of Barth's *Church Dogmatics*. Barth proclaims the word of God. He does not philosophically reason his way to it. He does not provide a bridge for the reader by means of which he can pass gradually from the world of man to the word of God. Instead, he plunges his reader into the world of faith without defensive introductions, which would necessarily have to begin by taking the standpoint of unbelief seriously and which therefore might end in unbelief. Reading a page of Barth is something like shock therapy because it introduces the reader or the listener to a frame of reference that attempts only to be true to itself and its sources and not to external demands that can be satisfied only by fitting the Church's message into their mold, a mold foreign to it and therefore necessarily distorting. Barth's work is also profoundly biblical in the sense discussed. Barth is listening to all the voices in Scripture and also the voices that speak in the Church postscripturally, and on their basis he attempts to say what he can as a function of what he hears. And in this process something more than scholarship must be at work. Because dogmatics is an activity of the Church and cannot exist independently, there must be at work in dogmatics the divine promise not to abandon the Church but to keep alive the gift of the spirit, without which interpretation is merely the work of man and not of God. Dogmatics is therefore the living self-definition of the Church by means of which and with divine grace it attempts continually to understand its mission and thereby bear testimony to the greater glory of God.

We have referred to Barth not because his understanding of theology (as we have already seen, Barth prefers to speak of *dogmatics*, though we will use *theology* to name the enterprise Barth calls *dogmatics*) is altogether novel but because it is the most elaborate formulation of a concept that, in some aspects, goes back as far as the church fathers and the medieval schools but which emerges most sharply in the Reformation. This new understanding of theology is nonphilosophical and profoundly biblical. It is rooted in the preaching function of the Church, as we have seen in our discussion of Barth. It is an attempt to understand the message of the Bible not with the intention of imposing questions and categories that are foreign to it but from within its own spirit. Because it takes the religious message of the Bible seriously, there is an underlying effort to make the biblical message a living word that can speak to the contemporary listener instead of becoming an object of antiquarian interest. It therefore continues Christian history in the very effort to understand the documents of the past. It is true that some degree of systematization is implied in such an undertaking, but it is not a philosophic but a theological systematization. It is also a rational enterprise because it is an attempt to shed light on the biblical message so as to understand it better, but as long as it is theology it seeks to find a rational structure that is not simply a reproduction of what reason is elsewhere but one that is appropriate to the word of God as a living and unique word that carries its own conditions of possibility with it and is prepared to yield these structures only to those obedient to its demands and not to those whose intellectual formation is derived from other loyalties and goals. Theology, understood in this sense, is prepared to enter into dialogue with philosophy, but not in a spirit of subservience, since it fears only God and never man. And because it fears God, theology must constantly test its formulations against the word of God because it is aware that all of man's handiwork is subject to divine judgment as sinful and disobedient.

We have already seen that philosophy in the sense of the tradition that started with the pre-Socratics, Plato and Aristotle, is a foreign enterprise as far as Israel is concerned. A certain amount of Jewish energy has been expended in bringing these two traditions into dialogue with each other, but no matter how legitimate and helpful that attempt may be, it must remain peripheral to Israel's destiny. Jewish theology must therefore look to its own resources for its impetus or, to put it more accurately, it must look to God for the truth it seeks. But here the problem and the divergence becomes very great. We have already said that Christianity deals with a completed salvation history that is more amenable to understanding because it is there, before us to be viewed and adored. In the Christian incarnation God appeared before man and was seen, not in the mysterious and dark way in which the Hebrew Bible speaks of seeing God, but in a far less dialectical and much more positive sense. The Church is a spiritual community constituted of the fellowship of the faithful who are members of that fellowship by virtue of a faith, an idea the proclamation of which and the witnessing of which is not only the task of the Church but its very being. From its earliest origins, the Church has prided itself on not being a biological but rather a spiritual community. For that reason, in attempting to define its faith in the theological sense, the Church seeks its own definition. It is true that the witness of the Church is also carried out by the lives led, collectively and individually, by its members and by its public worship, in which it thanks and praises God. But though there are these other forms of witness less self-conscious than the way of theology, they live in the light of theology because an idea is at the heart of the Church whether it manifests itself theologically or in service or worship. This is not true of Israel. To put the matter simply, there is more darkness in the existence of Israel than of the Church. This is expressed, and we shall return to this, in the incompleteness of Israel's venture. The redemption awaited by Israel has not yet happened and therefore Jewish existence is in hope rather than in knowledge. The question that therefore now looms before us is the question of knowledge in Judaism. Just what are Jews entitled to know? What do they need to know to perform their mission? Does Israel have a mission of witness and what role does proclamation play in that mission? Finally, how much light does Israel's covenant permit and what is the focus of Jewish reason and what is its nature? In short, what sort of reason, if any, can penetrate Jewish existence as a community obedient to God?

Chapter 3

THE PERSONALITY OF GOD

1. GOD AS PERSON

Again and again, as we think of the relation between Judaism and philosophy, we find ourselves discussing the dialectic of light and darkness. We are in a clearing illuminated by a sharp light, but we are also surrounded by darkness, from which shadows fall over the illuminated landscape. We are driven to equating ourselves with consciousness, whose order—and order is of the essence of consciousness—we call logos. But we also know that we dwell in our bodies, and we awake into consciousness from preconscious existence in darkness. The "I" that I know therefore extends behind itself into a preexistent darkness. Very much the same is true of the future. In respect to it, consciousness projects anticipation. The future dwells in the realm of imagination. In imagination, consciousness is not bound to the opaqueness and weight of the present but is liberated into a realm of light in which there is no constraint. But at the same time, the future is heavily burdened with the darkness of the unknown. Fantasy is free and unburdened, but it is also uncertain and therefore largely vain as an exercise in futility. The real future remains hidden until it is ready to reveal itself as reality.

We now face a decisive question. Is our anthropology of light and darkness a genuine philosophical portrait of the human condition or are we intellectual Marranos, secretly practicing Judaism while pretending to philosophize? Are the human and Jewish conditions fundamentally alike or are we reading the human condition from our Jewish standpoint, while in reality the two are not at all identical? In a formal sense, of course, Jewish existence is a subclass of human existence and everything that is true of the latter should also be true of the former. But such logical sequences are not always dependable guides in the realm of facticity. Jewish light may not be the same as general light and Jewish darkness may be different from other darkness. Is there something that can be called a Jewish logos, a Jewish understanding of rationality that would determine the kind of light shed by it? This question was touched on earlier when we spoke of the prominence of reason in the biblical world and the tradition of rabbinic thought, with its deductions and analogies, reflecting the conviction that the Torah has now been given to man for exegesis and elaboration. This is an unusual development because encounter with the holy usually shakes man's foundation and threatens his self-confidence. What accounts for the self-confidence of rabbinic thinking?

Jewish existence is existence before the living God. More accurately stated, it is existence before the Thou of the God of Israel. Reason, as usually understood, pertains to the realm of the I-It. The unpredictability of the genuinely I-Thou is evidence that the usual structures of reason are transcended in the I-Thou. The very act of thinking, the *Denken* of Heidegger,[1] presupposes an attitude of calm reflection most plausible after the event, when we can sit back in tranquility and think about it. In the directness of the encounter with the person who addresses me and calls for a response, thinking has no place. But if the withdrawal in thought is not possible when addressed by a human Thou, how much more impossible is it before the divine Thou? Jewish existence is lived before this Thou and yet there remains the foundation of the power of man to attempt what Buber considers impossible, the viewing of God as an It.

Is the God whom Israel meets totally immune to becoming an It? Buber's error is that he sees God as the eternal Thou who can never become an It, while every other Thou is condemned to a perpetual swinging from Thou to It. For Buber, this is the divinity of God, that he cannot be reduced to the level of an object, as can every other person. Buber breaks decisively with the God of the philosophers and affirms the living God of the Bible. Yet, without realizing it, Buber remains tied to the Jewish philosophic tradition, with its stress on the immateriality and unity of God, unity interpreted metaphysically so as to remove effectively the living God from the realm of human conception. This raising of God to lofty heights is accomplished by the philosophers with metaphysical stratagems culminating in the *via negativa* of Maimonides. Buber sees the pitfalls of this process and therefore clings to the God of dialogue. Nevertheless, the fatal elevation of God to ineffective heights is not completely avoided. The Thou who cannot become It, whose subjectivity is so powerful that we cannot make a thing of him, is another inconceivable God. Does God have all the power and man none? If man's power in the final analysis is the power to reduce subjectivity to thinghood, and if man totally lacks this power with respect to God, then man is not created in the image of God. In creating man, God does not destroy himself, but neither does he remain unaffected: God is now addressed by man and influenced by this address. The question of the personhood of God now requires our attention.

We cannot overlook a basic contradiction. The God of the Bible is a person. He is one of the characters who appears in the stories told in the Bible. He has a personality that undergoes development in the course of the story. He creates man with certain expectations, which are apparently disappointed, and he is then sorry that he has created him. He is subject to the emotions of anger and jealousy, among others. He is also filled with burning love, particularly toward Abraham and his descendants. He desires certain things and detests others. He is faithful in the sense of keeping his promises, even when for long periods of time it seems that he has forgotten them and has no intention of keeping them. Those who trust in him are not disappointed, especially if they are patient. At this stage, our purpose is not to draw any sort of character portrait of God but to point out that there is a personality in the Bible who is God and who interacts with the other characters in the biblical narrative.

Against this simple fact, Jewish philosophy has marshaled all of its resources. The personality of God had to be demythologized. How could God have human failings such as emotions and how could his actions have unexpected results? If God could not foresee the consequences of his actions, then he is not omniscient and a perfect God must be omniscient. The attribution of emotions to God was particularly unacceptable to Maimonides, who was firmly convinced that even properly rational men were ruled exclusively by reason rather than emotion. What was true of philosophers could hardly not be true of God. The biblical portrait of God had to be reinterpreted. The simple, human words the Bible attributed to God were to be understood in a sense different from common understanding. Perhaps it was appropriate for common people to take the Bible "literally," but it was not appropriate for intellectuals, who had to be taught, if they could not figure it out for themselves, that the truth about God was far removed from the simple picture that the common people were offered. Maimonides' full energy is expended on this enterprise of demythologization, of showing that the words of the Bible do not mean what they seem to be saying but something quite different. Maimonides perfects this deliteralization of the Bible, but he is not, of course, the first to make the attempt: Philo preceded him by many centuries. And gradually the philosophic God comes to permeate Jewish consciousness. The real God whom Adam feared and loved fades, to be replaced by a philosophical principle. The real estrangement between God and man has begun.

To some degree, the estrangement had already begun in the rabbinic mind. The focus of that mind is the Torah, the teaching that is God's gift to Israel, so that study of it constitutes man's clinging to God. It cannot be maintained that the rabbinic enterprise constitutes a demythologization of the encounter with the biblical God. There are too many rabbinic texts in which God thinks and hopes, plans and fails, and sometimes succeeds, in which his emotions influence his conduct. The rabbis were not philosophers and were not particularly upset by the anthropomorphism of the Bible. But they lived in a time of the silence of God. The prophetic "Thus sayeth the Lord" was no longer being heard. The divine teaching had ceased to habitually shatter human expectations and began to congeal gradually into a body of law that could be codified. Codification, as in the Mishnah, is the opposite of narration. Instead of the world of story, we are in the domain of the legal, where systematic relations become dominant. It is true that the first rabbinic codification, the Mishnah, does not reach the level of abstraction later found in Maimonides' Code. Compared to the Code of Maimonides, the Mishnah is a collection of cases often lacking conceptual clarification. But the difference is one of degree rather than principle. The development of the narrative midrashim proves this, if proof is necessary. The very fact that agadic literature tends to separate itself from the halachic indicates a modification of consciousness. Such separation is less prominent in the Bible than in rabbinic thought. Perhaps because of this separation, the agadic realm begins to lose its solidity. An atmosphere of proliferation develops, so that conflicting versions of the same events are permitted to stand alongside each other in an uncharacteristic spirit of toleration. It is true that in halachic literature divergent opinions are also recorded. But there is usually some indication of which view is to be considered normative. This is not so in the agadic realm, where the imagination is given free reign and we have the characteristic agadic exaggerations (*guzmot*), which stand in startling contrast with halachic sobriety. When narration is separated from law, the domain of imagination is born because seriousness is reserved for the halachic realm. At this stage there is no focus on the problem of anthropomorphism because the development in progress is not philosophic. But it prepares the ground for philosophic demythologization by creating the category of the legal detached from its narrative setting. Such a conception of law is an ideal medium of transition to the philosophic standpoint because it substitutes what is inherently systematic and abstract for the existentially particular and concrete of historical happening.

The rabbinic frame of reference is, of course, more than merely a transition from the biblical to the philosophic. It did not understand itself as such because it could not foresee Maimonides, who brought to fruition the marriage between philosophy and law. The fact remains that when the philosophic critique of anthopomorphism comes into its own, the reality of God recedes. It is to this problem that we must now turn.

2. GOD AS THOU

Buber's great contribution to the religious thinking of the twentieth century was the rediscovery of the I-Thou focus of the Hebrew Bible. From Buber's point of view, it would be misleading to speak of God as a person because the very concept of personhood is an I-It category, derived from an external classification of things, some of which appear as things and others as persons. The term *person* is not used in direct address; to address someone as "You there, person" is to court laughter. The crux of the matter, though Buber never puts it in those terms, is that the I-Thou attitude is not one of thought. Analysis comes after the lived moment, not during it. The I-Thou is never fitted into a broader framework; if it is, it is or has become I-It. In the reality of the I-Thou there is only the Thou who stands over against me and who addresses me, and whatever else there is exists only in the light of the primary Thou. It therefore follows that the living God is met only in prayer. All thinking about God is therefore doomed to failure. It is for this reason that a writer such as

Augustine begins in the mode of exposition and soon finds himself addressing God in prayer. But this does not come very easily. One is embarrassed to speak to a person who, after all, is not there in any obvious sense. Buber, therefore, did not write prayers but a book about the I-Thou relationship, which, according to its own categories, must be an I-It undertaking.

This did not hinder Buber from realizing the reality of the I-Thou encounter. The I-Thou became a reality for him in the human context. Those who met with Buber knew that they had his undivided attention, not as a result of an act of will on Buber's part, but because he was listening to the person who was speaking to him. Buber always insisted that the divine Thou was not another Thou alongside the human Thous of our lives but was the lines extended, the Thou lurking behind and through the human Thous we meet every day. By saying this, Buber did not mean to exclude talk to God directly; he only meant to exclude the withdrawal from total human commitment, considered essential by some religious traditions. Still, when it came to God, there are no prayers that Buber left behind, at least not in writing. One can, of course, only speculate about the reasons for this. Buber was estranged from the Jewish community of worship. Speaking to God remained difficult, perhaps easier to talk about than to do. And this also left its imprint on his thought.

The word *you* is the most concrete of all because it is addressed to the particular individual who stands before me.[2] Were I to characterize this individual in any other way, as a man or a woman, a tailor or a cobbler, I would be applying categories not unique to the particular person. But while the word *you* is indeed the most concrete of all, it is also the most universal precisely because it can be applied to any subject whatsoever, and this is not true of *tailor* and *cobbler*. There exist therefore a class of concrete terms or concepts that are simultaneously profoundly universal and abstract. This is true of Buber's I-Thou relationship. There is no abstract "I-Thou" that we can discuss. Every I-Thou is different. Every I-Thou must be different because otherwise it would cease to be an I-Thou. It should not and is not possible to compare one I-Thou with another because they cannot be fitted into a framework without instantly losing their I-Thou character. But if each I-Thou is different, the viability of the whole category is put in question because a category refers to a common element that unites diverse instances. The logos of the I-Thou is here at war with its content which cannot be captured by any concept. To take the concept of I-Thou seriously is therefore to transcend it in the spirit of Wittgenstein,[3] who proclaimed his teaching a ladder that must be discarded once it has served its purpose. But, in this case, what is left after the ladder is discarded? We can only conclude that the very act of formulating a domain of the I-Thou and contrasting it with that of the I-It is possible only from an I-It standpoint. The real I-Thou resists classification.

The difficulty with Buber is greater still. Even if we were to ignore the problem just posed and accept the I-Thou relationship as a valid discovery (which, to a degree, it of course is), we would still be forgetting that God is not just a Thou among others. Buber knows this of course, and he therefore devotes the third part of *I and Thou* to a discussion of the "eternal Thou," his expression for God. There are two basic differences that distinguish the eternal Thou from all others. First, "extended, the lines of relationship intersect in the eternal Thou." And second, the eternal Thou can never become an It. These two basic points need investigation.

"Through every single You," writes Buber, "the basic word addresses the eternal You. The mediatorship of the You of all beings accounts for the fullness of our relationships to them—and for the lack of fulfillment. The innate You is actualized each time without ever being perfected. It attains perfection solely in the immediate relationship to the You that in accordance with its nature cannot become an It."[4] There is therefore a very great degree of interdependence between man's I-Thou relationships with his fellow human beings and his I-Thou relationship with God. At the very least, it would be safe to assert that no human I-Thou relationship is just a human relationship. Wherever I-Thou happens, in some sense God is present. The divine presence in all genuine I-Thou relationships is one-half of the picture. The other half consists of Buber's belief that not only is God present in all human I-Thou relationships, but that no I-Thou relationship with God is possible independently of, or to the exclusion of, such relationships with human beings. Buber is particularly eager to reject Kierkegaard's claim that an absolute relationship with God rules out all essential relationships with human beings. For Buber, to reject the claim made on me by a fellow human being is to reject the possibility of relationship with God. It must be pointed out that the divine intrusion into human relations is not mirrored in the realm of human relations. There, it would seem, only one I-Thou relationship is possible at a time. In the I-Thou relationship the Thou fills all space and all attention must be concentrated on him; a third person can appear only on the periphery of the original relationship. But in the case of God it is different. He, as it were, lurks behind the human Thou who is encountered. If "extended, the lines of relationships intersect in the eternal You," then human relationships point beyond themselves to some presence behind the human Thou. And while the relationship with the eternal Thou is different from that with a human Thou, it must also be deeply continuous because the human relationship points to, or is fulfilled in, the absolute relationship. It might be asked whether this third presence in the human encounter would not constitute an intrusion or even a destruction of the human I-Thou relationship. Buber seems not to be disturbed by this possibility.

The second important difference between the human and divine I-Thou relationship is the impossibility of the I-Thou relationship with God turning into an I-It relationship.

> By its very nature the eternal You cannot become an It; because by its very nature it cannot be placed within measure and limit, not even within the measure of the immeasurable and the limit of the unlimited; because by its very nature it cannot be grasped as a sum of qualities, not even as an infinite sum of qualities that have been raised to transcendence; because it is not to be found either in or outside the world; because it cannot be experienced; because it cannot be thought; because we transgress against it, against that which has being, if we say: "I believe that he is" — even "he" is still a metaphor, while "you" is not.[5]

Here, in spite of all the differences, the philosophic tradition reasserts itself in Buber. God is beyond human conception. God cannot be grasped by anything available to man and no subterfuge is possible by grasping him as that which cannot be grasped. We cannot fail to detect the basic Maimonidean argument that insists that there are no predicates that apply to God because terms such as *just, good,* and *merciful* derive their meaning from the human context and the sense in which God is just, good, and merciful cannot in any way resemble the human understanding of those terms. The concept of God in Maimonides becomes rather indefinite. Motivated by the desire to protect God's divinity and the desire to shield him from human contamination, God is raised to such high conceptual levels that he drifts off into the philosophic stratosphere, leaving the human world

free to conduct its affairs without the need to reckon with any particular notion of God. This is the orientation that comes to the surface in Buber's removal of God from the world of It.

We must now connect the two respects in which human I-Thou
relationships differ from the I-Thou relationship with God. The difference, as we have discovered, is twofold: human I-Thou relationships point to God ("extended, the lines of relationships intersect in
the eternal You") and the eternal Thou never becomes an It. Viewed
from one aspect, the two differences are antithetical. The insistence
that the eternal Thou can never become an It removes God from the
human world because in the human world every Thou becomes an
It only to become a Thou again. The human standpoint is one of tension between the Thou and It and it is precisely because a Thou can
and does turn into an It that the moments of Thou are precious, as
they are not destined to last. The Thou that is immune to this dialectic cannot easily become a Thou that appears in the human world.
At the same time, Buber returns the eternal Thou to the human
world by integrating the I-Thou with God with the I-Thou with man
to the point that the two almost become one. Are all deep human
relationships really relationships with God? Is it possible to flee the
world of human relationships for the absolute relationship with the
eternal Thou?

And if this is impossible—and Buber seems to think so—why is it
impossible? Is it because God forbids abandonment of one's fellow
man for his sake? Does he then refuse to enter into relationship with
one who has so abandoned his fellow man? Or, as seems more likely, is it impossible to live with God without living with man because
all or part of God is in man and to abandon man is therefore to abandon God? These are some of the questions that come to mind, and
they remain unanswered. We can be certain only of a double movement in Buber's thought: as God is lifted into the remoteness of the
Thou who never becomes It, he also returns in the immediacy of
human relationship, which is haunted by the divine presence. The
concreteness of the relationship with God turns out to be the concreteness of human relationship, whereas what is most characteristic
of the relationship with God, that he can never become an It, recedes
from the concrete into an almost fictitious I-Thou possibility unlike
any other known to human existence. And because the I-Thou with
God is so different, so free of psychological ambiguities and tensions, it may not be an I-Thou at all.

Here we come to the heart of the matter. Buber's eternal Thou in *I and Thou*, he whom he calls God (and he hesitates before using the term because it is more concrete than an "eternal Thou," more laden with historical associations because it is the word men utter in their extreme situations), is not the God of Abraham, Isaac, and Jacob. It is the Thou men have addressed at diverse times and in many languages under many different circumstances. It is the universal aspect of "You" that Hegel discusses. We address one man as you and then another and in some abstract sense there emerges the category of the Thou, which merges them all in a great, universal You beyond this or that individual. But is it not the Thou in the most important sense that we have then lost? When I address my friend as You, it is he who I am talking to, with his face and intonation, his gait and opinions. It is so ultimately specific that his name rather than the Thou is required. The name specifies his particularity. That there are others with the same name does not alter anything because the others are not called by that name because of any universal trait that they all have in common. That is what distinguishes proper names from nouns: all cobblers and barbers share the word because they share some characteristics, while all the Jacobs of the world share only the name. The God of Israel is not just a Thou. *The God of Israel has a proper name.* There is no fact in Jewish theology more significant than this. And the tradition always understood the significance of this fact and so surrounded this name with endless mystery, so that it became an ineffable name because it celebrated the most terrible of all recognitions, the personality of God. To stand before God is to stand before him who is God and not another. This is what we must now comprehend.

3. Personhood and Emanation

To believe in God is to have a psychological relationship with God. A psychological relationship is more than a Buberian I-Thou relationship. It includes the It. The I-Thou characterizes the relationship at certain moments, not necessarily at very infrequent intervals. But a psychological relationship also includes "thinking about" the other. It includes some negative feelings: anger, jealousy, fear, envy, etc. As we open ourselves to others, they gain power over us, and this is never without pain and therefore hostility. To live with another is to become vulnerable to him and therefore to want to protect oneself. To have a psychological relationship with someone involves getting to know his orientation, what he strives for, what matters to him and what does not. But this cannot happen without the prominent presence of the I-It component. There is thus an immense absence of real writing about God in Judaism. This is not true of the Bible and not completely true of rabbinic literature because midrashic writing has many genuinely theological passages if by theology we mean the taking seriously of the reality of God as a person. But, as we have already pointed out, the process of the depersonalization of God begins in rabbinic Judaism by the separation of halachic and agadic materials and the dehistoricization of Judaism. And it is, of course, completed in philosophical Judaism of the Maimonidean variety. It is only in kabalistic literature that the personalistic and even physical description of God is kept alive. The kabalistic tradition, from our point of view, is a fascinating mixture of the most valid and the most problematic. An analysis of this mixture will shed light on our problem.

We must now embark on a slight terminological innovation. Henceforth we shall not speak of "God" but of "Hashem." The term *Hashem* means "The Name" and has long been used by Jews to refer to God by reference to the ineffable name of God, whose pronunciation is both unknown and forbidden. The term *God* is a neutral one. It is used by many religions to refer to the being or object worshiped and thus presupposes a class of Gods, as in the biblical exclamation "Who among the gods is like you, Hashem?"[6] The term *God* therefore has a built-in tendency toward the abstract because it focuses on the characteristics gods have in common rather than on the uniqueness of the God of Israel. To speak of Hashem is to speak of the one who is related to the people of Israel. The term carries within it an overwhelming intimacy because it is a secondary displacement of the ineffable name, which is first circumvented by *Adonoy* ("Master") and then by *Hashem*, since the first circumvention is still too holy for indiscriminate usage. In *Hashem* the Jewish people speaks easily about and to God, free of legal inhibition and the absolute deference that is the beginning of the expulsion of God from human reality. At times, nevertheless, we will speak of God when we wish to emphasize the more abstract aspect of Hashem. But the reality of God in the life of the Jewish people is Hashem.

We are now ready to return to the problematic of the kabalistic view of Hashem. Our attention is attracted by three features of the

kabalistic way of thinking: its air of mystery and secrecy, its
Neoplatonic emanationism, and its concrete, at times even material,
depiction of Hashem. These three features curiously reinforce and
contradict each other and thus reflect the totality of the problematic
that surrounds Israel's approach to Hashem.

No encounter with Hashem is possible without mystery. This is
the counterweight to Israel's intimacy with Hashem, rooted in
Israel's fear of God. But fear is only one component of mystery. It
is an important component. Without fear no relationship with
Hashem is possible. Fear is not only the inevitable consequence of
the recognition of Hashem's power. It is vital to distinguish between
the fear that is native to man when he finds himself surrounded by
the dark nature that imperils him and Jewish fear. Israel's fear is not
derived from its preexistence in nature. That fear can continue to exist not as a component of Israel's relationship with Hashem but only
to the extent that the covenant with Abraham has not taken root, has
not been heard. Once the election in Abraham has happened,
another fear appears. It is the fear of Hashem's striking out to punish
the people of election. Now this is not unique to Israel's relationship
with Hashem. Many people fear their gods. But the difference may
be this: that the fear of other people is limited by the overarching All
from which their gods have emerged and that therefore controls,
even if only very ultimately, the overwhelming power of those gods.
Those gods can therefore be guilty of excess, for which they must
pay. But the origin of the God of Israel is never discussed. He does
not emerge out of a primordial chaos, and to fear him is therefore
to face an unrestrained being over whom being itself exercises no
control. Elsewhere, the concept of being unites man with God and
ordains, in the deepest sense, a common fate for man and God. So
fear must not be dismissed, but it is not the only element in the
mystery.

The other element is the personhood of God. Kabalah is aware of
this personhood. But it is also afraid of it, and out of this emerge
both the emanation system built around the *sefiroth*, on the one
hand, and the materialistic descriptions of God on the other. The
emanation concept is, of course, a Neoplatonic one. For the
Neoplatonists, there is an Absolute that is altogether beyond con-
ceiving. This Absolute (the "Good" of Plotinus) is totally self-
contained and beyond the possibility of activity. Hence the problem
of the existence of the world arises: How could the world have come

into being, since it could not have been created by the Absolute, as creation is an activity and the Absolute, being self-contained, does not act? From the metaphysical point of view an even deeper problem arises. The being of the Absolute is an absolute being without limit. But if there were anything other than the Absolute, then the being of the Absolute would not be unlimited, since it would be limited by the being of the other, which it would not be. It would then seem to follow that nothing could be other than the Absolute. In its most rigorous form, this reasoning leads to a total denial of the reality of the visible world, a conclusion not unknown in Eastern thought but not fully acceptable to most Western metaphysics.

Western strategy revolves around the notion of emanation. The world is not a creation of the Absolute to which no activity can be ascribed but rather an emanation from the Absolute. Emanation is to be understood as an overflow. The fullness of the Absolute is so great that it overflows, and the trickling down of this overflow is the creation of the world. Two aspects of the concept of overflow or emanation must be understood if the proposed solution is to be grasped. An overflow is not an action. It is not a goal-directed undertaking, as creation is. God as creator must have had a purpose and if he had a purpose he was incomplete and therefore not perfect. But an overflow as a spontaneous discarding of unneeded excess does not constitute purposive action and therefore is compatible with a notion of the Absolute. But what is even more important is that such a discarding of excess does not diminish the Absolute. From its point of view, nothing has been lost and therefore nothing exists but itself. This, of course, is the Neoplatonic solution to the problem of how there can be anything beside the Absolute, whose being is absolute being. The Neoplatonic answer is that, in fact, and from the point of view of the Absolute, there is nothing other than itself. The world exists only from its point of view but is nonexistent from the point of view of the Absolute. The world is the refuse of the Absolute. It is as if a wealthy man discarded something that had no value to him but that constituted a treasure for the pauper who found it.

It is quite clear that this is the perfect antithesis of Hashem, who creates man, elects Abraham, and redeems the people of Israel from the land of Egypt. And yet this emanation theology is prominent in kabalistic thought. It is a fleeing from the directness of the God of Israel. It was otherwise for the Neoplatonists, who did not have to contend with the biblical God. But the kabalists were deeply pious

Jews whose world was that of the rabbis and the Bible. They were heirs to the rabbinic turning away from the directness of Hashem, which became the halachah, the vast system of exposition of the will of God in which the presence of God recedes as the system takes on a life of its own. The emanation system must therefore be understood as a function of the fear of God and his absence. It becomes acceptable to Jewish religious consciousness because it pretends to serve the cause of raising God to greater heights, of magnifying his name. We must praise God only as he wishes to be praised, no more and no less. If Hashem does not find his dignity impaired by being known as the creator of the world, the elector of Abraham, and the redeemer of Abraham's seed from the land of Egypt, then it is not the task of man to protect Hashem's dignity more than he wishes it protected. We must learn from the word of God which attributions constitute the proper praise of God and which do not. To heap the praise of the philosophers on God is to create a God in the image of man, be it in the image of philosophic man.

Deep down, the kabalah understood this. It could therefore not rest content with a system of emanation. The immediacy and personality of Hashem had to reassert itself because the kabalists were Jews who were intimate with Hashem, the God of their fathers. There therefore develops the physicalization of God that is strange to the modern mind and whose coexistence with emanation metaphysics is difficult to grasp. It is, in fact, an overcompensation. What emanation metaphysics has made so remote must now be brought very close indeed. The measurement of God's limbs becomes possible as a kind of reverse plunge into the concreteness of Hashem. We find the materialization of Hashem strange. It violates the axiom of Jewish philosophy that Hashem is, above all, nonmaterial. We are also repelled by the inevitable I-It character of such materiality, particularly of the irrelevancy of measurement of God's body. In some sense those who spoke in these terms meant what they said symbolically rather than literally. But it would be a grave mistake to radically demythologize such texts. Whatever symbolic meanings they were intended to have, we must not ignore the incarnation by means of which the symbolic meanings are transmitted. Such material kabalism is a particularly concrete form of I-It talk of Hashem, and it coexists with the highly metaphysical construction of emanation theology.[7]

4. THE BODY

But now we note something very curious. When we begin to think about the measurement of Hashem's limbs, a shudder of mystery comes over the Jew. It is sacrilegious. It is terrifying. That Spirit can be in body, particularly absolute Spirit, is terrifying. This is the terror of the dead body as such. Here is a person we have known. He talked and walked, moved his hands and feet. He was a person. And now he is dead. His corpse lies before us. There are many persons nowadays who have never actually seen or been with the corpse of a person they have known. It is clear that this is an experience we naturally flee. Judaism forbids the displaying of the corpse. Where it is not forbidden and where the corpse is shown, great efforts are made to deprive the corpse of its corpsehood, of the particular appearance of the dead. By means of skillful intervention, the corpse is given the appearance of a living person asleep. Thereby we can satisfy our desire to gaze at the dead, a desire that coexists with the simultaneous urge to flee from its presence, to avert our gaze from it. What is occurring in this attraction-repulsion dialectic? And how does it relate to man's relationship with God and the Jew's relationship with Hashem?

The corpse is naked. It is naked even when it is clothed. The corpse lies revealed before us. It cannot protect itself. The mobility of the other's living body limits our power over it. It can escape us. And even when it does not escape us, it exercises a countervailing pressure to ours. The subjectivity of the living person is contained in his gestures and in the expressions of his face, in the way he carries his body. Even in sleep, there is an activity that is being engaged in, sleeping. The sleeper is doing something, he is sleeping. And therefore mobility does not completely cease in sleeping as the sleeper breathes and his chest goes up and down and can be heard faintly as he tosses and turns in his sleep and is thereby confirmed as a living person. Sleeping is therefore one of the projects of the human condition. But death is not. The corpse is immobile. The eyes of the dead are perhaps the most terrifying of all because the eyes are the organs by means of which man thrusts himself ahead. In the corpse the eyes gaze into the distance as if without limit because there is no longer a need to limit the horizon to what is within the range of the rest of the body. The gaze of the dead is therefore fearfully empty, an impotent thrust into the beyond that returns into itself and only emphasizes the deadness of the corpse. We are therefore driven to closing the eyes of the dead, thereby confirming their death; otherwise the dead impotently protest their death. Death is thus a termination of subjectivity, and for this reason the corpse, to most people, is no longer sexually attractive. Sexuality is the dialectic between the hidden and the revealed, the revelation of a subjectivity that remains hidden in its revelation. But the dead no longer hide anything, and the corporeality of their bodies is therefore radically different from the corporeality of living persons. Were the two corporealities totally different, there would of course be no continuity and the corpse would then not be a corpse. But because corporeality is spatiotemporal continuity and because the face particularly is recognizable, the corpse does not cease being the person we have known in life.

We are both attracted and repelled by it simultaneously. It is the person we have known and loved. We want to see what happens to man in death because death is an irruption of the sacred into life. Even in the most secularized of environments, the dead are considered holy. They are treated with deference and circumspection. They are approached with awe, and an attitude of the ceremonial is naturally assumed. The attraction-repulsion dialectic is itself unmistakably reminiscent of the attitude to the holy, which is loved and feared simultaneously. The dead are the last vestiges of the holy because they are the incontrovertible witnesses of the vulnerability of man. If secularity is a function of man having come of age, then death reminds him that coming of age is a prelude to the return to helplessness that waits at the end. But there is no secularization that expels the religious from death. However successful secularization may be in regard to birth, marriage, or any number of other life situations, death eludes its grasp. The mausoleum in which Lenin is displayed has the atmosphere of a secular cathedral, an exercise in pseudoholiness. In the midst of the most consistently organized atheism the world has ever known, the holy appears in the corpse of a dead revolutionary leader. He was not always dead. And only because he was once alive is he now dead. Death does not apply to the inorganic, to that which never lived. Death is the immobility of the living, who retain a certain life in death. In Jewish practice, the corpse must be prepared for burial by being cleaned and washed. After they have finished their work, those who have performed it turn to the corpse and address it, asking it to forgive any acts of disrespect they may have shown it during the preparation. The subjectivity of the dead is thus not totally overlooked because the absent life is still mirrored in the shape of the body, a shape that transcends itself toward its activities and projects. Death is transcendence terminated, the longing to rise and the inability to do so.

Kabalistic thinking does not hesitate to examine Hashem, be it in terms of emanation, *tsimtsum*, or the measurement of Hashem's limbs. We have already spoken of the question that arises from the Absolute: How can anything else be if the Absolute is. Does not the Absolute fill all possibility of being, so that nothing else but it can be? Neoplatonism's answer to this, as we have pointed out, is emanation as a process of overflow, which, in effect, means that from the point of view of the Absolute there really is nothing other than itself. While in many respects the kabalah accepts emanation thinking, it introduces an interesting modification in the concept of *tsimtsum*. Originally, the being of Hashem fills all metaphysical space, so that nothing else but Hashem can be. But Hashem then withdraws (*tsimtsum* means "withdrawal" or "contraction") in order to leave an area relatively free of being so that creation can take place. The act of creation is still to be understood as emanation, but the point is that this must be preceded by a withdrawal so as to create the space into which the overflow is possible. That the kabalists found it necessary to make this modification in their Neoplatonism is, of course, interesting. It is difficult to resist the conclusion that *tsimtsum* Judaizes the emanation of Neoplatonism. Whereas in classical Neoplatonism the process of emanation is unknown to the Absolute and is therefore in no sense an undertaking on the part of the Absolute, Judaism cannot absorb such an impersonal process at the core of its faith. Before emanation takes place, there must be a prior divine movement to make possible the subsequent process, and this prior movement is purposive. Now we must remember that purposive action itself is contrary to the nature of the Absolute as understood by Neoplatonism. But here we are dealing not just with any purposive action but an action of contraction or limitation. To the Neoplatonist, any action, metaphysically speaking, is a limitation of the Absolute because action implies lack of completion and the desire for the attainment of a goal and therefore greater completion. But kabalah makes explicit what needed only to be implicit. It makes explicit an act of self-limitation, if not humiliation, on the part of Hashem. In order to make possible the creation of man and the world, Hashem abdicates his absoluteness so that something other than he can become.

So, against its will, and against its better judgment, the kabalah deals with, or at least leaves a place for, the personality of Hashem.

It is terribly frightened of this thought, and it therefore speaks of emanation and the measurement of Hashem's limbs, which is terrible enough but which, because of its self-evident implausibility, will be interpreted symbolically; yet, no matter how symbolically interpreted, this will leave a residue of horror in the Jewish mind. But we cannot play such games. For better or worse, we are modern men, heirs of the Enlightenment, refusing to leave in darkness anything on which light can be shed. We come up against the realization that God has a personality, is a person, has emotions and plans, makes calculations that sometimes succeed and sometimes fail. And if he has a personality, then this personality also has weaknesses, insecurities, neuroses. Traditionally, such thoughts have not been allowed to come to the surface. The time will come later to modify everything we say here, to emphasize that Hashem is, after all, the Absolute and therefore nothing we say of him can be interpreted literally. But for a while we must put the corrective moves out of our minds because they have been made so often and have ceased being the corrective and have become the original thesis rather than a necessary corrective to the biblical account of the personality of God. Who, then, is this God whom we meet in the Bible? What are his characteristics? What is his project? What is his psychological profile?

What does he look like? This is a peculiar and even impudent question, given the strength of the conviction in later Judaism that Hashem has no body. But this thesis is hardly crystal clear in the Bible. The Bible does not, of course, specifically say that Hashem has a body, but then again neither does it say that he does not. There is very little description of physical appearance in the Bible in general. We know nothing of the physical appearance of any of the biblical personalities except in those cases where some specific physical characteristic is germane to the incidents recounted, as, for example, the tallness of Saul. Epic literatures are primarily narrative rather than descriptive. They are intent on telling a story and waste no time, as do modern novelists, on elaborate descriptions of the physical appearance of the characters or the decor of the environment. Such description is a function of the conscious writing of fiction, in which details are invented by the author, who is not transmitting a received tradition but exercising the power of creative imagination. Classical literature transmits stories that have impressed themselves on the memory of a people and that therefore restrict themselves to the essentials required to tell the story in ques-

tion. Description of physical appearance is therefore extremely un-
common in the Bible and because this is so it is difficult to interpret
the absence of descriptions of the physical appearance of Hashem as
a calculated omission explainable by the biblical conviction that
Hashem cannot be described because he has no body. The fact is, of
course, that there are references to Hashem's front, which Moses did
not see, and his back, which he did. We are told, furthermore, that
no man can see God and live. Such statements are not to be read as
affirmations of the noncorporeality of Hashem. They intend to assert
the royalty of Hashem, that he is an exalted king on whom no com-
moner, in this case created man, may gaze. The frightened com-
moner who longs for a glimpse of his monarch might steal such a
glimpse of his back, since he thereby sees the king but is not forced
to come face to face with him, an encounter that is far too threatening. As citizens of the twentieth century, we live in a world of
republics and figurehead monarchs without power. But in the past,
kings were perceived as divine persons or, at least, as divinely ap-
pointed rulers from whom there emanated the majesty that is the
essence of royalty. The Bible is not reluctant to speak of God as
descending and walking in the garden, activities commonly associated with physical beings.

5. SOME TRAITS OF GOD

So we cannot inquire into the physical appearance of Hashem;
but we must not be misled by this into accepting as biblical the
dogma of the noncorporeality of Hashem. Without rushing to the
opposite conclusion and inferring that the Bible does attribute corporeality to Hashem, we note, somewhat more cautiously, that
Hashem is located in certain places at certain times and that men
meet him in these places when Hashem so desires. Hashem cannot
be seen,[8] not so much because he is not visible as because he is too
holy and therefore it is too dangerous to see him. But above all, he
is presence in the highest possible degree. His is total presence
because it produces total attention. It simply cannot be ignored. It is
not a nonspatial presence. Just as man is a dweller in a space and
his personality lives in a location, so there are locations in which
Hashem dwells. There are two aspects to the location of Hashem.
There is first his particular domain, which is his domicile: heaven
(shomayim). There he dwells surrounded by the heavenly hosts,

whose task is to minister to him. From time to time he leaves this abode and descends to the earth, where he appears at certain places at certain times. When he leaves his heavenly place of dwelling he descends to the earth. His place of dwelling is above the earth, high in heaven. Hashem is never beneath, in the earth below. He does not dwell below but above man. It takes little philosophic learning to insist on the demythologization of these expressions. Rudolf Bultmann had sound, gentile instincts when he found it necessary to erase the three-tiered universe of the Bible, the heaven above, the earth, and the *sheol* ("netherworld") below. Such localization must be prevented if the Bible is to be interpreted as mainly a document about the human condition and the problem of being. But the truth is that human nearness to God must be spatial because man is a spatial being. His greatest suffering is to be separated from those he loves. Even though man's thought can bridge continents and centuries, spatial separation from those he loves is a human misfortune. If it is man as man who is to have a relation to Hashem, if man is not to cease being man in spite of this relation, then Hashem must be able to enter space and to be near man wherever he is. And not only near man but in man, or more specifically, in the people of Israel.

Our purpose is to focus on the personality of Hashem, on the reality of his being as a person of whom a psychological portrait can be drawn. And yet we find ourselves drawn into a discussion of the people of Israel. This is a very significant fact. No portrait of Hashem is possible without his relationship to the Jewish people. The Bible never depicts Hashem alone, as he was before the creation of the world. One of the most significant facts about the biblical account of creation is that it is totally silent about the origin of Hashem and about his acts before he decided to create the world. The Bible does not even say that Hashem always was, that there never was a time when he was not. It does not deny this, of course, but it does not affirm it either because it refuses to deal with Hashem prior to the beginning of his creation. The Hashem we know is the Hashem connected with the history of this, our world. In that sense, we can say that Hashem is Hashem-of-this-world. And to say that Hashem is Hashem-of-this-world is to say that he is Hashem-of-Israel because, for the Bible, the human drama of this world centers about the drama of Israel. In a sense, everything in the Bible until the appearance of Abraham is prelude. With the appearance of Abraham, the focus remains on him and his descendants. Hashem's relation to man now flows through his relation to Israel, and his relation to Israel is in the service of his relation to humanity.

Hashem appears in the world as the God of Israel. There is no other way for man to refer to him, to particularize him, to distinguish him from other gods, except by calling him the God of Israel, a concept we express by the term *Hashem*. Hashem has chosen to dwell with this people. He dwelled with them in the Tabernacle before the Temple in Jerusalem was built and he chose the Temple in Jerusalem as his dwelling place after the Temple was built in Jerusalem. This is, of course, something of a paradox. We must remember that the gods of the ancient Near East were territorial gods. Their jurisdiction extended to a specific territory and ended at the boundaries of that territory. Hashem, from the first, had no territorial limitations. The people of Israel were under his rule wherever they were, and it is for this reason that they could not worship the gods of other people when they found themselves in the territories over which these other gods had jurisdiction. For the average non-Jew, to continue worshiping a god after one had left his territory would be as strange as it would be for a modern man to insist that the jurisdiction of one state extended beyond its borders into another state. The universality of Hashem, at least in terms of his jurisdiction, was therefore always well established. And from the idea of the universality of jurisdiction the notion that no space could contain him can be seen to follow. And yet the Temple in Jerusalem was his dwelling place, so that Solomon, in his famous prayer of dedication at the consecration of the Temple,[9] refers to this paradox when he points out that this house will be the dwelling place of Hashem even though heaven and the heaven of heavens cannot contain Hashem. And still, this Temple, the one he had built—his father could not build it because he had been a warrior—was the dwelling place of Hashem in the world, the place to which Jew and gentile could come when either wished to speak to Hashem. Hashem is therefore the God who dwells in Jerusalem on the Temple Mount.

But we cannot stop here. The Temple in Jerusalem is the dwelling place of Hashem and before that it was the Tabernacle, which the people of Israel carried with them. But Hashem was the God of Israel before either a Tabernacle or a Temple existed. The people of Israel becomes a people before it has a land, a location. Abraham is sent out from his place of birth and told to go to a place that God will show him,[10] not a specified place but an unspecified, indefinite one. While this people has a land because Hashem ultimately gives it a land and dwells in it, its peoplehood is not coextensive with the land, as is the peoplehood of others, who cannot survive as a people once they are separated from their land. It seems that the people of Israel is ruled by a God whose jurisdiction is not limited to any particular space, and therefore it is a people that is near Hashem wherever it is. This was the insight of this people after the destruction of the Temple when the Day of Atonement came and there was no sacrificial order for the forgiveness of sin, as there had been for so long. Then Rabbi Akiba could comfort Israel by pointing out that Israel is blessed because it is purified by its father in heaven.[11] Hashem is with Israel wherever it is because Hashem has taken up residence among this people and therefore in this people. The Jewish people is the dwelling place of Hashem. It is the people among whom he lives. The dividing line between *among* and *in* becomes very shadowy here. Hashem lives among and in the Jewish people, both individually and collectively. Perhaps in the first instance this is so collectively. Wherever three Jews gather the *shechina* ("divine presence") is present. It is the national or collective existence of the Jewish people that is the dwelling place of Hashem. There is no relation possible for gentiles with Hashem except in the context of their relation with the Jewish people. Conversely, every relation of gentiles with the people of Israel is a relation with the God of Israel, whether so understood or not. The pervasive hatred that has been directed at the Jewish people ever since it came into being is therefore first and foremost a hatred of Hashem, who is represented by the Jewish people and who can be gotten at only through the Jewish people.

But though our concern at this stage is with Hashem and not the Jewish people, we find ourselves drawn into a discussion of the Jewish people because of the immensely strong bond between Hashem and this people. With the exception of the events before Abraham and incidents such as the mission of Jonah, who is directed to predict the destruction of a non-Jewish city if it does not repent, almost all of Hashem's involvement with man is through involvement with Israel. This does not mean that Hashem is interested only in Israel. The very fact that the Bible does not begin with Abraham but rather with the creation and Adam, signifies the broader human significance of the story. The prophetic picture of the end of days envisages a reconciliation among the peoples of the world, so that the redemption of Israel is also the redemption of humanity. The election of Israel and the biblical focus on the history of Israel are therefore, in a sense, the means chosen by Hashem for the redemption of humanity. Nevertheless, the working involvement of Hashem is with the people of Israel. The others, for the time being, are in the background. Their presence makes itself felt and is never totally missing. But the people of Israel is in the foreground. It is the object of God's love. It is the people whose unfaithfulness hurts Hashem. It is the people who, when they sin, are the object of his powerful wrath, a wrath that, however, is as temporary as it is powerful. Such wrath is followed by a resurgence of the original love, perhaps intensified by the temporary interruption. In this, Hashem shows a vulnerability that is most significant. His anger is a function of that vulnerability. Such anger is known in human psychology only in the relationship of the rejected suitor or, perhaps to a degree, in the relationship between parent and child when the parent feels himself rejected by his child. And it is found in Hashem's relation with Israel.

6. PSYCHOLOGICAL DYNAMICS

We must now ask some psychological questions. What are the dynamics of Hashem's relation with man? Are they the same dynamics as those behind his relation with Israel? What are Hashem's needs? What is the nature of his love for man? Just how does his jealousy work? What is the effect of man's emotion on Hashem? What is the significance of the pattern of estrangement and reconciliation that we find in the Bible? Does Hashem have any insecurities and vulnerabilities that would help us understand the psychological quality of the relation? Such questions will sound strange to those accustomed to the usual respectful discussion about Hashem that passes for theology in both Jewish and Christian circles. But if we are to talk about the real God of Israel who has revealed himself in the Bible, then we must take seriously what we find in that book, and we find in it a passionate and concerned God who is a real rather than imaginary person and who stands in personal relation with many human beings.

Hashem is first the creator. He creates the world and everything in it, including man, and then he rests. He then places man in the Garden of Eden, which seems to have been designed in every way as the proper and satisfactory setting for man, in which all his needs are met. Man is given dominion over creation, he assigns names to the animals and thus imposes the logos of man on Hashem's creation with the approval and at the command of Hashem. But at the same time a potentially serious challenge is introduced. He is permitted to eat of all the trees in the garden except one that Hashem explicitly forbids. It is clear that we have here the potential for drama. Will man eat of the single forbidden tree or won't he and if he will, what will the consequences of doing so be? All eyes are now riveted on the tree and the first man and woman circling around it, filled with temptation and curiosity and desiring to taste the forbidden fruit in preference to the others, which are not forbidden.

But why is this prohibition introduced? Why create man, place him in an environment ideally suited to his needs, give him dominion over creation, and then forbid the fruit of one tree, the eating of which would give man knowledge of good and evil? We cannot avoid probing into what is not said but implied, into the psychological dynamics of the relationship.

Why did Hashem create the world? The Bible does not say but one point is clear: the creation of the world is but the prelude to the creation of man. Creation culminates in the creation of man and we hear very little about creation after the creation of man on the sixth day. The purpose of the creation as a whole is the appearance of man. But what, then, is the purpose of the creation of man? We are not told, but we must learn to read between the lines. In creating man, Hashem brings into being a creature rather similar to himself. We are informed of this similarity when we are told that man was created in the image of God, a statement that clearly establishes the resemblance. Man is given dominion over creation; he becomes the lord of the earth as Hashem is the lord of creation. Man is Hashem's representative on earth. Hashem's intention seems to have been to create a being not identical with himself but similar to him. When we are told of Hashem's conclusion that it is not good for man to be alone and of the resultant creation of woman, we cannot but wonder whether there was not a similar dissatisfaction with being alone that caused Hashem to create man who would become his companion. Such a partner, to be worthy of being Hashem's partner, would have to possess some marks of divinity, and this is precisely what we find to be the case. At the same time, another motif becomes inevitable. If this creature is to be worthy of dialogue with Hashem by possessing God-like qualities, is there not a danger that he will forget his creatureliness, his dependence on Hashem, his inferiority to him,

and begin to act as if he were his equal, if not his superior? The prohibition not to eat of the tree of the knowledge of good and evil is
thus the visible sign of the creatureliness of man, who is set into a
world over which he has dominion but a dominion that is limited by
the creator, who retains the right to forbid man to exercise unlimited
authority over Hashem's creation. The "thou shalt not" of the commandment limits the God-like dominion that is otherwise granted
man, especially because the prohibition is specifically said to prevent
man's becoming like God in knowing good from evil. The rest of the
story is, of course, well known. Man does not willingly accept the
limitation placed on him. He eats the fruit of the forbidden tree, he
builds the Tower of Babel and he asserts his sovereignty against the
divine prohibition. He does not succeed; in fact, he fails and suffers
greatly for his disobedience. But acceptance of his dependence on
Hashem and of the obedience that should follow from that dependence does not come easily to man. He is ever eager to test his
strength and his freedom against Hashem's authority.

What is Hashem's reaction to man's stubbornness? Does he play
the role of the wise parent whose desire is that his child grow up and
stand on his own feet? He does not. He insists that man obey him,
that he remember the limits of his strength in comparison with
Hashem's unlimited strength. He does not take kindly to man's
rebellion. He demands obedience and when it is not forthcoming, he
does not hesitate to punish man so as to impress upon him the needed lesson. There is a struggle for power here between two rather
tenacious partners. Man's setbacks are many because the power that
faces him is overwhelming. Yet he never seems to learn this lesson
permanently and no matter how often his rebellion proves futile, he
seems to remain unconvinced of the inevitability of his defeat and
therefore tries again at the next opportunity with some hope of
greater success. But what of Hashem? He is, of course, invulnerable.
However complicated the situation becomes, he remains in control
with the outcome never in doubt. That, at least, is the predominant
biblical line. But here and there we catch glimpses of something different. Perhaps it is the force of the divine anger that makes us
suspect vulnerability. Perhaps it is the depth of the divine hurt when
it is abandoned by Israel that makes us wonder what it is that Israel
has that Hashem needs and the withholding of which matters so
greatly to him. Man before Abraham and Israel after Abraham seem
to have some power that, at least to some extent, is a threat to
Hashem. His plans do not always work out as he expected. He learns

from his experiences and sometimes, in retrospect, he is sorry for what he did, from which we can infer that had he known the outcome of his actions, he would not have done what he did. Against the dominant motif of the Bible, which shows Hashem always in perfect control with the outcome never in doubt, there emerges a less prominent, but by all means noticeable, theme of a God embarked on an adventure whose outcome is not altogether certain because there are developments that Hashem cannot fully foresee or control. Man is thus not simply a puppet in the hands of Hashem. He is a participant in the relationship who makes his own decisions, which can interfere with Hashem's plans.

If man is not simply a puppet in the hands of Hashem, then a number of possible conclusions follow. How are we to understand this power of man? Does he possess it because Hashem gave it to him or does he somehow derive it from the strength of his being, so that, once created, he could not have failed to have this power? Is man's power to frustrate Hashem an ultimate power or is it temporary, with Hashem remaining in full control of the situation, so that the outcome is never really in doubt? But if that is so, is not Hashem playing a cat-and-mouse game, giving man the illusion of options without, however, any reality behind the illusions? Can the opposite be true, that man and Hashem are more evenly matched than would appear and that the outcome is therefore far more in doubt than has traditionally been thought? This set of questions is not independent of the earlier questions as to why Hashem created man. If we ever come to understand Hashem's purpose in creating man we might learn more about the nature of the relationship between the Creator and his creatures. But how are we to go about answering these questions? We must look at the biblical text as the basic source of the answer. We must look at rabbinic texts for their understanding of the situation. And we must think about it ourselves in the light of our reading of the texts, our experience of life, and our relationship (if any) with Hashem. It will not suffice to draw up a register of relevant texts and thereby define the options to be found in the tradition. Surely these texts must be in the back of our minds as we think about the questions. But not all truth that can be found is truth that has been found. The living God of Israel is not a God who acted in the past and then retired on his laurels. He exists and lives today and deals with Jewish destiny and Jewish religious sensibilities in the light of the recent past and the demands of the present. It was a philosopher who said that the only events we will ever observe happening are those events we antecedently consider possible. Similarly, we will find in the texts only those insights that are spiritually possible for us to hear. We cannot, therefore, avoid approaching this problem from out of our experience and sensibilities.

7. GOD AND MAN

We approach the problem from the point of view of the master-slave dialectic of Hegel.[12] Hashem is the master and man is the slave. The master rules the slave and the slave obeys the master. There is a relationship based on superiority and inferiority, of command and obedience. The dependence is one-sided: the slave depends on the master but the master does not depend on the slave. But truth is not static. It is complex because it is alive rather than dead. Truth generates developments out of itself, and developments are the domain of the story. We start with the master, who is not dependent on the slave, and the slave, who is dependent on the master, but we soon discover that the master is no master without a slave and thereby the independence of the master gradually takes on an aspect of dependence. But there is more to it than that. It is not only that the master needs the slave if he is to remain a master. We must also realize that the kind of master he is also depends on the kind of slave he has. A slave without subjectivity turns his master into a master over nothing. If he is to be a true master he must be a master over subjectivity, freedom, resistance, independence, all those characteristics a slave is not supposed to possess. But to possess a slave who is all slave is to possess no slave at all because the exercise of mastery is real only if it is exercised over a freedom that is enslaved. The need of the master is therefore for an enslaved freedom. He must therefore posit both the slavery and the freedom of the slave in virtue of whose being he is a master. Hashem therefore requires the freedom of man. A being for whom rebellion is not possible is not a slave worthy of Hashem. Hashem's sovereignty is over man and not only over beast, and Hashem must therefore have a free man over whom he is to rule. Man's rebellion must therefore, in some sense, be encouraged by Hashem even if only ambivalently. This is perhaps one reason that behind Hashem's anger lurks his love. It is almost as if, having become angry, he is overtaken by a guilt for having set up the situation that makes man's rebellion inevitable. How else can we explain Hashem's constant swinging from anger to love that the Bible describes? Hashem's forgiveness of the sins of his people bespeaks a secret admiration of the determination of this people to assert its humanity in the light of the intensity of its relationship with Hashem.

In stressing Hashem's desire that man and Israel be free, that their obedience be the result of a choice rather than an automatic effect of the divine command as its cause, we are not saying anything that is particularly original. The tradition has long emphasized that Hashem desires man's freedom because without it there is no virtue and therefore no merit in man's obedience. Only if man can disobey is obedience meritorious. But we are saying more than that. We are saying that man's freedom and the ability to disobey or to ignore the divine command that is thereby implied is not only a prerequisite for the merit of man, as if it were only man's well-being that were at stake here. It is Hashem's lordship that is at stake. Man's freedom is required if Hashem's lordship is to be exercised over a being whose enslavement makes Hashem a master over someone worthy of being enslaved, someone who has a will but whose will is made to yield to Hashem's will. But why does Hashem need a slave? Why must there be a will that is made to yield to Hashem's will? Why must Hashem be a master?

We cannot answer this question. We can only speculate. The striving after mastery is inherent in consciousness, we are told by Sartre.[13] Because consciousness is intentional, because it transcends the being of the one who is conscious, it fixates on that which it knows and immobilizes or objectifies it. When it is another consciousness that comes under the attention of consciousness (and only another consciousness is really worthy of the attention of consciousness), then a struggle is inevitable, which can only end by the objectification of one consciousness by the other. If God existed, says Sartre, man could not bear not being God. What he means is that if God existed, if there were a superconsciousness of the magnitude of the divine, then no other consciousness would have a chance against him and therefore all men would be destroyed because there would be no possibility of combat. But it is here that Sartre misunderstands the situation. The possibility for combat exists. The battle is not, of course, exactly equal. The divine consciousness that faces man is superior and even overwhelming. But it is a consciousness that needs its victory and therefore needs the possibility of combat. It is therefore prepared to yield enough so as to make the combat real and the victory meaningful but not enough to make victory doubtful. But this is a very difficult balance to strike. And it is not even certain that the balance must be left to Hashem to strike, because if it is, then the resulting combat is staged and therefore unreal. The logic of the situation pushes toward a true encounter between the divine consciousness and that of man, and that is, after all, the biblical record.

But the divine consciousness is not just another consciousness. Most readers of the Bible have been so paralyzed by the concept of God that they could not read the Bible with the realization that Hashem is a biblical character whose motivations and actions require analysis, as do those of other biblical characters. But Hashem faces problems that no other character does. What are some of these problems?

Above all, he is desperately alone. We have already noticed that Hashem creates man with a resemblance to himself that makes man a kind of God of the created regions. The possibility arises that Hashem wishes to create another God, equal to himself, because what other kind of creature can end Hashem's loneliness? But this cannot be. Is it because it is not possible (logically? ontologically?) for Hashem to create an equal to himself or is it that such a creation would be too dangerous, genuinely threatening Hashem's supremacy? In any case, it will not be. He whom Hashem has created is limited. He is to eat of all the trees in the garden, except of one, the tree of the knowledge of good and evil, from which he may not eat. His limitation is thereby doubly confirmed. He lacks knowledge of something that clearly is vital and he labors under a prohibition, a challenge to his freedom, a confirmation of his slavery. The creature thus brought into being is no equal to Hashem. And as soon as this is determined, Hashem declares that it is not good for man to be alone and he therefore creates for him a helpmate to become his companion. But why this juxtaposition? Why does the thought that man needs a helpmate occur to Hashem immediately after he has imposed the prohibition on man that seals his finitude and inequality with Hashem? The answer that suggests itself is that by determining the finitude and limitation of man, Hashem seals his own loneliness. If man, in spite of his resemblance to Hashem, is going to be a finite creature, then the loneliness of Hashem has really not been ended because there has not come into being a partner worthy of Hashem. And as this becomes clear to Hashem he thinks of the loneliness of man, who, like Hashem, has no partner. But the loneliness of man can be corrected, and so Hashem creates Eve, man's helpmate. As the loneliness of man comes to an end the loneliness of Hashem is confirmed both because the contrast between the curable loneliness of man and the incurable loneliness of Hashem is made sharper and, more significantly, because man's relation to Hashem is altered by his relation to a fellow human being.

That man would not be a proper companion for Hashem could have been foreseen from the outset. Nevertheless, as long as it was Hashem and man, there was some sort of companionship. While we must not forget the creatureliness of man, his finitude and limitation, we must also remember his divine image, which makes him a replica of Hashem and less than divine only in comparison with Hashem himself. Hashem and man were therefore destined as partners, the attention of each focused on the other in a life of true relation. Had there been Hashem and only one man, the two would have turned toward each other by necessity, in the absence of an alternative. But now the creation of Eve intervenes. Man has a fellow human being with whom he stands in a relation of equality. She is, of course, not identical with man. She is a woman, while he is a man, and this difference adds a particularly powerful dimension to their relationship. Hashem creates the sexual difference in the knowledge that he will be excluded from it. He observes human companionship, from which he is excluded. There is nothing that children find more painful than isolation from other children, having to live with adults and missing the companionship of other children. And when such a child is finally brought together with another child, the two run off in glee to play, to share their common childish natures. Must not something similar have occurred when man, whose previous companion had been Hashem, finds himself in the presence of a fellow human being? They are both finite and are in the same predicament. Death awaits them and therefore their choices have meaning because there are only so many choices that can be made, so many possibilities that can be explored. Their lives are therefore a shaping of something definite that will not go on forever and in which doors are forever closing, leaving unfulfilled possibilities. Human existence is an existence of farewells, a leaving behind of times, places, and meetings that will never happen again. And, above all, human existence is coexistence, a dwelling with another exposed to the nonbeing of absence and yet taking comfort in the presence of the other, equally exposed but yet together. From this existence Hashem was to be excluded because he does not need the protection of shelter and he therefore cannot—unless he joins man—experience human vulnerability.

Man therefore lives in two relations: his relation with man and with Hashem. Buber speaks of a continuity. If "extended, the lines of relationships intersect in the eternal You."[14] But do they? Do not men huddle with each other to escape God? Children are not happy when they are called from play, from communion with their fellow children. Hashem is forever calling man away from his companions. Is it not this that he demanded of Abraham, to leave the human beings with whom he had grown up and whom he knew and to go off to strange places where his only companion would be Hashem? Human dwellings, as they cluster in a valley or on the side of a mountain, nurture man. He takes satisfaction in his place, whose familiarity protects him from the terrors of nature. Is there not a choice to be made here? Must he not choose between an essential relation with man or an absolute relation with Hashem, which, in turn, necessarily excludes essential human relations? Kierkegaard knew this and made his choice, knowing fully what he was rejecting. Buber rejected this. For him, there is no such choice to be made. To reach God, he tells us, we must be present to our fellow man. Judaism has not approved of withdrawal, of the life of hermits and monastic isolation. Yet, when Moses was to be taught the Torah, he left the community to ascend the mountain to be alone with Hashem. It is true that he then returned, to share what he had learned with the people of Hashem. Nevertheless, the rabbis claim, only the first word of the Ten Commandments was heard by the whole people. The rest was uttered by Hashem to Moses on the top of Mount Sinai when the two were alone. The question then is the aloneness of man before the aloneness of Hashem.

For Kierkegaard, only the single one stands before Hashem. In the crowd, the word of Hashem cannot be heard. We become human as we learn to be alone. And when we are alone we find ourselves in the presence of he who is also alone, forever, permanently. It is as if he refused to meet man unless man learned to share his destiny of aloneness. In meeting Hashem, aloneness meets aloneness because the two partners are so mismatched that, in a sense, each remains alone. Is Hashem's aloneness ended by the presence of man? Can man understand what it means to be God? And can God understand what it means to be man? Kierkegaard used the parable of the king who falls in love with a simple girl. His problem is how he can reveal himself to her without overwhelming her with the grandeur of his majesty. The king loves a simple girl, and if she were transformed into a princess, she would no longer be the girl with whom the king fell in love. Similarly, Hashem must protect the humanity of man so that his partner is truly man and the relation is not of Hashem with himself.

We already referred to Sartre and his remark that if there were a God, he could not bear not being God. By saying this, Sartre expresses in his abrasive way the human longing for divinity, which is rooted in dissatisfaction with the limitations of the human condition. We shall return to the human longing to be God. But what of the divine longing to be man? There is, of course, a difference between a longing to become human and a longing to associate with human beings. Christianity speaks of the incarnation, of the God who became man. Judaism does not know such an event, but it certainly does know a God who seeks association with man. And we are therefore forced to ask, as we have been asking, why Hashem wants to associate with man. We have suggested loneliness as part of the answer. But we must now note a circularity in our argument. Loneliness is a human trait. The God who is lonely is already a God who has human traits. We could argue that in order to associate with men Hashem must take on human traits and he does so in order to associate with them. But why does he wish to associate with them? If it is because he is lonely, then he has human traits prior to his decisions to turn to man. Are the human traits that Hashem displays in the Bible therefore simply the face that Hashem shows man or are they true traits of his being in terms of which we can explain his turn to man? At this point in our discussion we cannot adopt the former alternative. Were we to do that, the rest of our discussion would not be serious. If the personality of Hashem is simply some sort of disguise, or face that Hashem puts on for the sake of man, then the Hashem to which man speaks is not the real God of his life. Perhaps later there will be reason to speak of the God behind God and to struggle with the problems that such a position raises. But here we cannot draw that distinction. We either stand in relation to Hashem or we do not. If we do stand in such a relation—and it is the basic message of the Bible that we do—then it is Hashem that we stand in relation with and not a mask that he turns toward us but that is not really he. He is not a total enigma to us because he created us in his image and we therefore have a basis for understanding and communication.

8. A PARTNER IN THE HUMAN ENCOUNTER

We can now return to our line of thought. It is loneliness that causes Hashem to create man. And having created him, Hashem finds something attractive about man, something that he perhaps misses in his divine being. We have already spoken of man's social nature, of his ability to share his being with his fellow man and therefore not to be alone. The finite meets the finite and human relation is established. From one point of view, the mutual finitude of men who meet makes coexistence in fellowship possible, something not possible in the relation of Hashem to man. But finitude is also corrosive of the encounter between man and man. Given the human situation, human meeting is surrounded by blackness, by death. For some hours during the night the lovers cling to each other, temporarily hiding from themselves the fate that awaits each one. But sooner or later the blind universe will erase traces of meaning. It will be absorbed into the eternal silence of a mindless universe that ultimately triumphs over all human meaning. How many loves (of lovers, of parents for children, of friends) have there been that are no longer remembered by anyone, swallowed without trace by death? If Hashem is inclined to envy the human situation because man can find a friend like himself, he need only remember the other aspect of the human situation. If man's meeting with his fellow man is not to be rendered meaningless, if a mindless universe is not to engulf and extinguish the meaning that man finds in his existence with other human beings, then there must be a divine presence in the meeting between man and man. It is that divine presence that gives human love its dimension of eternity. Lovers could not love if they did not have an ally against death, if the only certainty were the grave and silence. There are those who can love (and not all can) because the clinging of the lovers to each other takes place in a protected dwelling shielded from the onslaught of nonbeing. But how is such protection possible? Does the protection consist of a forgetting, a shutting out of the truth for the immediate moment, or is there more reality to the sense of protection? This is the question that grows out of human love.

This is the route by means of which Hashem becomes a partner in the human encounter. He enters it as its metaphysical protection against the inevitability of dissolution. He makes it possible because without his silent presence the power of destruction is simply too great. Once the magnitude of the power of destruction is understood, the destruction becomes self-destruction because, as the ultimate power, the power of destruction must be worshiped, and it can only be worshiped by a demonic *imitatio dei*, a participation in and identification with the power of destruction. In the better case this turns against the self and becomes self-destruction. In the worse case, it turns against the fellow man and becomes the murder camp of the Third Reich or the Soviet labor camp, in which both the other and the self are destroyed. In either case, the hopelessness of the human encounter as it faces death and nonbeing is exposed. And if it is not to be doomed to failure, if suicide or murder are not to be the inevitable consequences, then a protective presence that is more than human must be felt. This protection does not destroy nonbeing and does not eliminate the finitude of man. The God who enters the human relationship as a partner is a God who shares the human situation. To some extent he is also exposed to the power of nonbeing. He, too, has his disappointments. We are here talking of Hashem and not the Aristotelian Unmoved Mover. But we are still talking of Hashem, who is not man. He sanctions the being of man. Without his stamp, man would be of no value, as would the rest of creation. The image of God bestowed on man, carved into his features, introduces importance into his fate. It is identical with the image of man in animals. The suffering of animals is important because they are created in the image of man. The destruction of a rock or a piece of metal is merely an event in the universe without much meaning as such. But the death of an animal is an event of an altogether different magnitude. And this is so not only because animals suffer while rocks do not. The death of an animal without suffering is only a little less sad than with suffering. The fact is that animals resemble men and are therefore seen as quasi-human. This is particularly true of children, who tend to humanize animals to an even greater extent and for whom the suffering or death of an animal is often particularly painful.

Just as the animal derives the significance of his fate from his resemblance to man, so man derives his from his resemblance to Hashem. It is important not to spiritualize this excessively. Usually we are told that this refers to man's mind, the power of his reason. It does not, of course, exclude these faculties. But the word *tselem* is a rather visual one. It is related to the concept of shadow, a naturally occurring drawing of physical likeness. The dignity that is bestowed on man by the divine image does not cease with death, which would be the case if only the spirit of man had the divine stamp. Instead, a corpse remains holy or perhaps becomes more holy than ever. With life gone out of the human body, the divine image becomes startlingly sharper because it is no longer mediated by the invisibility of thought and speech. In death, the illusion of spiritual eternity is shattered, and yet the image of Hashem does not flee but remains sharply impressed in the human body. There is something horrible about the stamp of death inflicted on the divine image. And yet Hashem is present even in the human corpse.

Hashem is therefore present in all human encounter. Without his presence, love and compassion are not possible. Without his presence, human encounter would be driven to despair and murder. Without his presence, the other who faces me would have no significance. And if my fellow man had no significance, I would have none either. Nevertheless, the divine presence in human encounter is not without difficulties. Is the other human being not enough to arouse my concern and love? Is it the God in him that I love but not him? Is it permissible for me to extend the lines (in Buber's sense) behind my fellow man to reach the eternal Thou behind him? Do I not thereby make the human being invisible and force him to function as a conduit to Hashem? If we are not careful in our formulations we will find that all real relationship is with Hashem because relations with human beings turn out to be really relations with Hashem. This is the power of Kierkegaard's insight. His test case was Abraham's relation with Isaac. Abraham's willingness to carry out the dreadful command proves that his relation with his son is decidedly secondary to his relation with Hashem. Any man who has a relation with Hashem, we are told by this episode, is a potential murderer, ready at any moment to strike out against the human being he most loves when so commanded. Hashem's presence in human encounter is therefore profoundly ambivalent and ambiguous. On the one hand, without his protection, as we have seen, man is totally exposed to the meaninglessness of a nihilating universe indifferent to, and therefore destructive of, human significance. But when Hashem enters into man's relation with man, a certain displacement takes place. While man is sheltered, he is also in danger of losing his humanity and his ability to be related to his fellow men. He is overwhelmed by a partner who must become the center of human attention instead of his fellow man. And yet, man seeks the company of his fellow human being. Men look at each other and sense an understanding that is possible only among those who share the human fate of mortality and finitude. Hashem stands outside of this circle, yet without him the human circle is not possible.

The relation between man and Hashem is therefore ambivalent on both sides. From man's point of view, his need for Hashem is clear. He is weak and finite, threatened from all sides. Not being the ground of his own being, he is grateful to the source of his being and protection. But he is also resentful of his limitations. He is angry with himself for being dependent and therefore angry with the benefactor on whom he is dependent. He cherishes his humanity, which is both his sorrow and his pride. We must not think that his humanity is nothing but powerlessness. It surely is that, especially in relation to Hashem. But human being is also power and independence. This power is played out against a backdrop of inevitable death and defeat, but it is nevertheless power, perhaps greater for the setting in which it appears. A Mozart quartet or a Platonic dialogue represent the human condition. They represent triumphs against nonbeing and meaninglessness. They are not permanent triumphs. We cannot listen to the quartet or read the dialogue without remembering that those who created them have ceased to be. On the one hand, they live in their work. But, after all, this is only a figure of speech, a consolation to us who are still alive and cannot endure their nonbeing because it is also our nonbeing. We are therefore frightened both by the power of man and his powerlessness, each of which sharpens the grandeur of the other. If man cherishes his humanity and wishes to protect it against divine appropriation, it is in the light of the human situation that this wish must be understood. Usually, man's rebellion against Hashem is attributed to an illusion of power. The story of the Tower of Babel is paradigmatic here. To build a tower to reach to heaven is to be intoxicated with the potential of man, to forget the limits of human power. While there is an element of intoxication in human rebellion, we must not overlook the tragic element of the rebellion. Surely man knows, and the men of Babel must have known, that their efforts were doomed to failure. But man persists nevertheless. He hurls himself against his divine adversary in defiance. He will be defeated, but Hashem cannot rob man of his freedom to attempt to overthrow the presence he both loves and hates.

And how about Hashem's ambivalence toward man? His is also a love-hate relationship. Perhaps the hate is easier to understand. In a sense, the hate is the very affirmation of human being. In love, the one who is loved is drawn toward and into the being of the one who loves. In hate, the other is repelled from the self of the one who hates. But man can only be if he is not drawn into the being of Hashem. The natural tendency is for the divine being to absorb all other being. But if man is to be, then this must be resisted. A distance must be created between Hashem and man, and this distance must be nourished by a force of repulsion, which is perhaps the divine hate. And once man's identity is secured by the created distance, the divine nature of attraction reasserts itself except that it is now directed to the other than Hashem. The loneliness of Hashem has been ameliorated but so has his total hegemony. There is now a partner whose response Hashem seeks but of which he cannot be certain. He begins to understand the human predicament and its uncertainties. Suddenly, Hashem can be rejected. And the feeling of rejection comes to play a central role in the relation between Hashem and man. (Israel represents humanity in the dialogue with Hashem.) It is curious to note that the feeling of rejection, the emotion of the husband whose wife has been unfaithful, is an emotion frequently ascribed to Hashem in the Bible and rarely if ever to man. Man, after all, also at times experiences himself as forsaken by Hashem. Yet man does not develop the language of jealousy in his reaction. Hashem's feeling apparently is that man is capable of many loves and can therefore be diverted from the love of Hashem by the pursuit of other loves. But Hashem does not have that option. His relation is either with man or with no one. The divine jealousy is based on the recognition that man has many possible partners and, as we have already pointed out, is naturally drawn into the human circle and its rewards rather than into the encounter with Hashem. On the human level, the theme of jealousy is heard not from man toward Hashem but rather between man and man, particularly from the gentiles toward Israel. The special favor shown by Hashem toward Israel by its election is resented by the nations in the spirit of sibling rivalry. The resulting anger is directed primarily at Israel, but there is also an anger at Hashem that is perhaps somewhat below the surface but not absent.

And in spite of all this, but only after we have realized all this, there is Hashem's infinite, eternal, and absolute love for Israel. This is the central theme of the Bible. Nothing else ultimately matters. Everything else must be seen in its light. Only because it is true is everything else true. Only because of this love is there his anger. Hashem's humiliation at being rejected by Israel presupposes this love and cannot be understood without it. It is, of course, easy to be free of jealousy if one does not love. By being jealous, Hashem reveals his passion for Israel and his dependence on this people. But what is the quality of this love? Is it to be understood in human terms? Is it one of the loves of Plato's *Symposium* and how does it relate to the erotic? These are the questions to which we must now turn.

9. LOVE

There are few topics in the history of human sensibility that have received as much attention as love. In its various forms, it permeates human art. But this itself is misleading. It is easy to forget that love is intentional, that it necessarily has an object. One cannot love love itself. One loves a person, an object, an activity, or whatnot, but one does not love love itself. And therefore even to speak of love itself is strange because when we do, we tend to forget the object that is loved, since that varies from case to case and we focus on the love itself as if it could be understood apart from that which is loved. And when it is considered apart from that which is loved, it is self-love rather than love that is under discussion. The question that arises then is whether self-love is one of the forms of love. This is a question that must be answered with care. Ontologically, there is reason to promulgate a law of the self-preservation of being. This is perhaps most dramatically visible in the phenomenon of life, where we find the universal tendency of the organism to organize itself toward survival to be a rather acceptable definition of life itself. But the tendency to want to be, to persevere, to avoid the cessation of being is not restricted to living organisms. It seems to be the very nature of whatever is, such as solid matter, which obstructs penetration in varying degrees. It is less obvious with the liquid and gaseous forms of matter, which yield more readily. But in yielding, they do not cease to be. Their ability to yield more readily than matter in its solid state can indeed be interpreted as a more effective defense of its being against the forces of destruction. The matter that yields now lives to fight another day, while solid matter either succeeds in resisting or is broken. Because the human mind had this insight into the innate will to survive of that which is, philosophy from its earliest beginnings invented the theory of substance, which posited an underlying unchangeable and indestructible substratum that was behind change, so that change was considered an appearance rather than reality.

Given such a metaphysical foundation, love can easily be integrated into these parameters. To love is to want to incorporate what is loved into one's being. Love is the energy that draws being together. It is resistance to separation. It is, therefore, in a sense, being itself. Interpreted in this framework, all love is self-love because that which loves and that which is loved become one. Since becoming one, resisting separation and destruction is of the very essence both of love and being, the identification of love with self-love becomes a conceptual necessity. If any evidence of this is necessary we need only turn to the self-contemplation and self-love of the Absolute in the Plato-Aristotle-Plotinus system (in much of medieval philosophy the three blended into a unified metaphysics). The love of this Absolute is necessarily exclusively internal, since to deny this would be to forget that, from the point of view of the Absolute, only it exists. It must then be obvious that Hashem's love cannot be of this sort. The self-love of the Absolute, as we have seen, is turned toward its own being. But Hashem's love is between him and the creature. It does not destroy the creature by absorbing it into the being of Hashem but affirms it in its identity. In short, Hashem's love for Israel is a far more human love than that of the Absolute. And because of this, it cannot be understood apart from Israel's love for Hashem. What is the relation between these two loves?

Hashem loves Israel and Israel loves Hashem. Both are true. To assert the one without the other is to distort the truth. It is the practice of Christian theology to stress Hashem's faithfulness to Israel and to overlook Israel's faithfulness to Hashem. This Christian tendency is understandable. The climax of Israel's faithlessness by its rejection of its redeemer is a vital part of the Christian system and it therefore becomes easy to focus almost exclusively on the negative in Israel's history rather than on its positive. Furthermore, quite apart from the particularly Christian interest in the matter, it is true that there is much faithlessness in Israel's history. This is particularly true of the postpatriarchal period. The theme of disobedience seems muted with the patriarchs. One does not hear of sin in their lives. But by the time we reach Moses, Jewish disobedience is well established and habitual, ranging from the sin of the golden calf to dissatisfaction with the diet in the wilderness. Nevertheless, in the midst of all the faithlessness, there is always a continuity of obedience both in the form of a saving remnant and in the quality of the disobedience itself. Israel's disobedience is always followed by repentance once punishment is administered. Such repentance ought not to be lightly dismissed. It is easy to prefer obedience freely given and not prompted by fear of retribution. But there is also something very human in fear of retribution. It is something very real. The pure love of God is almost too good to be true. It would be appropriate for angelic emanations of Hashem, whose being is so rooted in Hashem that the very notion of command would be inapplicable to them, since they do not have the power of free response. The man who is not an angel has his own being to contend with, a being that makes its own demands in its own world. Fear of Hashem must therefore precede love of him. In fearing Hashem, we not only encounter the being of Hashem and his power but also our own being and its power, however much it is limited in comparison with that of Hashem. Israel's return to Hashem after it has sinned is therefore not inconsequential. It is not inevitable that the sinner return to Hashem after he is punished. Instead of narrowing the breach, punishment may widen it. It may poison the situation further, heaping hatred upon hatred. But when Israel suffers, it turns to Hashem. Such a return is evidence that it experiences its punishment as coming from a loving rather than hating source. And this is, of course, the decisive element that determines the significance of the punishment to the recipient.

In the love relationship between Hashem and Israel there is no question that it is Hashem who takes the initiative. It is he who elects Abraham. He commands Abraham to leave his place of birth in return for a promise that will be fulfilled in the future. Abraham thus gives up something very definite (his home, his rootedness, his security) for something rather intangible and unproven: the divine promise. And when Jeremiah proclaims that "Thus saith the Lord: I remember thee, the kindness of thy youth, the love of thine espousals, when thou wentest after me in the wilderness, in a land that was not sown,"[15] he probably has in mind the original Abrahamic act of trust—leaving the known for the unknown, which the people as a whole repeats in its Exodus from Egypt toward the wilderness of Sinai. While it therefore remains true that Hashem takes the initiative in the relation between him and Israel, Israel's response is not far behind. It is a response of trust. In this context, trust means two things. It means, first, that Israel believes that Hashem will fulfill his promise. And this is believed in spite of the fact that the evidence seems to point in the other direction, as when Sarah was getting old and she had not given birth to the son through whom the descendants of Abraham were to become as numerous as the stars in the heaven. But trust means more than the conviction that a specific promise will be fulfilled. It refers to a sense of protection that the individual or the nation has in the hands of Hashem. It is the feeling that Hashem knows what he is doing and that therefore the outcome will be to the good however much this is difficult to see at the moment. This attitude does not involve a love of suffering. The norm remains well-being. Because Hashem loved Abraham he bestowed on him much cattle and other wealth. That is the norm, the proper reward of love and obedience to Hashem. But when such reward is not forthcoming, when it is suffering that seems to be the reward of obedience, the sense of protection does not disappear. Nonbeing and meaninglessness do not erase Israel's basic sense of security. While facing the depth of the anguish, there is a deeper trust of Hashem's wisdom, which expresses itself in a hope that becomes a conviction: that the future will redeem the past and that the suffering of the present is not meaningless.

While it is Hashem who takes the initiative in the love relationship between him and Israel, it is in some ways man's (Israel's) love of Hashem that is the more problematic. This can be sensed from the Bible. Israel is commanded to love Hashem with all its heart, soul, and might. That this needs to be commanded with such a degree of emphasis is suspicious. What can it mean to command love? And why should man love Hashem? Can love and fear coexist?

The natural relationship between man and his gods is fear. The gods are thought to have immense power. Man is largely at their mercy and for this reason it becomes vital to propitiate the gods. Man's hope therefore depends on acquiring the knowledge of how to do this. He needs to know what the gods require. By satisfying these requirements there is reason to hope that the gods will refrain from harming man. Stated in these terms, this is a relationship in which each party attempts to satisfy the needs of the other in return for having his needs satisfied. But it is, of course, never as simple as that, not even in human relationships. In a relationship no partner simply remains alone, using the other as a means toward self-satisfaction. Because the self is no longer alone, a turning toward the other takes place, and such a turning must, to a degree, consist of attention to the personality of the other. Even if, initially, this concentration arises out of the need of the self for its satisfaction and is therefore only instrumental toward achieving that satisfaction, in time the reality of the other asserts itself with its own claims on the self. And this is so even in the case of fear. It is true that in fear there is concentration on the self. I fear for myself, for what will or can happen to me. But it is not I who am frightful. There is another who I am afraid of and who therefore appears frightful. Were I totally oblivious to the being of the other, I could not fear for myself, since I would not be aware of anyone to frighten me. Fear, therefore, involves a perception of the other and is therefore only secondarily related to the self. It is the other who appears frightful. Israel's love of Hashem must therefore grow out of the fear in the context of which the love became possible. It is difficult to say whether the element of fear ever completely disappeared. But it is certainly supplemented by something quite different from fear. That the love of Hashem was commanded proves not only that there is a natural human resistance to such love but, probably more important, that such love is possible. That it was commanded must be viewed in light of the rabbinic teaching that "greater is he who is commanded and does than he who is not commanded and does."[16]

Israel's love for Hashem cannot be separated from Hashem's love for Israel. This is what must remain with us in this chapter. We have not hesitated to explore the ambiguities of the relationship. We have avoided every idealization of it. It is a real relationship between a people and its God. It is the relationship of a much-suffering people whose election has been an ambiguous blessing for itself. And it is also a relationship that has had deep elements of disappointment for Hashem. His feelings have also been hurt by Israel's infidelities. And yet, there has been a love here compared to which all other loves vanish into insignificance. It is a love that has enabled a deeply injured people to retain its dignity and its sense of being protected by its God. But even this understates the matter. The measure of Hashem's love for Israel is the Jew's love for his children. Abraham's willingness to sacrifice his son is not understood if it is not seen to presuppose the uniqueness of Abraham's love for Isaac. The initial promise to Abraham that his descendants will become a great people must equally be seen in this light. This is not the reward that is offered the Buddha or that he offers his fellow men, nor is it the "good news" of the New Testament, which speaks of eternal salvation and the conquest of death. Abraham is not offered escape from death. Instead, what is offered to him is something good not for him but for his descendants, and Abraham is more than satisfied because the welfare of his children means more to him than his welfare. This is the kind of fellowship of the generations that is made possible in Abraham. It is a love of children that far surpasses in importance the conquest of death. And this becomes possible because the Jewish parent joins with Hashem in love of the Jewish people. No other people has received such love from its gods. The nations of the world are weary of their gods. Or they seek leaps of enlightenment by which they hope to cease to be who they are, to find their salvation not in the confirmation and redemption of their being but in the dissolution of their selves. This is the only possible salvation for a people not loved by its gods and faced with the reality of human suffering. The redemptive path of Israel does not abandon the human condition. Resurrection of the dead is redemption but also affirmation of human being in its physical and therefore decidedly human form.

In this chapter we have dealt with the reality of Hashem's personality as it reveals itself in interaction with Israel. To do so, we have left out of consideration the philosophic critique of such mythologization as well as the silence of God in the modern world. We must now turn to these problems.

Chapter 4

CREATED BEING

1. Being and Existence

We have attempted to reverse the depersonalization of Hashem that philosophic thought has imposed on Judaism. Hashem is depicted in the Bible as a living personality motivated, at least in part, by psychological considerations, and we have therefore attempted to explore the dynamics of the Hashem-Israel relationship within the circumference of, and with the categories applicable to, the relationship of persons. To some, such an approach will necessarily appear sacrilegious and demeaning to the Absolute, which must be saved at all costs from contamination by all genuinely understandable predicates. For us, the authority of the Bible does not permit such evasions. Man must not heap greater honor on Hashem than he commands, and if the Bible, as the word of Hashem, is willing to speak of him in terms akin to the human, then it is not for man to teach Hashem a lesson in the dignity that properly pertains to the divine. Our first priority is to save the reality of the human relationship with Hashem. The reality of that relationship is seriously eroded by the transformation of the living God of Israel into an ineffable Absolute who cannot be with man when he is in need, when he turns to the living God. Nevertheless—and without in any way retracting what has been said—it is also necessary to remember that Hashem is God, the creator of heaven and earth. He is therefore not just one personality in the biblical drama but the Creator who is Lord of the Universe and therefore the master of the world and of everything in it. It cannot therefore be altogether false to claim that Hashem transcends all human comprehension and that, with respect to God, silence is better than words.

The tendency has been to formulate this problem in terms of the inadequacy of human language to express the reality of Hashem's being. Fortunately, this problem can be solved by silence. This seems to have been the primary goal of Ludwig Wittgenstein, whose work is often understood as a far-reaching assault on the meaningfulness of the concept of God. It is easy to misunderstand this contention if it is interpreted extralinguistically to constitute an assertion about what is or is not. Wittgenstein intended no such assertion. He intended only to terminate the talk about God, which, he believed, was inappropriate because it demanded of language something it could not do. Once this is conceded, Wittgenstein's criticism is stilled. The realm of the "mystical" (the term Wittgenstein used for that which language cannot deal with) does not lose any of its importance for being beyond the reach of language.[1] One gets the impression from Wittgenstein that it is that which can be talked about that is inherently unimportant and to be beyond the reach of language is therefore perhaps a necessary condition for being genuinely significant in any but a purely linguistic sense. The ineffability of Hashem cannot therefore be the central problem in the encounter of reason with Hashem.

The real problem is the relationship of God to being. This relationship is a pervasive one. This is sensed even in the Bible at a point where the presence of philosophy seems to appear even on the non-philosophical biblical landscape: when asked by Moses for the name by which he is to be spoken of to the people of Israel, Hashem instructs Moses to refer to him as he "who will be who he will be,"[2] though the Hebrew phrase in question is commonly mistranslated as "he who am who I am." Whether the tense is future or present—and it is the future tense that is used in the text—it is clear that the expression speaks of being and that it utters a tautology. The reference to being reveals the significance of the connection between Hashem and being, and to those acquainted with Parmenides, who is the founder of Western thought about being, the puzzling appearance of a tautology will hardly come as a surprise. We will have occasion to elaborate this observation presently. Here our purpose is merely to note in a preliminary way the inherent relationship between God and being. And it is even worthy of note that this profound relationship between God and being is also reflected by the tenacity with which the question of the existence of God is raised. There is no other being about which the question whether or not it exists seems to be so pressing and so often repeated. There are many entities, ideas, or constructs about which the question of whether or not they exist can be raised. It is reasonable to ask whether time, the Freudian unconscious, a geometric triangle, or beauty exist, and while all these questions have, of course, been asked, it must also be noted that the question of existence is by no means as closely associated with them as with God. The question of being is *the* question that seems to be the archetype of all questions about God. It may be that the question whether God exists asks more than it realizes. What is asked is the question of the relation between God and being. At this stage we can only note the opinion that both the assertion that God exists as well as the assertion that he does not exist are unsatisfactory because neither existence nor lack of existence can properly be predicated of God. There is, therefore, a problem in the relation of God to being and it is this problem that we must now investigate.

If we are to achieve any degree of clarity in this matter, we must realize that there are three components to the problem facing us. There is, first, the cluster of problems around the notion of being as such. Secondly, there is the problem of predicating being of God. Connected with this second problem is the question of applying any predicates at all to God. And finally there is the Jewish component that we must reckon with. Are there any special considerations that Jewish theology must have in mind as it deals with this set of inter-related questions? While proceeding in a relatively orderly way from the first to the second and then to the third of our questions, we will keep in mind that they are interconnected and that all the questions must be kept in mind simultaneously even if, at any one time, primary attention is being focused on one of them.

What is the problem of being? Why is being any more of a problem than any other predicate? The basic answer to this question is that being (or existence: we shall use these terms interchangeably until further notice) is difficult to conceptualize. This can be demonstrated by a thought experiment. Let us proceed to think of a fish. The moment the word *fish* is pronounced, a definite concept forms in our minds. Let us then add the predicate *green* to the fish. *Green* brings into our minds another definite concept (or essence, in the older terminology) and *green fish* therefore corresponds to a clearly thinkable concept. If we now add the concept of dead, we have a still more definite concept since *dead* introduced another definitely thinkable concept to the previously understood concept. Let us now add the predicate *existence*: we now have before us an existing, dead, green fish. Previously, each time a predicate was added, a definite thought appeared and was inserted into the picture. But what appeared before us when we were asked to add *existing* to the picture? It is hard to say. *Fish* stands for something definite. So do *green* and *dead*. But *existing* is different. In what does an existing dead green fish differ from just a dead green fish? What is the difference between an existing coat and a nonexisting coat, which is just imagined? It is tempting to answer that an existing coat will keep an existing person warm while a nonexisting coat will not. But it is also true that a nonexisting coat will very nicely keep a nonexisting person warm and thus the difficulty has merely been shifted rather than solved because we now inquire what the difference is between an existing and nonexisting person. We seem not to be able to define existence. When we are tempted to identify it with hardness—an example of another thinkable predicate—we realize that there is existing hardness and nonexisting hardness and that hardness is therefore not identical with existence. Existence, it would seem, resists being turned into a concept.

Kant invented a quaint little argument to drive this point home.[3] He pointed out that if an existing object contained one more predicate than merely the concept of the object, then the concept would not be a concept of that object, since the concept would have one quality less than the object and therefore be an inadequate concept of the object. Since adequate concepts of objects are possible and common, it must therefore be the case that an adequate concept of an object is not missing one of the qualities of the object. But since it is nevertheless the case that the object exists and the concept does not (as object, though it does, of course, exist as concept), the existence of the object cannot be one of its qualities, since all of its qualities are reflected in the concept but existence is not. To say that existence is not a quality or a predicate is to say that existence cannot be thought as qualities such as green or dead can. Existence is just there. It is the ground of all qualities. When qualities inhere in an existing object they are existing qualities, but we cannot think the existence that adheres to the qualities and to which they adhere. We can also express this by saying that when we think existence, we are thinking the thought of existence but not existence itself. The older terminology spoke of existence and essence with essence corresponding to what we have called concept or thought. Existence referred to the fact *that* a thing was, while essence designated *what* it was. Everything that existed had an essence because if it existed it was something and therefore the question of what it was could legitimately be asked. But what about existence? Could it be asked what it was? Here a problem is seen to emerge. If we were to ask what existence was and answer the question, we would be defining the essence of existence and that is not what we were looking for. The essence of existence is just another essence, whereas it is existence that we were asking for and not its essence. It would therefore seem that existence could not have an essence and this, in turn, meant that existence was not knowable, at least not in the ways other things are known through a grasping of their essences.

Existence thus emerges as something opaque that cannot be penetrated by the light of understanding, which operates through the grasping of essences. Once this is understood, a number of other aspects of the question of being become understandable. It has long been observed that it is difficult to cope with the question why a thing exists. Normally, we proceed from the premise that a thing is and inquire why it is the way it is and not some other way. Our inquiry is normally directed toward the "what" of the thing and not its "that." In its sharpest form, we experience the mystery that attaches to being when we are asked why is there anything rather than nothing. When this question is asked we experience a dizziness, as if the ground beneath us had lost its firmness. One of the reasons this is so is that, as we have already seen, we rarely question *that* a thing is but rather *what* it is. The question why is there anything rather than nothing does not ask why is this or that aspect of the world the way it is but rather why is there anything at all and not just nothing. Part of the strangeness of this question is a result of its posing the possibility of there being nothing instead of what is the fact, that there is something rather than nothing. We will soon speak of the problem of nothing, with which the question of being is deeply intertwined. Here we focus on another aspect of the mystery that attaches to this question. The "why" approach seems not to work when directed to existence. The "why" orientation seems ill equipped to cope with the opaqueness of existence. Existence defies the why by its sullen being. It just is and seems to wrap itself in a peculiar contingency that just has to be accepted without justification or argument. On the human level, this fact is reflected in the emergence of consciousness out of a base of being that precedes it. When man begins to think, he finds that he already is and has been quite some time prior to the emergence of his consciousness. Consciousness is therefore precluded from examining and deciding its own coming into being. This decision has been made for consciousness before it appears on the scene and constitutes the guidelines within which it must operate. The result is that there is a free-floating quality about consciousness that is related to the primordiality of existence, out of which consciousness emerges and which it can therefore never fully grasp.

2. NONBEING AND THE ONE

We must now turn to another of the problems that cluster around the notion of being: that of nonbeing or nothing. The emergence of any concept is naturally accompanied by the simultaneous emergence of its contrary. When we think of the human, we think with it the nonhuman. And the same is true of any other concept. This is not just a form of psychological association. That is, of course, also operative. But there is more to it than that. The very thinkability of a concept depends on its limits. It is not only psychologically the case that when I think the idea of chair my mind will drift to a comparison with whatever is not chair. The point is that to think the concept means to delineate it from the domain that is not included in the concept, the nonchair. The concept of nonchair excludes from its domain what is chair and thus crystallizes chair as a concept. The negative is thus the defense of the identity of the concept.

All this is nonobjectionable and nonproblematic until we come to the concept of being (in spite of the difficulty in turning being into a concept, we cannot avoid speaking of it as such). The only contrast that is available to being is nonbeing, and then the wild dance begins. If we have difficulty grasping being, we have even greater difficulty grasping nonbeing. What are we thinking about when we are thinking of nonbeing? We are, it would seem, thinking of nothing, but if we are thinking of nothing, are we still thinking? The likelihood is that the average person will think of empty space if asked to think of nothing. But is space not something? If it is, then it cannot represent nothing. But the question of the thinkability of nonbeing does not exhaust the problem. To speak of nothing, even in the absence of the ability to think it, is to make nonbeing the subject of a sentence to which predicates are added. The structure of predication, it can be argued, involves the attribution of being. To say that the house is green is to say that the house *is* a green thing.

To say anything at all about nonbeing, then, involves attributing being to nonbeing and that is an obvious self-contradiction. For this reason, at the very outset of Western metaphysical thought, Parmenides emphatically declared that nonbeing must not be thought about or spoken of.[4] It must be excluded from the domain of thought because it is excluded from the domain of language. But to say this is itself a contradiction, since to say that nonbeing cannot be thought about or spoken of is both to think about it and to speak of it. We thus find ourselves enmeshed in contradictions that cannot be escaped, since every escape attempt only enmeshes us more deeply by forcing us to utter and think more self-contradictory sentences and thoughts. Finally, it must be remembered that if nonbeing is unthinkable, so is being, since the unthinkability of the negation of a concept leaves the original concept without boundaries and therefore without meaning.

We thus meet the convergence of two lines of analysis that started independently of each other but are now found to converge. We first found existence beyond the reach of concepts because it was not a predicate and could not be conceived. We then found nonbeing beyond the reach of conceptualization, and the same would have to be true of being. For various reasons, then, thought is found to be inadequate to being. It must be noted, however, that until now we have spoken of existence and being interchangeably. We have assumed that to exist is the same as to be, and so, to a very large extent, it is in common usage. Yet we find ourselves saying that existence is not a predicate and that nonbeing (rather than nonexistence) cannot be thought. In the back of our minds some distinction seems to be operating, and it would be desirable to discover what that distinction is.

To some extent, the distinction between existence and being—if a distinction must be made—is a matter of stipulation. Kierkegaard inaugurated the practice of reserving the term *existence* for the mode of being that is man's and applying the term *being* to the being of all things other than man.[5] Heidegger, in turn, followed Kierkegaard's practice of reserving *existence* for man's being,[6] but he does so in the context of a more fundamental distinction between the being of things that are and being as such. He finds this distinction of the greatest significance. In a sense, it is the distinction that defines the philosopher. The common man fixes his gaze on the things that are. His vision is restricted to that which is. The "is" that attaches itself to the things that are is a derivative and objectified being because it is bound to an object that is. The philosopher's gaze, on the other hand, is fixed on being as being, in the freedom of its determination and unencumbered by the objects that are. Stated in these terms, the distinction is parallel to one that runs consistently through the thought of Plato.[7] We have in mind the distinction between a thing and its "idea": the green chair and the idea of greenness, the beautiful thing and the idea of beauty. It was also Plato who insisted that while common people perceive this or that beautiful thing, the philosopher ascends to a knowledge of beauty itself, and once this takes place, the fascination with individual beautiful objects all but disappears because beauty is the eternally unchanging, while beautiful objects come into being and go out of being. And yet Heidegger does not dwell on the Platonic parallel. Being as such as distinguished from the being of the things that are, seems to him a far more fundamental distinction than that between a thing and its Platonic idea. We must come to understand the significance of this fixation with being.

There is one other aspect of the being problem that we must note before we are ready for our next step. The focus on being tends to erase difference from the conceptual vocabulary. This follows from the fact that to the extent things are, they are one. They are not one to the extent that they are the specific things that they are. Chairs are different from tables and tables from chairs to the extent that they are chairs and tables. But viewed simply as beings, as things that are, they are all the same. Were it possible to restrict the unifying force of being merely to being, the metaphysical consequences of the unifying effects of being could be contained. But being cannot be localized. Being is the foundation of every predicate, each one of which must be if it is to be an operative predicate. Only to the extent that predicates, or that which predicates express, have being can they be applied appropriately. The result of this is that the unifying effect of being collapses the apparent diversity of things into the undifferentiated unity of being that was first proclaimed by Parmenides.[8] The ontology of being is caught up in an irresistible monism that sharply denies the reality of difference and therefore of the world revealed to man's senses. It is for this reason that there has been a historical affinity between ontology and mysticism. Mysticism stresses the unity of all things from the experiential point of view, while ontology tends to do so on intellectual grounds. In its most consistent form, as in Parmenides, the ontological point of view results in the total denial of the existence in the world of diversity and change. It particularly excludes time from the realm of the real simply because time is inconceivable without diversity. Time is expressed in the before and after, which are the essential determinants of motion and change. Ontological monism therefore rejects time, motion, and change as illusory. In the case of Plato, the purity of this position is diluted and instead of an absolute denial of the reality of time, change, and motion, a lesser degree of being is accorded to them. But at its core, Plato remains in the Parmenidean camp because time, motion, and change are denied to true being and permitted only to apply to lower realms of being where being is mixed with nonbeing. When we come to an assessment of the role of ontology in contemporary thought, we will have to notice that as ontology is resurrected by Heidegger, it is an ontology that not only comes to terms with time but introduces it into the very heart of being. Here we only wish to note that classical ontology has always found it necessary to exclude time from the realm of being.

3. HEIDEGGER AND THE A PRIORI

One of the most striking features of Heidegger's resurrection of the centrality of ontology for philosophy (or perhaps we should say for "thought," since philosophy may already be a degenerate form of thought) is the sense of rediscovery that permeates the new ontology. Western thought, according to Heidegger,[9] began the turn from being as early as Plato. Only the pre-Socratics were still in the abode of being. While the turn from being to the consciousness of the subject as the point of departure for thought culminates with Descartes, who explicitly makes the "I think" the ground of the "I am," this process began with Plato. Being is, after all, by no means as central to the thought of Plato as it is to Heidegger. Plato's ethical interest is probably as strong as his interest in being, and while it may be argued that when Plato's ethics is understood properly it turns out really to be ontology, the fact that Plato feels compelled to reconcile ontology and ethics and even to start with ethics rather than with ontology indicates an attempt to take seriously the ethical focus of Socrates even if Plato finds it necessary to integrate it with the cosmological and metaphysical direction of Greek philosophy before Socrates. The result is that, from Heidegger's point of view, being has been forgotten and needs to be rediscovered. The old wells that had become covered up must be reopened.

Heidegger's need to return to the pristine form of thought before

things took a wrong turn cannot be fully appreciated without understanding those characteristic philosophic attitudes he finds objectionable and therefore wishes to avoid at all cost. One of these is the
conformity theory of truth:[10] the view that truth consists in the conformity of the judgment with its object (*adaequatio intellectus et rei*).
The other is the philosophy of values:[11] the view that there is a sharp
distinction between normative and descriptive statements because
being is valueless and values are introduced by the observer and are
not to be found "objectively" in the things that are. Fundamentally,
Heidegger objects to both of these opinions on phenomenological
grounds. Both of these views locate crucial events in the subject
rather than in the object. Truth is something that happens when the
subject's judgment is adequate to, or corresponds to, what is. Value,
on the other hand, is even more subjective because here it is not
even a question of adequately or inadequately reflecting what there
is but of actually introducing something into reality that is not there
before the subject puts it there. The result is that man becomes the
master of being. It is he who values (or disvalues) being and it is he
who judges adequately, thereby creating truth. Heidegger detects
the arrogance of manipulation lurking very near the surface of this
attitude, which is the technological attitude. The technologist is the
master of creation. He will not let things be as they are but must
bend them to his will. His will creates the values he wishes to attain
and his theory creates the truth by means of which his created values
are realized. Phenomenologically, this is false because it overlooks
the intentionality of consciousness. Consciousness is transcendental
in essence. It is never consciousness of consciousness but of an object that is a constituent part of consciousness. Both truth and value
must therefore appear in some way in the objects that appear to consciousness. An object or event does not first appear to consciousness
without value (such as beauty or goodness) only to have a value added to it subsequently. In the case of beauty, for instance, the very
first thing we notice about a beautiful person or a landscape is that
it is beautiful. We notice this before we notice anything else about
the phenomenon. The theory that beauty is not in the phenomenon
but added by the subject to the phenomenon contradicts experience
and is advanced for theoretical reasons rather than fidelity to the appearance of beauty in experience. And the same is true of truth.
Truth is also an appearance of phenomena. True judgment reflects
that which appears. Heidegger speaks of truth as an unveiling of being. This unveiling is not a willful decision of man whereby he

wrests being's secret to himself but as much an initiative of being as it is a receptivity of listening man to the revelation of being. The emphasis is thus shifted from the subjective construction of man and its presupposed solipsism to a man-being continuum that avoids both ungrounded subjectivism and mindless objectivism of the materialist sort. Man stands in relation to being, which is his ground. Man is not the author of being, he is not his own ground. But neither is he an ontologically uninfluential observer who has no share in the happening of what is. He dwells in the domain of being and being dwells in him. Human being is thus ontologically grounded without gaining manipulative control over being.

We conclude this brief exploration of the problem of being with a glance at its relation to the *a priori*. It is in the thought of Kant that the *a priori* came to be central. Rationalism before Kant had, of course, been concerned with the truths of reason, having made these truths the cornerstone of its philosophy. But rationalism takes a decisive turn in Kant in two interconnected respects. There is the shift to judgment as the decisive domain of philosophical thinking. This is the reason that the notion of the *a priori* makes its appearance. Coordinated with this is Kant's Copernican revolution: the explanation of the possibility of the *a priori* in terms of the contribution of the knower's mind to the judgments of experience. Kant thereby solves a mystery: How can a finite knower who is not the author of the objects of his experience possess knowledge that seems to go beyond experience? If all knowledge comes to the knower from the outside, then any knowledge possessed by the knower should be subject to revision by further experience. Yet the fact is that there are propositions (e.g., every event has a cause) that are known to be true with certainty and that no conceivable experience could dislodge. Kant's explanation for this mystery is that this sort of knowledge cannot be dislodged by experience because it does not originate in experience. It is the contribution of the human mind to experience. Human knowledge is a composite of two elements. The bulk of knowledge, more specifically, its content is derived from experience. It comes to the knower from the outside through his senses. But knowledge also requires a knowing mind and this mind has its own constitution, which leaves its imprint on the resulting composite. The *a priori* is therefore, in a sense, self-knowledge because it is knowlege of the categories of the human mind that the mind imposes on experience. Knowledge can therefore never claim to be knowledge of the "thing itself," of the world as it is in itself but only of the world as known by a mind having the particular structure that the human mind does. The certainty of *a priori* knowledge is thus gained at the price of a profound subjectivization of human knowledge, of a turning inward of the observer on himself and the categories of his mind.

It should be clear by now that this is a maneuver Heidegger cannot accept uncritically. It represents for him a form of ungrounded solipsism, of which we have just spoken. It is by no means a coincidence that being is not a central question in the thought of Kant. Other than the argument adduced for the view that existence is not a predicate, there is very little concern with being in Kant. The Copernican revolution in his thought turns his attention away from being to the consciousness of the subject and its categories. Yet Heidegger maintains an abiding interest in the Kantian perspective. The basic reason for this is the Kantian focus on the finitude and temporality of man, which needs to be reconciled with the possibility of *a priori* knowlege. The presence of the *a priori* in man is a trace of the absolute, which needs to be reconciled with the fact that man is not the ground of his being but dependent on something other than himself. In Heidegger's interpretation, Kant is struggling with the relationship of temporal man to being, though of course Kant does not understand this himself and thinks he is dealing with the conditions of human knowledge rather than the problem of being. But what becomes of the *a priori* in Heidegger's interpretation of the Kantian perspective? Can the *a priori* be interpreted nonepistemologically and if so, how?

A priori categories for Kant are the universal conditions of human experience. They determine how that which can be known will be known. For Heidegger, the focus is not on the conditions of human knowledge. It is on being and its manifestations. The *a priori*, therefore, ceases to be a characteristic of certain propositions and becomes, instead, the ground of the possibility of beings, the ontological support for the ontic. In its simplest and most direct form this expresses itself in the insight that only because there is being can beings be. Being is prior to beings, not in the temporal but in the ontological sense. Being is the ground of the possibility of all things that are and it is in this sense of *prior to* that we encounter the *a priori* in Heidegger. In understanding the actual functioning of the Heideggerian *a priori* we must realize that Heidegger's basic purpose is to give the conditions of human existence an ontological ground. To give an ontological ground means to explain dimensions of human existence such as being-in-time as functions of human being itself. Time is not something that man "has" but must be traced back to something that man "is." The ontological ground of temporality is therefore found in the extendedness of human being into nonbeing, in the basic ontological fact that man's being does not simply coincide with itself but that it is extended, that it projects into nonbeing, and that man both is what he is but is also not what he is. Another way of saying this is that man has to become what he already is. This ontological constitution of human being makes possible his temporality and this, in turn, makes possible the invention of such derivative determinations of time as clock-time which is measured by timepieces such as clocks. And the same is true of human consciousness. Instead of just accepting as a given fact that man has consciousness, Heidegger is far more interested in an ontological interpretation of consciousness. What kind of being, he asks, is conscious being? While the answer to this particular question is far more developed by Sartre, whose existentialism, in the Cartesian tradition, focuses heavily on consciousness, it is implicit in Heidegger. Consciousness is a mode of being that reaches out to that which it is not. Nonconscious being is contained within its being. It is bounded by its limits and does not extend into what it is not. Conscious being, on the other hand, by its nature ranges far beyond itself to reach things it is not. Temporal and conscious being is thus not a contingent fact of human existence. It is a necessary consequence of the mode of being that is human being and is therefore an *a priori* of human existence.

4. GOD AND BEING

Up to this point, we have been exploring the cluster of problems that group themselves around the problem of being. If, at times, it has seemed that we were intent on exegesis of Heidegger for its own sake, this has been so because Heidegger has put the problem of being in the center of his thought at a time when the problem of being had all but disappeared from philosophic thought. We are now ready for the next stage of our investigation. What is the connection between being and God? We have already remarked that the most widely discussed question in connection with God seems to be whether he does or does not have being. God is the one being whose existence or nonexistence is most widely debated. Once this is realized, the next problem follows naturally. The term *being* or *existence* is most often used in a material context. For the common man, to say that something exists is to say that it can be touched, that it has weight and dimension. But those who assert that God is, very rarely mean by it that he is a material being. God is conceived as a spirit and while Christianity speaks of incarnation, the very fact that such an expression came into use implies the presupposition that we are dealing with a being that is initially not material but became so at a certain time, a fact that is understood to be the justifiable ground for the deepest wonder. But once we realize that our idea of God is that of a nonmaterial being, the question naturally presents itself as to just what kind of being God does have. What is the meaning of non-material being? Does God exist in the way that ideas do? If that is the case, then would that be equivalent to saying that the idea of God exists but not God? But this clearly comes very close to saying that God does not exist as mermaids and centaurs do not, all of which are ideas that lack being.

These relatively simple and simpleminded (though not without a certain force) questions are adduced to make clear that the relation between being and God is problematic from the outset. The problem becomes far more sophisticated and exciting in the ontological argu-ment for the existence of God, one of the most significant points of contact of faith and philosophy. The ontological argument is both an intellectual thicket and a crisis point for faith, as is demonstrated in Karl Barth's important study of it in the form advanced by Anselm.[12] That the ontological proof is of considerable philosophic significance is demonstrated by the attention paid to it by philosophers since its appearance. Many, if not most, of the problems that surround the concept of being come to a head in the ontological proof. The result is that if a list of the most famous philosophers since the time of Anselm is drawn up, it would show approximately half of them sup-porting the ontological proof, with the other half opposing it as un-sound. It is true that most philosophic discussion of the ontological proof turns on such questions as whether there are degrees of being and whether being is a predicate, questions that do not go to the heart of the theological problem raised by the ontological proof. On the other hand, there is little doubt that, properly understood, the ontological argument plays a crucial role in the dialectic between God and being.

The heart of the ontological argument is the claim that to think God as a concept lacking existence is self-contradictory. This is not so in the case of other concepts (essences) whose nonexistence can be thought without much difficulty. There is no problem in thinking a mermaid to be a concept without existence. But to think God as a concept lacking existence is self-contradictory because God is defined as the most perfect possible being and to say that the most perfect possible being lacks existence would be as self-contradictory as to assert that the man who owns all the oranges in the world does not own a particular orange. The conclusion is that the idea of the most perfect possible being is the idea of a being who cannot lack existence and we have thus discovered the one concept in which existence is inextricably contained in the very concept itself, prior to the question of being having been raised at all. The opponents of the proof argue that it demonstrates nothing more than the incontrovertible truism that if a predicate (in this case, existence) is contained by definition in any subject, any proposition that attributes that particular predicate to the subject will be necessarily true by definition. But all this is so only as long as the matter is kept on the level of propositions that can be made necessarily true by stipulating the proper definitions of the terms in question. But, continue the opponents of the ontological proof, this cannot be used to guarantee the actual existence of anything. The game of definitions and of the necessarily true propositions that follow from them cannot prescribe what does or does not exist in reality. The proponents of the argument reply that what has just been said would be true if existence were stipulatively introduced into a concept. Thus, it would be silly to stipulate as the definition of mermaid a being half human and half fish possessing existence and then to argue that such a being does, in fact, exist because it would be self-contradictory to assert that it does not exist. This would be silly because existence has been gratuitously introduced into the definition of *mermaid* and this stipulation is then used as a basis for arguing that mermaids do actually exist. But, argue the defenders of the ontological proof, existence is not introduced into the definition of the most perfect possible being as a sheer act of caprice. In fact, it is not introduced at all. Instead, it is contained automatically in the very concept of the most perfect possible being. If actual existence is successfully extracted from the concept, this is a totally unique procedure, which works only in the case of this one concept that is unlike any other.

Our purpose here is not to evaluate the ontological argument but to understand its significance. What are the forces at work in this argument? Why is it so sound and yet so questionable that it convinces some but not others? What is the theological significance of the ontological proof?

The ontological proof deals with the relationship of God to being. The question it attempts to answer is whether God does or does not have being. Is God one of those entities that have being (like the Empire State Building and the Eiffel Tower) or is God to be included among those concepts (like mermaids and centaurs) that are only thoughts but have no being? The answer that the ontological proof attempts to give is clearly that God is to be included in the former category, i.e., among those things that possess being. If the ontological proof is successful, then God would be one of the things that have being. It would then be the case that the Empire State Building is, and the Eiffel Tower is, and God is. *There would then be a concept above God that would embrace God and all other entities possessing being. Being would then be an umbrella concept covering God and many other things.* God would thus be dethroned and being would become the ruling concept. It could then be asked when and how God came under the coverage of being or, in other words, how he came into being. This is a question that most mythologies do not fail to ask and to answer. They speak of a primeval chaos out of which the gods emerged. However this chaos is conceived, because it represents the wider context out of which the divine beings emerged, they are subject to fate because there is a framework that they did not create and over which, therefore, they do not rule. It is quite otherwise with Hashem. There is not a word in the Bible about his origins. We meet him in the process of creating the world and we are told nothing about his coming into being or about his condition before he began the act of creation. There are rabbinic texts that speak of Hashem creating and destroying many worlds before creating the present world.[13] But even here it is Hashem as creator (and destroyer) that we meet, but never is the question of Hashem's own origin raised. This silence is of basic significance. Being does not rule over Hashem. He is not one of the many beings that are. He is not a being who has come into being and who therefore will cease to be. He is not subject to being. *He is the Lord of being.*

What is the significance of the philosophic concentration on being? We have seen its centrality in the thought of Heidegger. Heidegger claims that it is a concept (if, indeed, it can be spoken of as a concept) that has been forgotten and that must be reinserted into the center of philosophy. To some extent, Heidegger is right. He is not completely right because being does figure prominently both in Plato and Aristotle (it is central to Aristotle's *Metaphysics*) and is not completely forgotten in medieval and modern philosophy either. But it is not *the* problem of philosophy. In modern times, perhaps starting with Descartes, the problem of knowledge, particularly the search for certain knowledge, receives more attention than the problem of being. In the case of Aristotle, his scope is so broad that it is difficult to identify one theme as central in his philosophy. While being plays an important role in Aristotle's thought, the biological, organism-directed orientation of Aristotle is so pronounced that being cannot occupy any position of pronounced centrality because the logic of the being argument (as we have already seen), points away from development and growth to a more static and less dynamic metaphysics. In the case of Plato, the ethical and political compete with being for Plato's attention. It can be argued with some justification that the ethico-political focus in Plato should not be taken at face value and that behind the political point of departure of a work like the *Republic* there lies a contemplative vision in which being is central and toward which the political plays only an introductory role. But the introductory role—if it is that—played by the political for Plato is prominent enough to deprive being of the centrality that Heidegger believes it deserves. And Heidegger is much more clearly correct in the modern period. There, being is hardly in the running. Here, man and his consciousness are at the center of philosophy. Descartes' formula "I think, therefore I am" speaks of being as the conclusion toward which the "I think" functions as a premise. The analysis of consciousness could have been followed by a thorough analysis of being. But this does not happen. Descartes' dualism circumvents being. His attention is directed toward delineating the differences that obtain between the two kinds of substance, the mental and the material. We are told that it is of the essence of mind to think and of matter to be extended in space but we are not told what these two kinds of substances have in common. What they have in common, of course, is being, but this is precisely what Descartes ignores.

We cannot here write a history of modern philosophy from the point of view of the problem of being. Were we doing that, we would certainly have to discuss Spinoza, a thinker all but ignored by Heidegger. And we would also have to discuss Hegel, for whom the tension between being and history is central. The question that we must face—and we do so after our preliminary discussion of the problem of subsuming God under being—is the significance of the problem of being in the philosophic enterprise, particularly in the context of Western thought. Why is it that being was far more the problem of Greek philosophy than of modern philosophy and what is the significance of its resurrection in Heidegger? Is this simply a matter of a Heideggerian obsession with being or is there a set of philosophic considerations that establish the priority of this or that question in philosophy? When we begin to philosophize, how do we determine which question comes first and which second?

There is no philosophic way of determining the priority of philosophic questions because to attempt to do so is to become enmeshed in a flagrant circularity. To attempt to demonstrate that this or that question has philosophic priority involves appealing to some considerations that must already be assumed as established, and it is then these that are primary and not the question whose primacy these principles are alleged to support. Let us illustrate this by reference to the debate about whether the problem of knowledge or that of being should be the point of departure for philosophy. On the one hand, it is argued that the problem of knowledge deserves clear priority. In raising any question, we are seeking knowledge and it is therefore crucial that we understand what knowledge is and how it is obtained before we are entitled to engage in a specific search for any particular knowledge. Without such clarification, any result we obtain will be automatically suspect in respect to its pedigree as knowledge. On the other hand, the problem of being can also be advanced as the proper candidate for prior consideration. Every question and every statement predicates being. A question asks whether this or that *is* or *is not* something else. Without knowing what it means to attribute being, we simply do not understand our assertions, all of which posit being in one or another sense. It would therefore follow that to raise the problem of knowledge without prior clarification of the problem of being entails a positing of being at a time when the significance or even the meaning of such positing is not understood. And finally, both the priority of the problems of knowledge and being can be questioned in light of the case that can be made for the priority of the problem of language. All problems are both raised and answered in language. But how does language function? Are there characteristics inherent in language that determine what questions we raise and the terms in which we raise them? Such questions designed to gain insight into the nature of language can be argued to deserve priority over either knowledge or being as the point of departure for thought. It is also worth noting that each of these three problems is involved in a circularity apparently endemic to fundamental questions. In the case of knowledge, to ask, "What is knowledge?" is to seek knowledge without prior clarification of what constitutes knowledge and how it is obtained. In the case of being, to ask, "What *is* being?" is to use the concept of being before it has been clarified. And to ask, "What is language?" is to use language in the process of trying to determine what language is. The circularity involved in raising any of these problems indicates that they are profoundly fundamental problems, none of which can easily be given priority.

It is therefore not possible to conclude that Heidegger's focus on the problem of being is dictated by purely philosophic considerations that grow out of the logic of the problem. What, then, is behind the obsession with being? Is there a hidden agenda that needs to be uncovered if we are to understand the project before us?

5. Ontology and Human Being

We have already pointed out in a preliminary way the tension that obtains between God and being. Being arches over God. Being reduces God to the status of a being among all others, a reduction that is inherently fatal to the transcendence and dignity of God. Heidegger is of course aware of this tension between God and being. Even if it is not his intention simply to dethrone God and to substitute being in his place, in many respects, that is the effect of his thought.

Relationship to God requires faith, whereas being is grasped by thought. "Theology," writes Heidegger, "is seeking a more primordial interpretation of man's Being towards God, prescribed by the meaning of faith itself and remaining within it. It is slowly beginning to understand once more Luther's insight that the 'foundation' on which its system of dogma rests has not arisen from an inquiry in which faith is primary, and that conceptually this 'foundation' not only is inadequate for the problematic of theology, but conceals and distorts it."[14] Being does not require faith. It is the object of thought. Being must, of course, not be confused with particular beings that are ontic and not ontological entities. Being is thought in the sense in which Heidegger speaks of thought as the return to the primordial. Nevertheless, the positivity of being cannot be evaded. This positivity is not everlasting. By the time Heidegger finishes his analysis of being, it is found to be permeated by temporality and therefore negativity to a far greater extent than traditional metaphysics would have dreamed possible. But in spite of all this, being retains an initial positivity that makes it a viable approach to the holy in a secular age. That the positivity of being is relative rather than absolute is shown by the fact that being has been forgotten. But being can be thought anew by means of a human effort, whereas God appears when he sees fit and not when men summon him. Perhaps the matter can be summarized by saying that ontology is the theology of those without faith. Ontology is natural theology if we reinterpret natural theology not so much as an encounter with nature but rather as the domain of human existence in the absence of faith but in the presence of a tenacious bias in favor of human rather than nonhuman existence. This is not the inherent direction of ontology. But it is the direction that it takes with Heidegger.

Two pairs of concepts thus emerge and we must locate man among them. On the one side there is being and thought, the enterprise of Heidegger. On the other side is Hashem and faith, the enterprise of Judaism. And then there is man, who attempts to understand himself in the setting provided by these concepts and in light of the tensions generated by them.

From the purely philosophic point of view, man is our point of departure. It is man whom we know. It is man who we are. We either consider these facts decisive or we do not. If we do, then man is the metaphysical center of the universe. Human categories are then given ultimacy either directly or metaphysical categories are so prepared as to give human categories ultimacy. The fact is that such a philosophy has never been created. Socrates was perhaps the man who came closest to it when he proclaimed that man is the proper business of man rather than cosmology or anything else. But he has survived only in the Platonic form, and in that form the metaphysics of being (even if not satisfactory to Heidegger) overwhelms the human. Because what is most human is the life man lives, it is perhaps inevitable that life rather than literature is the medium of expression of those for whom man remains at the center of reality. Because man is ephemeral, man's most characteristic expression should also be ephemeral. Philosophic writings and works of art outlive their creator and therefore resemble more closely the eternity of being rather than the mortality of man. It is therefore possibly inherent in the writing of philosophic dialogues and essays that the very form, the escape from life into a medium of persistence, brings with it a turn toward being as that which lasts, as will the written word. Those who remain in the human condition speak, and speech disappears once it is spoken, leaving the speaker no option but to begin again if he is not prepared to be ignored. In life, the situation is always changing and we never know the truth until we die because something could always transform us and the truth of yesterday could become the error of today. Socrates could therefore only survive in the Platonic form, and if anything of Socrates actually does survive in Plato, its message can only be that we must live and find our own truth, as did Socrates.

It is therefore Kierkegaard who is the philosopher of man. His ideal, of course, was Socrates. Unlike Socrates, he not only lived but also wrote, and we can therefore read what he wrote, which we cannot do in the case of Socrates. But Kierkegaard was also embarrassed by writing. He hid behind the pseudonyms, thereby creating one of the mysteries of philosophic scholarship. But the mystery is not difficult to fathom. Kierkegaard was ashamed of writing. He was ashamed of freezing a doctrine as if it represented the truth for him. The truth was fragile and could not be preserved in nonwritten form. He therefore hid behind the pseudonyms, thereby proclaiming clearly and loudly to the world that the living Kierkegaard was not in them but that these were the thoughts of fictitious creatures, writers who had once lived but were now dead. To be a genuine philosopher of man is therefore to be a very strange kind of philosopher, perhaps not to be a philosopher at all. To be a philosopher of man requires as much negation as positivity. This can be achieved in various ways. As we have seen, one can refuse to write at all and only speak, and perhaps not even speak but remain silent (which is probably what Wittgenstein had in mind). Or, if one must write, one can do it ironically, a powerful technique of distancing oneself from what one says. This is the second, and far more important, technique used by Kierkegaard in the service of man. Irony is transcendence, the cancellation and going beyond what has just been said. It is therefore, strictly speaking, intellectually irresponsible because one either believes what one says or one does not. But the law of the excluded middle is not a human law. It contradicts human reality, which lives in doubt and uncertainty and in which there are layers of belief and disbelief that can not be significantly separated one from the other but that interpenetrate one another in a most confusing way. We are therefore told by Heidegger that Kierkegaard unfortunately never became an ontological thinker but remained an ontic one. And there is little doubt that Heidegger is right.

To become an ontological thinker is to leave the condition of man. Being is the widest possible concept. It is the widest possible perspective because it leaves nothing out, it embraces everything that is. The embrace we speak of here has the potential of smothering whatever it embraces because the concentration on being, as we have seen, eliminates difference and therefore individuality, which produces the undifferentiated oneness of the being of Parmenides. If difference is to remain real, then being must not be the center of thought. Thought centered on being is not human thought, i.e., not thought in which the categories of human existence retain both primacy and ultimacy. And it is in this connection that Heidegger's *Being and Time* is so interesting. Its attention is concentrated on being as the primary focus of thought. Heidegger's primary intuition is the centrality of the problem of being, which, as we have seen, has been forgotten since the time of Socrates. At the same time—and this is where the matter becomes most curious—*Being and Time* concentrates on human being. Heidegger justifies this on the ground that human being has a special ontological status because man is the being through whom being comes to be. Our first impulse is to demand a clarification of the claim for the ontological primacy of man. In one way or another, such a claim must rest on the observation that man is the only being who thinks being. Even if this claim is conceded, no special ontological status would accrue to man were we to maintain a fairly strict separation between being and thought. It would then not follow that because man is the only being who thinks being, being happens in the thought of man. But Heidegger does not separate being and thought very sharply, and while he vigorously denies all charges of idealism, a certain idealistic undertone is not difficult to detect. While he carefully avoids all discussion of consciousness, his analysis of human existence in its various modes such as anxiety and temporality is clearly, at least in part, a phenomenology of human consciousness. Yet, Heidegger's interest remains being, so that the phenomenology of human consciousness is not intended for its own sake but as a means toward the unveiling of being. It is well know that *Being and Time* remains incomplete and that the promised analysis of being was never provided. Heidegger's thought, at least in the framework of *Being and Time*, remains tied to human being rather than being in general.

It is true of course that the later Heidegger, though not the Heidegger of *Being and Time*, speaks extensively of being and not only of human being. But the sharpness of thought that characterized *Being and Time* is now lacking and we have the sense that a profound spiritual transformation has taken place in the period after *Being and Time*. There is relatively little spirituality in *Being and Time*. In the later Heidegger, the holy becomes far more central. The serenity of the later Heidegger is rooted in his reaching beyond the limits of human existence to a decidedly more cosmic notion of being no longer rooted in the human predicament. Anxiety and resoluteness (translated by Paul Tillich as the *Courage to Be*) are now calmed by the presence of a nonhuman cosmos in which being unveils itself in the celebrating word of the poet.[15] Language, the medium of poetry, ceases to be an extension of human being, man's means of taking hold of the world, and becomes the dwelling place of man, that in which he is encompassed and whose goals he serves. Instead of being an extension of man, language becomes the shadow that being casts before it as it unveils itself to man. The essential point is that thought does not provide a smooth transition from the being of man to being in general. There is a serious discrepancy between the human condition and the being of the cosmos. The cosmos is the setting of human existence. It is man's dwelling place, upon which he imprints his presence. In *Being and Time* Heidegger focuses on the world of tools, which are shaped to conform to human contours and which therefore testify to the human presence in the world. But there is relatively little discussion of the rest of nature which remains oblivious to man's presence. Heidegger is never aware of the separation that looms between human existence and being. In this respect, the poet is the savior because he permits himself to be seized by being, which uses him toward its ends. The true poet, for Heidegger, becomes a medium through which language and being speak. He is the prophet of being, similar to the biblical prophets who are sent by God to deliver divine messages.

But the transition from the mode of human existence to being is never made. Thought deals with being but not with human existence. Being is not surrounded by anxiety. Being is not faced with death. And the question then becomes one of ultimacy. How serious are these human concerns? Do they take place in the midst of a cosmos indifferent to them because it is not capable of understanding them or does human concern find its setting in relation to one who hears, sees, and understands the human situation even if he is silent when man wants him to speak? The cosmos in which being is the ultimate is not a cosmos that lends weight to human destiny. Being always is and always will be. It is unperturbable. It is the principle of nature that covers the gullies of Babi Yar with grass and the Warsaw Ghetto with the pleasant feeling of spring in the air. This must not be misunderstood. There is a liberation from the terror that is human existence in cosmic ontology. If being is indifferent to the concerns of men, if the seasons and the cosmic cycles go on no matter what happens to me and to those I love, then, strangely enough, a certain comfort can be drawn from this fact. A kind of serenity becomes possible because the problem of human existence is seen in perspective as something passing rather than permanent, as something that will ultimately leave no mark on the eternal face of being. There is thus a certain sort of redemption to be had in cosmic ontology. But it is not the redemption of man in the human condition. It is not an affirmation of the seriousness of human existence as that existence knows itself in its situation. It is a redemption based on a denial of the seriousness of human existence. The serenity that attaches to cosmic ontology is, in the deepest sense, a serenity of resignation. Human concerns shrink into insignificance when seen against the backdrop of a cosmos in which the human upsurge is one event among the infinite events of the galaxies that have happened and continue to happen, unrecorded and unremembered because only man records and remembers. It is for this reason that Heidegger was not able to continue *Being and Time*. In the portion that he did publish, man emerges at the center of being. The ontology of *Being and Time*, or of that portion of it that is available, is an ontology of man. And it would have been possible for Heidegger to complete his ontology by an interpretation of being as the being of man. In some respects, he approaches this option when, as we have seen, he assigns to man a privileged ontological status as the being through whom being comes to be. But in the final analysis, it was not an option he could embrace because to do so would force him to make the human condition far more ultimate than he is prepared to do. The ultimate must be being that is far beyond the beings that are, even if they are human beings. The ultimate cannot be the absolute person, as is the God of Israel. It can only be being, which is not person.

It is interesting to note that while Heidegger is extremely reluctant to speak of God, he is far less reluctant to speak of the gods. It has been said, not altogether in jest, that the one God of Israel is the last station on the road to atheism. First, it is claimed, there were many gods who were reduced to one God, and the next logical reduction is a world without any God. Underlying this witticism is the assumption that if one God is good, many gods must be far better and that, therefore, the thinning out of the ranks of the gods is an assault on the very presence of divinity in the world. What is overlooked, however, is that if there are many gods, then there must necessarily be an overarching principle behind or above them in the light of which they are deprived of all ultimacy. We have seen that, to a degree, this problem also besets the one God, who can be interpreted as a being and then fall under the jurisdiction of ontological being. But the matter is far more serious when there are many gods whose nonultimacy is far more evident. It is for this reason that an ontologist such as Heidegger whose ultimate loyalty is to being is far more at ease talking of the gods than of God. The gods can be no competition to being. The gods are clearly beings, even if more powerful and potent than other beings. While subject to the fate that ontological being imposes on all beings, the gods also illuminate in and participate in the holiness of being, which assumes historical reality through the gods. But they do not and cannot threaten being. Only the God of Israel can do that.

Hashem is powerful enough to threaten and conquer being and he is person enough to confirm the humanity of man so that it is not made meaningless, as in cosmic ontology. Our remaining problem then is Hashem's relationship, on the one hand, to being, which he created and over which he is lord, and to man, whom he created and over whom he is Lord but who threatens his ultimacy far more than being does.

6. THE LORD OF BEING

We must now look more deeply into the tensions that are generated by the relationship of Hashem to being. The basic problem, as we have seen, is that Hashem can be interpreted as a being among beings and being is thus elevated to the status of the overarching principle logically and metaphysically higher than Hashem. Once this happens, we have argued, it becomes possible to ask when and how Hashem came into being and it becomes possible to view Hashem as subject to fate, a force that rules over all beings in the name of the power of being. We have also come to understand that it is extremely difficult to extricate Hashem from involvement with being both because of the prominence of the question whether God exists and the long tradition of philosophic proofs for the existence of God, particularly in the form of the ontological proof and the structure of language as the predication of being, which seems to make possible the interpretation of all statements about God as predications of being. In analyzing Hashem's involvement with being we must attempt to distinguish those elements of the involvement not unique to Hashem but true of all things that are, and those elements unique to the relation of Hashem to being. Among the latter, the primary issue that is unique to the relationship between Hashem and being is the question of the existence of God, which is raised in connection with God far more persistently than in connection with anything else. The uniqueness of the question dealing with the existence of God is further underlined, as we have seen, by the ontological proof, which is a unique proof for the existence of God and which is viable only as a unique proof. This is so because it is essential to demonstrate that it is not possible to prove the existence of the most perfect possible object (e.g., typewriter, automobile) by arguing that since an existing typewriter is more perfect than a nonexisting one, the most perfect possible must, in fact, exist. Since it is known that the most perfect possible typewriter does not, in fact, exist, the ontological proof for the existence of God would be discredited if no viable distinction could be drawn between it and ontological proofs for the existence of various things other than God. The necessary distinction, fortunately, soon presents itself. In the case of God, we are talking about the most perfect possible of everything that is. Since this being must, of necessity, have all possible perfections, among the perfections it has must be existence. But the most perfect possible typewriter, however perfect it may be, is only the most perfect possible typewriter and may therefore lack some perfections, namely, those not appropriate to a typewriter, even the most perfect one. But if, admittedly, it lacks some perfections, it may also lack existence. But the most perfect possible anything, i.e., God, can lack no perfection and must therefore also possess the perfection of existence.

The ontological proof thus expresses an insight that we must now make explicit. The heart of the ontological proof is that existence is an inextricable part of the essence of God, so that whereas every other essence can be thought as either existing or not existing, God cannot be thought as nonexisting, since to do so would be to think a contradiction. The concept of God therefore implies his existence in an *a priori* way. In the case of all other things that are, their natures are subsumed under being. When they are so subsumed they are, and when they are not so subsumed they are not. One might say that they drift in and out of the temple of being as they emerge from nonbeing to being and then return to nonbeing once again. There are, of course, grave intellectual difficulties with this way of putting things (though it is difficult to think of another way). To speak of something that lacks being acquiring it later is to think of it as being before it acquires being, and that seems self-contradictory. One of the great difficulties of ontology has therefore been the explanation of change, particularly the most profound change of all, the coming into being from nonbeing. It is because of the difficulty of making coming into being intelligible that much of Western philosophy has been forced to deny its reality by positing some version of the notion of an eternal substance that always was and always will be. Accordingly, change is never a coming into being from a state of nonbeing but merely a modification from one state of being to another. Whether it is possible for something that lacks being to acquire being or whether all things that are have always been and the appearance of change is merely a rearrangement of elements that have always been into new complexes is not a question we need settle here. We need only point out that all things that are, are subsumed under being.

It is the insight of the ontological proof for the existence of God that this is not so for God. It is not the concept of being that implies the concept of God but the concept of God that implies the concept of being. Being, according to the ontological proof, is a necessary attribute of God. So is every other attribute that is a perfection or that increases perfection. All this flows out of the essence of God. The essence of God is perfection: nothing greater can be imagined. This essence, claims the ontological proof, can be understood before it is understood that existence is implied in it. The dialectical foundation of the ontological proof is that the essence of God must be admitted even by the atheist to be thinkable, since otherwise he would have no way of identifying what it is whose existence he denies. But once it is admitted, according to the ontological proof, that God can be conceived, the existence of God follows with logical necessity. Psychologically, it is therefore clear that the thought of God must come first, and the result of an analysis of this concept is that existence is seen to follow. But is it logically and metaphysically first?

We insist that it is. The ontological proof demonstrates that God is the Lord of being. By means of the concept of God, we reach behind being and give it a foundation. This enterprise of reaching behind being is fraught with great difficulties. Ontologically, it is in the context of nonbeing that the reaching behind we refer to has taken place. If being is to be thought, it must be bounded by that which delimits it, which can only be nonbeing. But nonbeing cannot be thought. It was therefore rejected in the Parmenidean tradition as being as unsuitable topic for discourse, the result of which was the expansion of being into an unbounded absolute that displaced the being of beings of the more modest sort. Such rigor could not be maintained for long and soon adaptations to reality began to appear. While being itself was left uncontaminated and uncircumscribed by nonbeing, nonbeing was permitted to return and function on some lower level of the ontological scale. The uncompromising ontological monism of Parmenides was thereby avoided but his basic insight of the unthinkability of nonbeing was maintained on the level of ultimate reality. In revisionist Parmenideanism (the term can be applied to Plato and the Neoplatonists) we see a limited attempt to outflank being, though not on the level of ultimate reality. The difficulty of such a compromise is that it is difficult to hold the opposites together and one is pushed into embracing one or another of the contesting positions. We have already examined the Parmenidean side of the alternative. It consists of a metaphysical monism in which neither individuals nor time has a place. This view is difficult to fault on purely philosophic grounds. The rigor of its logic is impressive and is the ultimate triumph of the criterion of consistency, since, by its rejection of negativity, it destroys the ontological foundation of the possibility of inconsistency, a concept that is unthinkable without some essential forms of nonbeing such as negativity and contradiction. But pure Parmenideanism is also deeply at odds with the reality of human existence, for which nonbeing in the forms of finitude, temporality, guilt, etc., are pervasively operative. The outflanking of being therefore becomes urgently necessary.

The accomplishing of this task requires the descent into nonbeing. It is a descent that has never been accomplished. It has never been accomplished in the sense in which Parmenides was an ascent into being. Even Heidegger, whose thought is certainly not oblivious to nonbeing, makes being the official object of his search. The intensity of his interest in being is suspect. It is an interest in being suspended over the abyss of nonbeing. But it is nevertheless a grasping at being, not a full descent into nonbeing. Such a descent is ruled out by the whole tradition of Western philosophy if not by the very condition of man himself. Thought is the celebration of that which is. The biological foundation of human existence is a surge toward preservation of self and species. One hardly knows where to begin to adducing evidence for the supremacy of being over nonbeing in human existence. Sexuality is an affirmation of life over death. The structure of language is rooted in the predication of a predicate of a subject, the affirmation that a subject *is* a predicate. However this *is* is interpreted, it remains a predication of being. From the phenomenological point of view, the very intentionality of human consciousness is a reaching out toward being, since consciousness is empty without an object for it to grasp. And the same is true of the social dimension of human existence. The communities and institutions among which man lives protect him from the threat of nonbeing. They lay out for him modes of existence that he need not create from out of nothing but that have existed for a long time and therefore lend stability and continuity to his existence. Finite human being is thus absorbed into structures far less finite, even if ultimately not infinite. The same is true of the search for knowledge, particularly in its modern form as the search for certainty. Certainty is the reflection of being in knowledge. It is the appearance of stability in the medium of consciousness, a medium that is profoundly time-bound and therefore in particular need of a stabilizing presence. In these and in many other ways the direction of human existence is toward being and away from nonbeing.

But nonbeing cannot be avoided altogether. It lurks behind and around every structure of being. There is always a horizon of darkness that surrounds the clearing in which man lives. The surface of the visible is not pure facade. What is visible has depth and what has depth can be seen only partially because the surface reveals itself but also hides what is underneath it, what is behind the surface. The human enterprise therefore becomes one of penetration, of shorter or longer incursions or penetrations into the unknown. The biological thrust toward life does not avoid death and nature seems more concerned with the survival of the species than its individual members. All knowledge comes up against the contingent, the discovery that somewhere in our system we have no other choice but to accept that this is how things are and not otherwise. Heidegger realizes this when he poses the question, "Why is there something rather than nothing?" It is not the kind of question to which an answer is possible. For some philosophers, the impossibility of answering this question destroys its standing as a legitimate question and turns it into a pseudoquestion. The positivist-analytic school insists that only those questions that can, at least in principle, be answered are legitimate questions. But this view reflects a profound misunderstanding of the ontology of questions. By means of the question, negativity enters the world. To ask a question is to break with the immediacy of the given. He who asks a question affirms that he conceives of an alternative to that which is. To ask why is to perceive that things could be otherwise than they are and therefore an explanation is demanded for their being the way they are and not otherwise. Heidegger's question, "Why is there anything rather than nothing?" is just a radicalization of the conceived alternative to what is. When we ask "Why do men walk upright?" we posit the possibility of an alternative to what is, their not walking upright. To some extent, therefore, nonbeing makes its appearance because to conceive an alternative is to conceive the nonbeing of the present state of affairs and the being of another state of affairs. Nevertheless, nonbeing is veiled because the alternative that is conceived is another state of being. Heidegger's question is more radical because the alternative it conceives is not another state of being different from the current state but just nonbeing itself. This is the reason that the question produces a sort of intellectual dizziness, a grasping for something to hold on to that one cannot find. But the difference between this question and other questions is not an absolute one. All questions undermine the solidity of being. They drive cracks into that solidity that have the potential of growing and plunging being into chaos. By means of the question, nonbeing appears in the world.

But the question is only the harbinger of nonbeing, it is not an embracing of it. Behind the question lurks the possibility of an answer and the answer silences nonbeing. When it becomes a basic tenet that only those questions whose answers are on the horizon (that can be answered "in principle") may be asked, then the holding on to being is obvious. We are then told that the only river we may attempt to cross is one whose opposite bank is visible before the crossing is attempted. We must never let go of being when there is no further being in sight to take its place. But even when such timid rules are not imposed, the very possibility of an answer is a groping for being. And even when that possibility is not overly apparent, as in Heidegger's question, the ground of being is not altogether abandoned. Two modes of ontological redemption loom indistinctly in the darkness. One is the possibility of an answer, however difficult it may be to imagine a satisfactory answer to such a question. And the other is the reflex action of a return to the being that is, from which Heidegger's question has temporarily alienated us but to the security of which we return when the dizziness threatens to exceed tolerable limits. Thought is therefore a groping for being, even when thought does not prematurely silence questions, even the most difficult questions. Thought is not oblivious to nonbeing. Nonbeing may even be the secret energy that drives thought in its undertaking. But thought, even questioning thought, is not the embracing of nonbeing.

7. DEONTOLOGY

The embracing of nonbeing is violence. In violence, being is turned against itself, toward its own destruction, toward nonbeing. We must therefore investigate the deontology of violence because we have now left the realm of ontology for the ontology of nonbeing, or deontology.

The first truth of deontology is that the whole enterprise cannot be conducted within the realm of thought. In thought, being must triumph. This is inherent in the nature of thought because it is inherent in the nature of language. The significant moves of deontology must therefore be made in action rather than in thought. And because this is so, our discussion of deontology must necessarily be brief. An elaborate theory of deontology is a contradiction in terms, a shallow attempt to tame the power of nonbeing by exhibiting it as a specimen of thought. Deontology is therefore not a participant in the dialogue of thought but a presence in the dialogue as a fallacy. Medieval thought referred to it as the *argumentum ad baculum*, the fallacy committed when one appeals to force or the threat of force to cause acceptance of a conclusion. Traditional logic did not have the slightest difficulty in categorizing such an appeal to force as a fallacy of relevance and dismissing it with the contempt it deserved. From the point of view of the realm of discourse and therefore the ontology of being, logic was, of course, perfectly right. The appeal to force is a fallacy of discourse, as long as we stay in the realm of discourse and refuse to venture beyond it. At the same time, there is obviously something quite shortsighted, even if not intellectually fallacious, in this procedure. The purity of relevance is maintained by the expulsion of violence from within its domain, but at the same time reality has been ignored. The reality that has been ignored is not the reality of metaphysics but of that which lies outside discourse. To some extent, such a realm makes itself felt even in ontology. We earlier had occasion to note that existence has often been understood as a given that could not be absorbed into any system of concepts without being converted into an essence, which is precisely what existence is not. For thought, the difficulty of coping with existence is hardly comparable in magnitude to its difficulty in coping with nonbeing. Nonbeing, unlike being or existence, is corrosive of discourse and therefore drives man out of the realm of discourse into that of action. It is important not to understand this as primarily an intellectual process. The unthinkability of nonbeing is not a particularly difficult concept to grasp. Nevertheless, since most men are not metaphysicians, it is not a familiar problem to them. But the temptation of violence is grasped much more directly. It is an elemental mode of human being in the world. Violence, as Sartre has pointed out, is rooted in the very essence of consciousness. The thrust of consciousness is toward the objectification of the world. The object is the powerless recipient of consciousness' fixating gaze. The vitality of consciousness penetrates the inner being of the object, which has no way of protecting itself from the gaze of consciousness. The sexual analogy implicit in this interpretation is reflected in the biblical practice of referring to sexual intercourse as a "knowing," as when "Adam knew his wife Eve and she gave birth."[16] The violence implicit in the sexual encounter is not restricted to those instances when the "consent" of the sexual partner is not obtained or when sadomasochistic practices are introduced to heighten the sexual pleasure. To the body of the other there always attaches the atmosphere of objectification, and it is this objectification that introduces violence as an essential component of sexuality.

It is for this reason that violence is such an essential mode of human being in the world. We have spoken of the question as an irruption of nonbeing into the realm of being. Hidden in the question is the negation of that which is because when a state of affairs becomes questionable, the possibility of its nonbeing or of its being otherwise becomes apparent. The question is also often the opening gambit in the thrust toward objectification because, once the question is asked, the temptation to extract an answer by the forcible unveiling of the object becomes very great. Nevertheless, both question and answer are in the realm of discourse and therefore the full power of nonbeing remains muted. But it is otherwise with violence. In violence, being can be smashed. The smashing of being takes place when the integrity of the object's being is dissolved into unrelated component parts. This is most obvious in the transformation of the living into the nonliving and it is for this reason that the most pristine form of violence is killing, the reduction of the living to the nonliving. The irruption of nonbeing into being is most visible in this instance because the ontological discontinuity between the living and the nonliving is so sharp. When a rock is smashed, a certain degree of disintegration of being takes place simply because the big rock represented a greater cohesion of being than the many small rocks. When a machine is smashed, a greater disintegration of being takes place because the resultant parts are not only smaller in size but lack the coherent purposiveness of the whole. But while machines have a degree of integrated purposiveness, it is the living organism that manifests being in its fullest. Life is the perpetuation of being in the form of a plastic solidity that preserves its identity not, as in the case of inanimate matter, merely by solidity but, more significantly, by preserving its identity in the context of purposive interaction with its environment: that which is not itself is incorporated into the unity of the organism and used to maintain or strengthen its identity. The dynamism of the living being participates in time and, in so doing, maintains a degree of identity that transcends the individual of the species and incorporates it into a continuity of ancestors and descendants stretching far in both directions of temporality. The triumph over nonbeing thus achieved is obtained at the price of a vastly increased vulnerability to the danger of destruction. The nonbeing that is conquered by life takes its revenge by introducing the possibility of death, a form of nonbeing unique to the living and therefore the purest form of nonbeing phenomenologically available. The dead Pierre (to use Sartre's friend, whose absence from the café makes nonbeing phenomenologically manifest) is far more absent than the absent Pierre.[17] The absent Pierre is not where he was expected and therefore his absence is visible. But the nonbeing of Pierre is far more visible in his corpse, which was his body and which formerly manifested his being and which, as corpse, manifests his nonbeing. The continuity between body and corpse is crucial in this connection. The difference between the two is so great because it is so small. The features of the dead Pierre are those of the formerly living, and yet the difference is so great that the nonbeing of the living person impresses itself on us with incomparable force. Death is the termination of the power of being itself and not merely of one or another of its manifestations. It is for this reason that killing is the purest form of deontology.

And it is for this reason that Nazism is the deontology of Heidegger. Heidegger's deep involvement with Nazism has been the single greatest philosophical scandal of this or perhaps any century. How could, it is asked, the greatest philosopher of the twentieth century support the most monstrous ideology of murder ever to appear in human history? The mystery is deepened by a number of extremely curious ancillary facts. References to Nazism as such are almost totally missing from Heidegger's published work. Even the infamous *Rector's Speech*,[18] which comes as close as Heidegger ever does to endorsing national socialism outright, does so without explicitly mentioning it. Yet the fact is that Heidegger was a member of the Nazi party and delivered many speeches enthusiastically supporting the program of the party without publishing any of these speeches. Our knowledge of their content comes from local newspaper reports that summarize their content without printing the actual texts.[19] Another noteworthy fact is that Heidegger never, in the postwar period, expressed any regret for these actions. In a brief note he takes cognizance of the fact that the dedication to Edmund Husserl,[20] the Jewish founder of phenomenology, was deleted. Heidegger explains that although Nazi authorities had demanded that all references to Husserl in the body of the work be deleted as well, he had adamantly refused to do so. The compromise that was arranged, he claims, was that the dedication to Husserl be deleted while all references to him in the body of the work be kept intact. Other than this brief attempt at self-justification—an attempt that hardly deals with the core of Heidegger's Nazi activity—there is no attempt in any of Heidegger's published work since the end of World War II to explain his attitude toward Nazism in retrospect.

The main problem, of course, remains Heidegger's Nazism. Is it an inherent part of his philosophy, so that Nazism is somehow the natural consequence of his ontology, or is it an accidental idiosyncrasy with no real connection to his philosophic enterprise? Much of the work of the French Jewish phenomenologist Emmanuel Levinas has been devoted to a deep, if largely implicit, polemic against Heidegger's deep, if implicit, amoralism. This amoralism expresses itself in a number of ways, among which perhaps the most striking is the centrality he assigns to notions such as guilt and conscience while insisting that these notions are not to be interpreted in any ethical sense but rather in an exclusively ontological one. This deethicization of clearly ethical concepts is probably unparalleled in philosophic literature. But the real tragedy is the silent presence of

Nazism in the thought of Heidegger, a presence that never becomes part of the argument but that speaks more loudly than words. This silence is his deontology. His ontology is what can be put into words, and to the extent that nonbeing can be put into discourse, Heidegger does so by orienting his understanding of being toward temporality and other modes of extendedness that dilute the undifferentiated positivity of being with large doses of nonbeing. But, however strenuous and ingenious the attempt to incorporate nonbeing into ontology, the final result must be a notion of being rather than nonbeing. Real nonbeing can be realized only in destruction outside of discourse, and that is the role played by Nazism for Heidegger. The essence of the Nazi movement was rage, a powerful and unspeakable hatred of many peoples and ideas but most particularly of Jews. In the uninhibited expression of such rage, the foundation of being is undermined and ontology meets its only worthy opponent. As long as the struggle between being and nonbeing is restricted to the realm of language, being has little to fear. But the picture changes radically when the debating platform is replaced by the field of combat. The famous remark attributed to Herman Göring to the effect that when he hears the word *culture* he reaches for his revolver, expresses this realization. And the same is true of Nietzsche's fulminations against Jewish and Christian psychological warfare, whose purpose is to inhibit and render impotent the natural strength of the superior man by imposing on him moral inventions designed to serve the interests of the weaker, who are meant to perish at the hands of the stronger. From this point of view, the whole philosophic enterprise, to the extent to which it is a reflective rather than active one, can be interpreted as a Jewish deflection into thought of what should be life rather than the endless, self-conscious intellectualizations of philosophic thought. Philosophy here turns against itself because it has caught a glimpse of the power of nonbeing and therefore finds itself unhinged, driven out of the realm of discourse into violence.

The nonbeing that properly circumscribes being is therefore not nonbeing as it is thought but nonbeing as it is translated into action in the mode of violence. This does not mean that the conceptual ballet that ensues when being is pitted against nonbeing in purely conceptual terms lacks significance. Quite the contrary. The paradoxes engendered when nonbeing is discovered to be the subject of predicates prepare the ground for the leap out of the realm of discourse by straining the limits of discourse so that acts of discursive violence precede the violence of action. Nor need we maintain that only nonbeing in the form of deontology forces on man a leap into action and away from discourse. Being also has its active correlate, as in all acts of making, building, creating, strengthening, and preserving. But just as in the realm of discourse being and nonbeing imply each other so that we cannot have the one without the other, so in the realm of action building requires destruction because, as Plato understood, opposites arise out of each other and imply each other. Yet each realm has a primary foundation: for the realm of discourse that foundation is being and for that of action it is nonbeing and violence. Discourse is the proper realm of being because action cannot be adequate to being. The finitude of all human existence dictates that all human creation is transitory, vanquishing only temporarily the cosmic forces of destruction that lie in wait for it. In a way, the power of human creation is thereby magnified because the work stands out as a defiance against its inevitable fate of destruction and disappearance. However powerful such a posture can be, it remains doomed to failure. But in the realm of discourse, being fares much better. This is so because the unique gift of man that is language is, as we have seen, rooted in predication and therefore in the positivity of being. The result of this is that when language attempts to listen to and speak of nonbeing, nonbeing is transformed into the positivity of being as it is spoken of and thereby divested, one is tempted to say, of its essential being as nonbeing. From this man can only conclude that discourse can only yield a fraudulent image of nonbeing that can only be truly embraced in destruction or self-destruction.

8. GOD BEYOND BEING

After this excursion into deontology and its expression in violence, we are now ready to return to the question of God. Traditionally, God has been far more closely allied with being than with nonbeing. The ontological proof, as we have seen, makes existence an essential characteristic of God. Images of building, creating, strengthening, and preserving quickly come to mind when God is thought of. Paul Tillich speaks of God as the "ground of being"[21] and not the ground of nonbeing. The very act of creation associates God with the forces of being. God speaks of himself as "I will be who I will be,"[22] and even if this is somewhat weaker than the mistranslation of "I am who I am," the association with being remains prominent. At the same time, as we have seen, it is not easy to formulate God's relationship to being. Is God a being among other beings, is God being itself, or is God beyond both being and nonbeing? It is these three possibilities that we must now explore in greater detail.

We have already spoken of and rejected the first option as inappropriate to Hashem, the God of Israel. It is not inappropriate to the gods of the nations, to whom even Heidegger finds it possible to refer. The gods of the nations are many and their powers are limited. They are subject to fate and therefore it is necessary to explain how they came to be. They, like all other beings that are, live under the universal umbrella of being as beings that are but not as being itself. It therefore can be asked how they came to be, but it cannot be asked how being came to be because being is the totality that permits no vantage point outside of itself from which questions about it can be asked. Since no questions about the origin of Hashem are ever asked in Jewish faith, Hashem cannot be a being among other beings. At the same time, as we have shown in the previous chapter, Hashem is not the unfathomable God of the philosophers. The Bible depicts him as a living person who can be addressed by man and who addresses man. He is a being about whom psychological considerations are not irrelevant, but no one has yet explored the psychology of being. While we must therefore reject the option of Hashem as a being among beings, we cannot do so without reservation because we must not sever the link to personhood that connects man with Hashem and that makes possible the biblical drama of man's interaction with Hashem. We must keep this reservation in mind, but it cannot obscure the basic truth that Hashem is not ruled by being.

The next option is to identify God with being. "By God," writes Spinoza, "I understand Being absolutely infinite, that is to say, substance consisting of infinite attributes, each one of which expresses eternal and infinite essence."[23] Spinoza had no hesitation in applying the word *God* to being. More recent philosophers are less eager to do so, for various reasons. The most important of these is that while the existence of God is considered a highly dubious proposition, the existence of being is the least dubious. In a world in which speech about God is no longer felt to be a viable option, being can be assigned the task of assuming some of the aura that had previously been borne by God. From the point of view of traditional empiricism, this is a most lamentable regression into metaphysical obscurantism that should have been left behind long ago by the impressive advances scored by positivistic, analytic, and logical techniques. But there remains the minority for whom the "theistic" God is beyond resurrection but who also cannot reconcile themselves to the total absence of the holy in the scientifically understood universe. It is for these that being becomes the focus of quasi-religious attention. Being has the potential for fulfilling a religious function because it is a limiting concept of reason. Being is not a predicate, as we have seen, because all predicates divide the universe into that portion to which the predicate properly refers and that portion to which it does not. Predicates therefore define themselves by that which they exclude, but being excludes nothing and it cannot therefore be either a predicate or a concept. Being is thus the only all-inclusive term available to reason, and the all-inclusive has a natural majesty akin to the holy. From the finitude of the human situation, reason attempts to find a vantage point from which it might view the all-inclusive as something that can be grasped. But the moment an attempt is made to grasp it, the limits of the all-inclusive begin to appear on the horizon and the all-inclusive ceases to be the all-inclusive just as it comes into the sight of reason. If the term *universe* is applied to the all-inclusive, the question that is asked is whether there can be anything "outside" of the universe or whether there can be more than one universe. If it is maintained that there cannot be anything outside of the universe and that there can be only one universe, the mind wonders what is beyond the universe, what is beyond the furthest limits of space, and this wonder is a sort of religious wonder that can yield a form of natural piety.

But being is nevertheless not God. To be more precise, being is not Hashem. The word *God* has a certain plasticity about it. It includes the supreme being of many peoples and cultures and is therefore necessarily an abstraction. As understood in the Western tradition, God is modelled on Hashem, who is the primary model for the Western notion of God. And Hashem is not being. *He is both more and less than being.* He is less than being because, as we have already pointed out, he is a person with a psychology to whom we can speak and from whom we can ask and either receive or be refused. He is a being who cares for the welfare of man and of his people. Jewish existence has been possible because the people has felt this divine protection in spite of the many horrors of its history. Israel's experience has been of the humility of Hashem, of his closeness to those who suffer and call on him. It would be ludicrous to ask being to forgive our sins, relieve our suffering, and grant us eternal life.

Common usage therefore comes to our rescue because the word *God* has a fair degree of definition in common usage and almost none of it is interchangeable with *being*. And it is also common usage, though perhaps less directly, that reveals God as more than being. God is the creator of the universe. Before God created the universe, there was no universe. But if the universe includes everything that is and if God existed before he created the universe, then the universe must have existed before God created anything. By not asking this question, Judaism makes an ontological statement. *It declares that being is created being.* To identify God with being is therefore to identify him with one of his creatures, which is the very meaning of idolatry.

We have thus reached our third option: God as beyond being and nonbeing. To reach the standpoint that is beyond both being and nonbeing, we must first traverse nonbeing. Being is what it is because it is not nonbeing. Nonbeing is the contrast by means of which alone we can grasp being. That which is totally without contrast cannot be understood and therefore the solidity and illumination of being must be surrounded by the emptiness and darkness of nonbeing. The quasi-religious awe that surrounds being is an awe at the realization that there is something rather than nothing, that there is not just nonbeing. The all-inclusive is therefore not all-inclusive because it does not include nonbeing. And there cannot be another, more inclusive all-inclusive that also includes nonbeing because nonbeing cannot be included in anything, since it is nothing. Nonbeing therefore undermines the possibility of a philosophic totality, and with the undermining of this totality the sovereignty of both reason and discourse come to an end. Reason and discourse are thus seen as islands of being in an ocean of nonbeing. But in order to perceive the contours of the island of being, the observer must station himself in the nonbeing that surrounds being and this cannot be done. Heidegger, as we have seen, went as far as is possible to go in this direction. The descent into time as the essential vantage point for the viewing of being is precisely the descent into nonbeing because time is the "not yet," the dimension by means of which man is ahead of himself, projected into that which he is not yet. This is the basic root of Heidegger's preoccupation with being: the more completely temporality and nonbeing are faced, the more necessary it becomes to hold on to the defiance of nonbeing that can emanate only from being. Heidegger understands that human existence is condemned to finitude through temporality and that being itself cannot remain uncontaminated by time. The temporalization of being is thus a reconciliation between the nature of man and the ultimate nature of being, which now comes to assume something of the nature of human existence. But this reconciliation cannot be successful because being is either absorbed into human existence or it retains its metahuman and metatemporal solidity. If it is totally absorbed into the temporality of human existence, then being is destroyed and nonbeing has, in effect, taken its place. If, on the other hand, the absorption of being into temporality is not carried through to its conclusion, then not only is the chasm between the existence of man and being not bridged, but the remaining solidity of being prevents the grasping of being because it deprives the thinker of the only possible vantage point from which he can attempt such an understanding. This is the reason for the necessity of an "early" and "late" Heidegger. In the early Heidegger the human condition is taken seriously and the doctrine of being that is hinted at though never developed is a fully temporalized being. But as this is not metaphysically feasible, since being cannot be fully temporalized without ceasing to be being, there simply does not appear a doctrine of being, but instead there does appear a doctrine of man. In the later Heidegger, being suddenly appears, and while it cannot be said that the being of Heidegger's later writings is totally nontemporal, the very shift away from the focus on man to the focus on being enables Heidegger to ignore the corrosive work of nonbeing and to celebrate being with the awe traditionally reserved for metatemporal being.

9. CREATED BEING

The final result of a purely philosophic analysis, then, is that thought drives man to the concept of being and that being drives thought into nonbeing and finally out of thought into deontology or violence. The wonder that there is something rather than nothing cannot fail to be a passing phase. Such natural piety cannot stand up to the power of nonbeing, which is corrosive to the highest degree both intellectually and existentially. Against nonbeing, human knowledge, art, and culture cannot survive. Death awaits both the fool and the wise man and all is vanity of vanities. In the struggle between ontology and deontology, the former cannot win.

It is at this point that Hashem speaks. Being, we are told, is not its own master. And neither is nonbeing. Being is created. It is not its own foundation. It is brought into being out of nonbeing not by nonbeing but by Hashem. But if that is so, then Hashem was before he brought being into being out of nonbeing and therefore there was being before Hashem created it. But that would constitute the triumph of ontology over Hashem, while the truth is that Hashem is the Lord of being. The being of Hashem before he created being could therefore not have been the being of being. It could only have been Hashem. Hashem's being is not existence added to his essence. In the case of all created being, essence and existence are not the same. Created beings may or may not exist. Their contingency separates their being from their nature and therefore being becomes possible because it is something that some natures have and others do not. The existence of Hashem, we learn in the ontological proof, is not separate from, or added to, his essence. His nature and his being are one and the same. *But if that is so, there is only his nature and nothing added to it.* Hashem is therefore beyond being. As created beings whose very understanding is subject to the dialectic of being and nonbeing, we apply the language of being to Hashem. This cannot be avoided. Only in the light of creation and therefore of being can we speak and think. We thereby bring Hashem into his own creation alongside us and therefore in partnership with us. And Hashem does not mind this, since in creating us he created himself as our partner so that he can participate with us in our history. But he is what he is and will be what he will be before being and nonbeing were created. It is for this reason that the ontological proof is both so persuasive and empty at the same time. Interpreted as proving the existence of God in the sense in which existence applies to creatures, the proof is justifiably rejected on the ground that existence is always contingent and can be known only empirically. But this is true only of contingent being, which is being that is bounded by nonbeing, the very definition of its contingency. Necessary being, the kind of being the ontological proof attributes to God, is being that is not bounded by nonbeing, the very meaning of its necessity. The most important philosophic conclusion which thus emerges is that necessary being is not a species of being. It is rather a being that is beyond being and nonbeing. Created being is juxtaposed with nonbeing, whereas the creator of both being and nonbeing is beyond his creation and therefore beyond both being and nonbeing.

We are thus left with three options. The first is positive ontology. Here being conquers all, nonbeing is eliminated, as in Parmenides, and being becomes the totality of everything that is. Positive ontology is inherently nondialectical and is therefore forced to dispense with all possible forms of otherness and, as we will see in the next chapter, with the ethical, which demands the reality of the other and the reality of the demand, whose being as demand is dialectical being and not the full being of positive being. In Descartes, it is positive ontology that is at work. That his point of departure is doubt would lead us to think otherwise, but the easy dispelling of his doubt demonstrates the merely tactical rather than strategic nature of it. Having demonstrated the indubitable certainty of his own being as a thinker, Descartes next moves, by means of the ontological proof, to the being of God, whose necessary being he interprets in very clearly positive terms. While Descartes is not the author of an ontology, to the extent that an ontology is implicit in his thought, it is not one that takes proper cognizance of nonbeing. The same, of course, is true of Spinoza. The ignoring of nonbeing is related to an ignoring of the limits of reason, as well as of language. The recognition of such limits is foreign to the rationalism of Spinoza, Descartes, and Leibniz. Philosophy, for such thinkers, is an illumination of darkness, which cannot be permitted to retain any of its secrets, of which nonbeing is the deepest. The self-confidence of rationalism is thus ultimately rooted in its ontology of being and its refusal to take seriously the dark side of being: nonbeing.

The second option is the far more serious and dangerous one. Here nonbeing is not ignored. Here the limits of reason and language are reached and the transition to the action of nonbeing is made, as we have explained, in the mode of violence. Nonbeing here acts as a source of tremendous vitality, as a creative, or, more accurately, destructive darkness that energizes the work of thinkers like Nietzsche and Kierkegaard. In these cases, the power of nonbeing is put to work with extraordinary effect, but because it is nonbeing, it results in an ultimately destructive achievement. And this is not only a matter of the paradoxicality of the thought, which appears rationally defective to the positive ontologist but is far more a matter of the life of the thinker, which does not remain outside of the ongoing upheaval. It is not a strange eccentricity of existential thought that the thinker must risk himself, that he must appropriate his thought into his existence, and that he must be prepared to put his life where his mouth is. The surge into life and risk constitute the breaking out of the positivity of thought and its virtues which are proof, certainty, and sobriety. The nonbeing the deontologist takes seriously shatters these forms, as it must shatter all forms, if not the very existence of the thinker.

Superficially considered, the third option—the turn to God—has far more in common with the first than with the second option. There is a positivity associated with God we saw reflected in the ontological proof for God's existence. The association of God with being is ancient and so Paul Tillich can speak of God as the ground of being and not seem utterly ridiculous. But we must now point out the other and more interesting aspect of the picture: the relation of Hashem to nonbeing.

It must first be observed that being is bounded only by nonbeing, as we have seen. But we have also spoken of Hashem as the creator of being. Hashem therefore also bounds being. It is, of course, not the same bounding as that of nonbeing. Nonbeing is a correlative of being, a complement of being implicit in the very notion of being. Hashem is the creator of being, and this is not implicit in being in the same sense as nonbeing is. When Tillich found it necessary to reach beyond being he reached under it to its foundation. The ground of being is that on which being rests. It is therefore, if anything, more like being than being itself because the movement of Tillich is toward the solidity of foundation and therefore toward greater positivity. But Hashem is not the foundation of being: he is the creator of being. Creation here does not mean the bringing into being of being out of the being of Hashem. That is the strategy of Platonism and of Neoplatonic emanation. The world is not the effluence of the being of Hashem. The being of the world is not continuous with the being of Hashem. Hashem created the world out of nothing. Before he created being there was no being. There was only Hashem. And in saying this, we are not asserting that before Hashem created being there was being, namely, the being of Hashem. The statement that Hashem was or that he is, is a statement made outside of the framework of ontology. And it is at this point that the kinship of Hashem to nonbeing becomes apparent. In speaking about nonbeing we are also drawn into the paradox of apparently attributing being to nonbeing. Parmenides therefore commands silence about nonbeing, as we have often been advised to be silent about Hashem. In both cases, however, these are commands we cannot obey. In the case of being, the logic of thought about being makes it necessary to think and speak of its complement, nonbeing. In the case of Hashem it is otherwise. There is nothing implicit either in ontology or deontology that forces the move to Hashem. The dialectic of being and nonbeing excludes the possibility of a totality and therefore of a relatively closed system in the manner of a Spinoza or Hegel. The philosophic drive toward necessary being is thus doomed to failure. Philosophy is therefore left with being bounded by nonbeing, or contingent being. But this does not force reason to invent the idea of creation. The only form of creation that reason can understand is the coming into being out of a previous mode of being. Being is possible only if it is already actual because out of nothing only more nothing can emerge.

The createdness of being is therefore not philosophically demonstrable. What is philosophically demonstrable is the contingency of being, that there is no philosophic answer to the question why there is something rather than nothing. But that does not dictate the idea of creation. The idea of creation cannot be grounded because creation is the idea of the ungrounded. Emanation is grounded creation. Emanation conceives the emergence of being out of a fuller, more solid being. The coming into being of the world is interpreted as an overflow of the fullness of being, which never misses what it loses. We have emphasized that Hashem's creation is the bringing into being of the world by Hashem, who is not a preexistent being but who is beyond being and nonbeing. To think of Hashem as a being is to think of him as one of the beings in the world he created. But, in the first instance, he is not such a being. The rabbis commonly use the word Mokaum (Hebrew for "Place") to refer to Hashem and they explain that the world is not the place of Hashem but Hashem the place of the world. There is no totality, according to the rabbis, that can contain Hashem but Hashem is the Lord of all totalities. In speaking of Hashem as the place of the world, it is important to note the spatial metaphor invoked. Hashem is not a substance that underlies the world. He is not the ultimate being of which the world is one manifestation. He is the space in which the world is enveloped. Space is a representation of nonbeing in the material order. Hashem is therefore not the ground of being, for which Place would be a very poor metaphor. Hashem is the transparency, lightness, and freedom that envelops being. Hashem is the principle of hope, which is not the ground but rather the future of history. And Hashem is ungrounded, unwarranted hope. Restricted to the realm of being, we would be condemned to basing our expectation of the future on our experience of the past, which is the proper grounding of all such reasonable expectation. In this sense, Jewish faith, like creation, is ungrounded. It is a trusting of Hashem that he will fulfill his promises even though the evidence indicates the contrary. The nature of Jewish faith is therefore rooted in the nature of the God of Israel. Were Hashem subject to ontology, were being the overarching concept uniting the world and Hashem, then creation would have to be grounded in the nature of being and there would be direct logical and ontological continuity between the being of the world and Hashem. Because there is no such continuity, faith is the proper mode of the knowledge of Hashem. Faith is the corresponding freedom of human movement toward Hashem that reflects the freedom of Hashem's movement of creation *ex nihilo*, out of nonbeing.

10. DEMYTHOLOGIZATION

Finally, how can we reconcile the thrust of this chapter with that of the previous chapter, in which we argued for the personality of Hashem? Is not the framework within which the Bible speaks of Hashem the framework of creation and is it not wrong in principle to put Hashem into his creation instead of realizing that no categories appropriate to the created world are appropriate to Hashem? It is the desire to save God from being dishonored anthropomorphically that has generated various attempts to demythologize the Bible by extracting its inner, existential meaning and discarding the "literal" garb in which this meaning appears. Tillich, as we would expect, has little sympathy for those who resist the necessary demythologization. He writes:

> The radical criticism of the myth is due to the fact that the primitive mythological consciousness resists the attempt to interpret the myth of myth. It is afraid of every act of demythologization. It believes that the broken myth is deprived of its truth and of its convincing power. Those who live in an unbroken mythological world feel safe and certain. They resist, often fanatically, any attempt to introduce an element of uncertainty by "breaking the myth," namely, by making conscious its symbolic character. Such resistance is supported by authoritarian systems, religious or political, in order to give security to the people under their control and unchallenged power to those who exercise the control. The resistance against demythologization expresses itself in "literalism." The symbols and myths are understood in their immediate meaning. The material, taken from nature and history, is used in its proper sense. The

character of the symbol to point beyond itself to something else is disregarded. Creation is taken as a magic act which happened once upon a time. The fall of Adam is localized on a special geographical point and attributed to a human individual. The virgin birth of the Messiah is understood in biological terms, resurrection and ascension as physical events, the second coming of the Christ as a telluric, or cosmic, catastrophe. The presupposition of such literalism is that God is a being, acting in time and space, dwelling in a special place, affecting the course of events and being affected by them like any other being in the universe. Literalism deprives God of his ultimacy and, religiously speaking, of his majesty. It draws him down to the level of that which is not ultimate, the finite and conditional. In the last analysis it is not rational criticism of the myth which is decisive but the inner religious criticism. Faith, if it takes its symbols literally, becomes idolatrous! It calls something ultimate which is less than ultimate. Faith, conscious of the symbolic character of its symbols, gives God the honor which is due him.[24]

But who is to decide what "the honor which is due him" is? Is that to be a decision made by philosophy or by him whom we wish to honor?

The problem of demythologization is a philosophic problem. Historically, it is a problem that arises when the religious consciousness encounters philosophy and when it attempts to express itself in philosophic categories. We have already seen that being is the point at which philosophy meets religion. Being is, in a sense, the philosophic equivalent of God, and when philosophy and religion meet, God and being tend to shade into each other, as we find with Tillich, where God becomes the "ground of being." The problem of demythologization is rooted in this quasi identification of God with being. The enterprise of demythologization revolves around two foci. One of these is the mythological god or, more accurately, the mythological gods, who are subsumed under being and therefore are subject to fate and whose coming into being out of nonbeing is explained. The other focus around which demythologization revolves is being into which the mythological gods are demythologized. Demythologization is therefore bound to the ontology of being as circumscribed by nonbeing. Neither prior to demythologization nor subsequent to it do we ever escape the domain of noncreated being, whose positivity, in spite of its contact with nonbeing, reduces the gods to the level of beings among other beings and then demythologizes them into the impersonality of being, against which only deontology in the form of violence can prevail. All this is irrelevant for the God of Israel. He does not require demythologization because he is the Lord of being. As the creator of being, he is not subject to his creation and therefore no account of his coming into being is required. Furthermore, as the Lord of being, he circumscribes being, not in the mode of nonbeing that must translate itself into violence but in the mode of the trustworthy promise, which is the power of nonbeing transformed into the principle of hope. Being itself lacks this power of overcoming nonbeing. Being is able only, as in Parmenides, to deny nonbeing as a possibility of thought and therefore covertly to affirm its reality in existence or, as in deontology, to exploit the power of being against itself in the mode of destructive violence. It is quite otherwise when being is created by Hashem, who remains its master and never becomes its servant.

And we can now understand why the Bible can speak about the actions of Hashem without getting entangled in problems of literal versus symbolic meaning and the broader problem of the function of language in relation to God. Just as with being we found that there was danger that Hashem would be subsumed under being and be subject to its dialectic, so it is with language. We either consider the structure of language as determinative in respect to what can be said of Hashem or we consider Hashem the Lord of language, who, as the creator of language, determines what language can or cannot say about its creator. If we choose the first option, then we must first learn the structure and dynamics of language; only after that has been accomplished can we address ourselves to the question as to what we can say about Hashem. But if we choose the second option, then we learn what language can say about Hashem by listening to what Hashem says about himself in and through language. The limits and interpretation of the speech of Hashem about himself and his relation to his people is thus not to be derived from a theory of language: a theory of language, particularly of language about Hashem, is instead learned from the actuality of the divine speech about himself. The possibility of such speech is derived from its actuality instead of its actuality being made dependent on its possibility, which, in turn, is derived from an *a priori* analysis of language understood in its own and therefore uncreated terms. The lordship of Hashem over language once again introduces a nondestructive negatvity into the nature of language. Instead of being contained by rigid structures of possibility, language is created toward the function that its creator assigns to it. Language then becomes the servant, rather than the master, of meaning. And just as created being is circumscribed by Hashem and not by nonbeing, so created language is circumscribed by the task assigned to it by Hashem and not by silence. Where it is silence that circumscribes language, as in Wittgenstein, the most significant dimensions of reality remain outside the domain of language and the being of language is then undermined by the nonbeing of silence. Against silence, the power of Hashem acts through the language of revelation, and hope conquers the despair of silence.

Our aim in this chapter has been to understand being as created being. As the creator of being, Hashem cannot be considered a being or even being itself, since to do so would be to include Hashem into the realm of being. Instead, Hashem creates being and prior to his creation there is no being. We have had to compare Hashem's relation to being to the relation of nonbeing to being. We have found that there is a certain parallel between the role played by nonbeing in regard to being and that played by Hashem in respect to being. Other than Hashem, nonbeing is the only power that can be thought to limit being and to serve as the ground out of which being arises and from which, by means of contrast, it receives its identity. In spite of these similarities between nonbeing and Hashem, the difference between the two is the difference between death and hope. The lordship of Hashem over being and language is a creative and fulfilling lordship by means of which being is fructified and prevented from destroying itself either in the mode of Parmenidean autonomy and the death of identity or by succumbing to the corrosive power of nonbeing and the silence of the void. Hashem's creation affirms being in the power of its finitude as contingent or created being.

Chapter 5

ETHICS AND JEWISH EXISTENCE

1. JEWISH THOUGHT

Our enterprise is Jewish thought.

It could have been Jewish theology. But Jews have not been comfortable with *theology*. Theology examines the logos of God. The logos of God then takes its place alongside the other logoi (of life: biology; of the universe: cosmology; of man: anthropology, etc.). These logoi disclose the rational structures of realms of being. Logoi are rational structures translated into the mode of the visible.

Jews may not see God.[1] To see God is to die. God can only be heard, and what he says cannot become an object of analysis. To analyze the word of God is to extricate oneself—if even for a moment—from the demand the word makes. It is for this reason that Israel replied "We will do and we will hear" when it heard God's demands.[2] Only obedience responds to the word of God as demand, so that a proper hearing can only come after the doing. But God is never seen, and where the Bible flirts with the seeing of God it does so with the greatest of reserve (e.g., "and you shall see my back but my face shall not be seen" [Exod. 33:23]). Because God is not seen, there is no logos of God. And it is therefore difficult to speak of Jewish theology.

But Jewish thought is possible. Thought does not have to create a system. It does not have an object before it at which it casts its glance. It does not interrupt its obedience to explore the rationality of the command. Thought probes here and there, always presupposing a living organism that does not suspend its life for the sake of the probes. The results of thought will always be partial, incomplete, even fragmentary. And most important, it will not shed more light on its subject than is warranted.

To think is to shed light, to create a limited clearing. But the clearing is always surrounded by darkness and it is easy to forget the darkness and to see only the light. But Jewish thought cannot lose sight of the darkness. This is so because Jewish thought is on the way. The Jewish story is incomplete. We do not see the outcome. The redemption has not as yet happened. It is not a question of uncertainty. The redemption has been promised by God and therefore will come. But because it has not as yet come, the story of Israel is still happening and cannot therefore be laid before us as an object of contemplation. Before faith lies the darkness of the future and therefore no logos of God is possible. At least not to man. And not now.

2. JEWISH THOUGHT AND THE JEWISH PEOPLE

In the nineteenth century, Samson Raphael Hirsch left the organized Jewish community because he found it impossible to coexist with Reform Judaism in the same community. Intellectually, he was right. Reform Judaism rejected the authority of the Torah that had guided Jewish life since talmudic times. More specifically, it reserved for itself the right to pick and choose, retaining those portions of the Torah that agreed with modern sensibility and rejecting those that did not. For the traditional view, all of the Torah was the word of God. These two views were clearly incompatible and, in the view of Hirsch, the two communities had to separate.

But the divorce was premature. If Judaism had been a system of ideas, the separation would have been necessary. Since even a cursory examination of the two systems would have revealed their incompatibility, the need for separation would have been obvious.

But Judaism is not a set of ideas. There are ideas that are specifically Jewish and that can be presented as the teachings of Judaism. But they do not constitute Judaism. Separated from the Jewish people, nothing is Judaism. If anything, it is the Jewish people that is Judaism.

It is therefore possible to agree or disagree with the teachings of this or that interpretation of Judaism but it is not possible to ignore the Judaism of any Jew. Judaism is the election of Abraham and his descendants as the people of God. The house of Israel is therefore not a voluntary association defined by acceptance or rejection of a set of propositions.

Because this is so, the people of Israel is always one people, each part of which affects every other part. Each Jew is responsible for every other Jew, whether or not he shares "membership" with him in any particular humanly created association. Hirsch therefore attempted the impossible: to separate himself from those Jews whose beliefs he found unacceptable. Before God, there is only the one Jewish people, from which no Jew can resign.

But this situation also affects Jewish thought. A Jewish thinker cannot simply formulate a teaching as an interpretation of Judaism. Because Judaism is inconceivable without a particular people, i.e., Israel, Jewish thought must serve two masters: God and Israel. It must not serve them equally. God is the Lord of Israel while Israel is the servant of God. Nevertheless, God appears in history as the God of Israel and there can therefore be no thought about God that is not also thought about Israel. And if a large portion of the Israel of our day no longer thinks of God, this fact, too, must find its way into the Jewish thought of our day. In attempting to understand Jewish consciousness, we must think of it as a composite of the vast diversity of Jewish manifestations of modern times. Each one of us as a Jew is a replica of the consciousness of the whole people. If we are believers, somewhere in us also lurks the nonbelief of our nonbelieving brethren, and if we are nonbelievers, the belief of the believers is also in us. It is to this complex and fragmented consciousness that the Jewish thought of our time must speak.

3. A CARNAL ELECTION

Judaism is a carnal election.

God did not formulate a teaching around which he rallied humanity. God declared a particular people the people of God. He could have brought into being another kind of people of God, membership in which would have been a function of the individual's faith and/or virtue. This is how the Church came to understand its election. As the new Israel, it saw itself as the people of God that had replaced the old Israel. Whereas membership in the old Israel was bestowed by birth, membership in the new Israel was open to anyone who embraced the message of the Church.

But this is not the nature of Israel's election. This election is that of the seed of Abraham. A descendant of Abraham, Isaac, and Jacob is a Jew irrespective of what he believes or how virtuous he is. Being a Jew is therefore not something earned. This reflects the fact that the initial election of Abraham himself was not earned. It is true that in rabbinic literature Abraham is depicted as having "discovered" the one God when it occurred to him that a complex world could not have come into being by chance. But none of this is mentioned in the Bible. We are simply told that God commanded Abraham to leave his place of birth and to go to a land that God would show him. He is also promised that his descendants will become a numerous people. But nowhere does the Bible tell us why Abraham rather than someone else was chosen. The implication is that God chooses whom he wishes and that he owes no accounting to anyone for his choices.

Israel's election is therefore a carnal election that is transmitted through the body. And to many, this is a scandal. Is it the body that makes someone dear to God or the spirit? Shouldn't we evaluate a person on the basis of his character and ideas rather than his physical descent? These are difficult questions to answer but we cannot evade coping with them.

We must first understand that we cannot sit in judgment over God. It is not incumbent on him to justify his actions to man. It is not for us to teach God what is fair but for him to teach us. If it was his decision to make Abraham his beloved servant and the descendants of Abraham his beloved people, then it is for man to accept God's will with obedience.

Having said this—and it is this that remains the fundamental answer—we can also go just a little further. Why do we recoil at a carnal election? Because we have been taught to respect the spirit and to have contempt for the body. The roots of this lie in Greek philosophy, which sought the unchanging and eternal. It contrasted this with the material that was subject to change and therefore not altogether real. Here is the basis for the Gnostic spiritualization that sees man as spirit fallen into the shadowworld of the material from which he seeks desperately to extricate himself. And if he does not so seek to extricate himself, then this is only because spirit has sunk so low that it has forgotten its origins and has come to see the material world as its home when it is the world of spirit that man really needs.

Judaism rejects this bifurcation of spirit and matter. Both were created by God and both are good. In the Bible it is not at all clear that the image of God in which man was created refers only to his spirit and not to his body. Man is a unity of spirit and body and it is for this reason that death is real. If the essence of man were his soul and the body only an outer and unessential garment, then the shedding of this garment in death would be no calamity. In fact, it would be a welcome liberation of the soul from the shackles of the body, which is precisely Socrates' interpretation of death.

Because the body is not an extraneous outer garment, Judaism views death as a calamity. If we are not convinced of this, we need only compare the calm and detached death of Socrates with the agony of Jesus' very Jewish death.

The carnal election of Israel is not unconnected with Judaism's view of the body. God chose to embrace a people in the fullness of its humanity. But this had to include the bodyness of this people alongside its national soul. God therefore loves the spirit and body of the people of Israel and it is for this reason that both are holy. The enemies of God who strive to destroy God by destroying his people cannot rest content with the destruction of the Jewish "religion" or Jewish "culture" but must also, or perhaps primarily, destroy the body of Israel.

Had God chosen a people on the basis of purely spiritual criteria, such a people could have abandoned its election by rejecting the teachings that were the basis of its spiritual election. But God chose a carnal people, whose physical being in the world is a sign of the existence of God. This people is in the service of God no matter what ideas it embraces or rejects. It cannot escape the service of God because its face is known in the family of man as that of the people of God.

4. HISTORICITY

The carnal election of Israel is intimately related to the historicity of Judaism.

The realm of history is the realm of the public life of nations and of the interaction of nations with each other. History is therefore preeminently the history of politics and international relations. Consequently, history is often related to the land because the identity of a nation is most commonly derived from the land it occupies. History is thus a reflection of the carnality of human existence.

Pure thought is ahistorical. This can be illustrated by the law of noncontradiction. Perhaps the most elementary dictate of pure thought is that a proposition and its contradictory cannot both be true. This is one of those *a priori* truths of reason without which no thought is possible. But the dimension of time complicates the matter. While contradictory propositions cannot both be true *at the same time*, they can both be true at *different* times. Time thus seems to erode the absoluteness of the law of noncontradiction. Pure thought and time have therefore traditionally been at odds with each other. From the point of view of pure thought, time is a lower domain of reality into which pure thought cannot, and indeed need not, penetrate.

What we have called pure thought can also be called philosophy, and the position we have ascribed to pure thought is the Platonic and Neoplatonic position. In its religious form, this is the position of Gnosticism. More broadly speaking, this is the position of all spiritualizing religion. The spiritualization of religion takes various forms. We can emphasize the prophetic over the cultic. We can deny the reality of nations and adopt an internationalist stance. We can lay stress on the ethical in religion to the exclusion of everything else. Finally, we can lose interest in history and focus almost exclusively on the inwardness of spirituality. These are some of the strategies of spiritualizing religions, and Judaism will have none of them.

A good example is the difference between the way redemption is understood in Judaism and in the Gospels. In Judaism, redemption is a religious-political concept. During the first century, this meant the throwing off of the Roman yoke in favor of a genuinely independent Jewish commonwealth. The hoped-for Messiah was therefore inevitably a religious-political figure who could not avoid being a threat to Roman rule. While Jesus was crucified precisely because he was perceived by the Romans as a figure threatening their rule, in the Gospels this political dimension of the Messiah is not emphasized. The kingdom of Jesus is not of this world because it is a spiritual and not historic kingdom. In spite of recent attempts to create a "liberation theology" out of Christian sources, the attentive reader of the Gospels must conclude that Jesus considers the blemishes of historic existence of small consequence. He counsels women to obey men and slaves, their masters. The social station to which we are assigned in this world is of little importance compared with the spiritual tasks assigned to us in this life. We are thus dealing with a profound spiritualization of Judaism, and once this is accomplished it is almost inevitable that this version of Judaism can no longer remain tied to the religious-political destiny of the Jewish people but instead becomes a fellowship of faith open to persons of all nationalities.

Judaism rejected such spiritualization. It did not sever its tie to the body and therefore to a people, a land, and history. Redemption was an event that had to be awaited amidst the political realities of history. The realm of government was not abandoned as the realm of Caesar which was beyond redemption. Israel thus remained in history.

5. BIBLICAL AND RABBINIC ETHICS

But Israel remained in history only in theory. In reality, after the destruction of the Temple in A.D. 70, Israel was no longer in history. Most Jews no longer lived in the land of Israel. The institutions of national sovereignty had been destroyed, and even if there was some self-government, as in Babylonia, it was by indulgence of the host nation, which could withdraw this privilege at any time.

The Judaism that came into being with the loss of sovereignty and the exit from history was rabbinic Judaism. We can exaggerate the discontinuity between biblical and rabbinic Judaism or we can ignore it. We must do neither.

Karaite Judaism rejected the very foundation of rabbinic Judaism. For it, only the written Torah was authoritative. While Karaite Judaism was a posttalmudic development, it had a parallel of sorts in the Sadducees, who also emphasized the written Torah and rejected the oral Torah and the principles of rabbinic hermeneutics, which laid the foundations of what has come to be post-Temple Judaism.

Because of the Karaite challenge, rabbinic Judaism has ever since been very sensitive to any attempt to separate biblical from rabbinic Judaism. It has insisted on the unity of the written and oral Torahs, never failing to point out that the written Torah is not self-explanatory but presupposes interpretation beyond what is given in the text (e.g., the passages dealing with *tefilin* do not detail how the *tefilin* are to be constructed).[3] There is no doubt that Judaism as we know it today is not based only on the written biblical text but owes much to talmudic elaboration. Any attempt to reduce the significance of the rabbinic component of Judaism in favor of the biblical constitutes a fundamental revision of Judaism as we have known it for two thousand years. It is indeed vital to understand the nonviability of a nonrabbinic Judaism.

While fully honoring the centrality of the rabbinic component of Judaism, we can't be so nonhistorical as not to notice significant differences between the biblical and rabbinic climates. This difference can probably be best expressed by saying that biblical Judaism is historical, while rabbinic Judaism, in the main, is the Judaism of a people outside of history.

To take one example: war. In biblical Judaism, war is not missing. In fact, it is one of the major domains of revelation. Wars that produce Jewish victories are taken, again and again, as signs of God's faithfulness to Israel as his chosen people. The victory of Israel, as it were, proclaims to the world the power and glory of the God of Israel. Rabbinic Judaism is far more irenic. R. Yohanan b. Zakkai's departure from a beleaguered Jerusalem to surrender to the Roman forces is characteristic of the rabbinic attitude. Judaism, the rabbis apparently believed, can survive under foreign domination. It can be transformed into a teaching perhaps even akin to the teachings of the philosophic schools of the ancient world (it is interesting to note that Josephus goes to great lengths to portray Judaism as a kind of philosophic teaching). The rabbis, of course, were right because Judaism did survive in many different countries under many different foreign dominations. But it would be dishonest to fail to note that the greater irenicism of rabbinic Judaism as compared with its biblical predecessor is related to the greater powerlessness of rabbinic Judaism.

This is true of the ethical realm as a whole. The ethical concern of rabbinic Judaism does not, of course, emerge from nothing. The Bible is full of commandments dealing with compassion for the poor and powerless, the orphan and the widow. But alongside this unusual moral sensitivity, the Bible is also quite amoral. The commandment for the destruction of the previous inhabitants of Canaan is a relevant example.[4] And so is Saul's loss of his throne because he did not obey God's command to tear Agog, king of the Amalekites, to pieces,[5] an incident Martin Buber found necessary to deny precisely because it did not correspond to his ethical sense.

It was Hegel who pointed out that private morality is not coextensive with the morality of the state. To the century that has experienced Hitler, such teachings stick in the throat. But the truth cannot be avoided. People who lead states—as we have learned since the emergence of the state of Israel—make difficult decisions that inevitably lead to the deaths of many, including many innocent.

Interpretations of Judaism that focus almost exclusively on the ethical, such as those of Hermann Cohen and Emmanuel Levinas, are therefore no longer adequate. Judaism is once again living in history and therefore the ahistoricity of rabbinic Judaism must now be supplemented by the historical Judaism of the Bible.

6. THE ETHICAL SECEDES

Ethics is the Judaism of the assimilated.

We must begin with the negative moment. The Judaism of the last two centuries is the Judaism of self-liquidation. For the past two centuries, Western man has been freeing himself from his bondage to God. There are many aspects to this liberation (or perhaps rebellion), among which the triumph of science plays a central role. In the midst of this general secularization, Jewish secularization took on a special intensity because the liberation from Judaism represented the end of Jewish exclusion from European society. But the process of liberation from Judaism raised many problems. Primary among these was the self-image of the liberated Jew. In the background of the liberated consciousness lurks the Dostoevskian recognition that if there is no God everything is permitted. The break with a life lived under the judgment of God should, if clear thinking is a value, lead to a Nietzschean break with Judeo-Christian slave morality. But the newly liberated Jew cannot accept this. He is the heir to thousands of years of spirituality. His self-image must remain noble so that his break with his faith will not be interpreted as a reversion to the animal in him. It is here that ethics rushes in to fulfill this task. The liberated Jew remains an ethical being. If anything, his ethical standards even rise as a result of his liberation. Is not ethics, after all, the essence of religion? And doesn't liberation from God constitute a purification of the ethical? The ethics of the religious, it is maintained, is an ethics of fear of punishment. But without God, the ethical is obeyed for its own sake, and this is surely a higher stage of the ethical. Furthermore, the religious history of the people is replete with many incidents of very questionable ethical value. The liberation of the Jew enables him to disavow the ethically problematic features of his past for a new, pure ethics.

In addition, the ethical component of Judaism is the component most acceptable to the gentile. The specifically Jewish practices like *tefilin* (phylacteries), the *kashruth* laws, *tsitsith* (ritual fringes), etc., embarrass the Jew who is on the path to assimilation. But allegiance to morality is quite different. Here is a commitment that does not set him apart from his neighbor but brings him honor instead. And this is especially true because the anti-Semite's stereotype of the Jew sees the Jew as the dishonest merchant. What better way is there to cease being distinctively Jewish and at the same time salvage the most important component of Judaism than the ethical? Furthermore, by adopting the religion of the ethical or by converting Judaism into ethics, the assimilating Jew retains a certain spiritual self-respect, which was threatened by his guilt at abandoning the faith of his fathers. When we add to this the gentile respect earned by an ethical stance, we have an inevitable strategy for the assimilating Jew. All this is, of course, not a conscious calculation. It is something that grows in the recesses of the mind and the soul, partly understood by the subject but partly covered by Sartrean bad faith.

The strategy we have just described is an old one, going back at least as far as Spinoza, who named his major work *Ethics*. But in its most pronounced form it appears among German Jews, whose commitment to honesty and truth is legendary. One of the most serious grievances harbored by German Jews toward eastern European Jews who had come to live in Germany was that the newcomers were not quite as honest as their German coreligionists. German Jews were deeply acculturated and therefore embarrassed by the far more obvious Jewishness of the immigrants from the East. The final blow came when one of the eastern European medieval relics, not satisfied by the humiliation his very presence caused his assimilated fellow Jews, attracted attention by some ethical misstep. Then all the accumulated rage would explode, justified by righteous indignation at the alleged moral transgression.

The ethics that was torn from its setting in the faith of Israel and from the context of the covenant and the historic reality of the Jewish people has thus become another strategy for Jewish self-alienation.

7. JEWISH DISOBEDIENCE

We must think about Jewish disobedience.

The overwhelming majority of Jews in the world today are not

Torah-observant. The creation of the state of Israel was the result of the secularization of Jewish existence. While Jews said "Next year in Jerusalem" for two thousand years, nothing much happened until Theodor Herzl, a secular Jew, conceived of the Zionist idea as a form of modern nationalism. He concluded that the cause of the "Jewish problem" was that Jews were aliens where they lived and this could be cured only by the creation of their own national home. As a modern, secular person, Herzl took it for granted that in politics nothing happens that human beings do not make happen, and he therefore founded a political movement to achieve what two thousand years of prayer had not achieved.

It is, of course, not necessary to insist on the total secularism of modern Zionism. There was always a religious wing to the movement, though it was always a minority. And even among the nonreligious components of Zionism, religious forces could be detected as, for example, in the Uganda incident, when Herzl learned that not just any piece of territory would do. From the broader point of view, therefore, in spite of its dominant secular, socialist outlook, Zionism must be read in the context of Jewish messianism and of the whole drama of exile and return as foretold by the prophets of Israel. Nevertheless, the secular self-understanding of Zionism cannot be ignored. Nor can we ignore the basic fact that the great majority of world Jewry today is not Torah-observant. How is this to be interpreted?

The history of Israel, was, like the history of man, from the beginning, a history of disobedience. The election of Israel was not unconnected with mankind's disobedience. It is almost as if God chose Israel because of his disappointment with mankind as a whole. At the beginning, all mankind was to be God's people. But the sin of Adam and the corruption of humanity that led to the Flood convinced God that his only hope lay with the selection of a smaller segment of humanity to which God would devote most of his attention and that would thus become an example to the rest of humanity with the final goal remaining the reconciliation of all of humanity. But here, too, things did not work out as planned. The special attention paid to Israel, while not without some effect, still left a deeply disobedient chosen people. Israel thus turned out to be more like the rest of humanity than envisaged. But what was God to do now? Reject Israel and look for another people? Would it not seem probable that the same drama would be repeated with the new Israel? So God was stuck with Israel, for better or worse. The covenant was irrevocable, and Israel and God had to live together to the end of time, in spite of all the ups and downs of a very stormy marriage.

The point here is not to document Israel's disobedience. The Bible does this very adequately, from the laughter of Sarah, who refused to believe the messenger's announcement that she would bear a child in her old age, to the golden calf and the many other instances of Jewish disobedience. What is the significance of Jewish disobedience?

We have already spoken about an alternative model of election: the election of a virtuous elite. Had God chosen that method of election, he would not have had to bear the disobedience of the elect, since the individual who became disobedient would thereby cease being a member of the elect who would consist, by definition, only of those obedient. But God did not choose this manner of election. He chose to elect a biological people that remains elect even when it sins. God is therefore involved with the sins of the elect, since the elect people become immersed in sin and purified in repentance.

How does the sin of the elect manifest itself both as sin and as sin of the elect? If the Jewish attraction to Marxism was sin, it was the sin of the elect because it took the form of thirst for righteousness. And the same is true for Jewish secular liberalism. If secular Zionism was sin because it rejected God as the source of Jewish redemption, it was the sin of the elect because, however secular its rationale, it was a longing for the holy soil of Israel. Even in sin, Israel remains in the divine service because the spiritual circumcision that has been carried out on this people is indelible.

Christian theology has always stressed Israel's disobedience. And it was right to do so because it is a truth carefully recorded in the Bible. But it is not the whole truth. There is also Israel's obedience, its stubborn faith in the promises of God in spite of the apparent hopelessness of it all. "Go and cry in the ears of Jerusalem," says Jeremiah (2:2–3), "saying, Thus saith the Lord: I remember thee, the kindness of thy youth, the love of thine espousals, when thou wentest after me in the wilderness, in the land that was not sown. Israel is holiness unto the Lord, and the first fruits of his increase, all that devour him shall offend; evil shall come upon them, saith the Lord." To go after God into the wilderness, into a land that was not sown, is the very definition of Israel's faith. In contrast with the *eros* of philosophy, which aims for certainty, the faith of Israel is existence lived into the unknown, the unexplored, the dark. And this leads us to the disobedience of Orthodox Judaism.

8. THE LAW

Orthodox Judaism would find it very painful to be classed among the disobedient.

Above all, Orthodox Judaism upholds the law. There was a time when Jews spoke about the Torah. But in recent years one speaks about the halachah, the legal portions of the Torah. The halachah is the operative part of the Torah. It, and only it, is the relevant part because only from the halachah can we learn what we have to *do*. Disputes in the nonlegal (agadic) portions of the Torah need not even be adjudicated because they make no practical difference. But halachic disputes must be settled because one must know how to act and therefore one must choose one of the alternatives. Occasionally, it is argued that agadic disputes have halachic implications. It is also argued that Jewish "theology" must itself be based on halachic sources and from time to time the theological enterprise is almost validated when based on halachic sources or when shown to have halachic implications.

Interestingly enough, it is such a theory of halachic primacy that Rashi, the most famous medieval Bible commentator, had in mind when commenting on the first verse of Genesis. He refers to a Rabbi Isaac who said that the Torah should not have started with an account of the creation but with the first commandment, which does not occur until Exod. 12:2. This being so, why then did the Torah start with the creation account? Rabbi Isaac replied that the creation account was included to justify God's taking away the land of Canaan from its inhabitants and giving it to the people of Israel. Since God created the world, he has the absolute right to dispose of it. The train of thought just summarized illustrates the primacy of the halachic. It is the halachic that constitutes the essence of the Torah, while the inclusion of the agadic requires explanation.

Although Orthodox Jews currently constitute a minority of Jews in the world (estimates range from 10 to 20 percent), Orthodox Judaism cannot simply be considered one of the branches of Judaism. In a profound sense it *is* Judaism because it is the form of Judaism most continuous with rabbinic Judaism as it has been practiced since postexilic times. While there is a broad spectrum within Orthodox

Judaism itself ranging from the most uncompromising to the modern branches of Orthodoxy, as a whole Orthodox Judaism is the continuation of historic Judaism, in relation to which all other forms of Judaism must be understood.

Precisely because of its stubborn adherence to Torah as halachah, Orthodox Judaism would find being criticized as disobedient difficult to grasp. To understand the argument against Orthodoxy, we can do no better than to listen to Martin Buber. Buber's epoch-making work *I and Thou* distinguishes between the primary words *I-Thou* and *I-It*. The world of I-It is the world of objects perceived in time and space and constituting a casual network subject to human knowledge and control. The Thou, in contrast, is never experienced as one object among others. When the Thou addresses man or when man addresses his Thou, there is only that one Thou that exists and everything else exists in its light. Unlike the It, the Thou cannot be known, nor can man gain control over it. And, above all, there is no security in the I-Thou relationship.

Security is a function of knowledge, which, in turn, is necessarily derived from the past. Experience has taught us the nature and characteristics of the things in the world. We assume that they will remain constant and that things will remain as they have been. But this is not applicable in the I-Thou relationship. If we perceive the other in terms of the past and attempt to determine his character traits, which we assume will continue in the future, we are not relating to a Thou but are studying an It. The Thou is alive in the present moment, and if the present moment is real, the Thou can surprise me, tell me what I did not expect on the basis of past knowledge. To live under an unchanging law is therefore to freeze God's living presence as the Thou of this moment into an objective system of demands from which the living presence of God must have departed long ago. In one of his most critical passages, Buber writes:

> O you secure and safe ones who hide yourselves behind the defence-works of the law so that you will not have to look into God's abyss! Yes, you have secure ground under your feet while we hang suspended, looking out over the endless deeps. But we would not exchange our dizzy insecurity and our poverty for your security and abundance. For to you God is one who created once and not again; but to us God is he who "renews the work of creation every day." To you God is one who revealed himself once and no more; but to us he speaks out of the burning thorn-

bush of the present . . . in the revelations of our innermost hearts—greater than words.[6]

What significance need we attach to this critique? Can it be dismissed as a kind of "higher anti-Semitism" or must it be taken seriously as an inherent problem of Orthodox and therefore classical Judaism?

Buber's difficulty is not unrelated to the classical Christian critique of Judaism. This is based on Jesus' polemics against the law as practiced by the Pharisees and to perhaps even a greater extent on the Pauline attitude to the law as understood in Christian tradition (we add this qualification because it is likely that Paul was misunderstood). In his book on the relation between Judaism and Christianity, *Two Types of Faith*,[7] Buber places the responsibility for the break with Judaism on Paul. Nevertheless, most curiously, he never comes to grips with the similarity between Paul's view of the law as classically understood and his own. Buber seems to be repressing the Christian flavor of his critique of the law. The Christian and Buberian contempt for a religion of law can, with considerable justification, be dismissed as another instance of false spiritualization. The romantic imagination has no patience for details. It insists on spiritual breakthroughs (e.g., the law of love or the I-Thou encounter) in the wake of which only the most prosaic philistine can still insist on detailed legal prescriptions. When we remember the teaching of contempt for Judaism inherent in much of Christianity, we are entitled to refer to the foundation of this teaching as anti-Semitic.

And still, it would be a great mistake to leave the matter there. Buber's basic thesis is that revelation is never law. Law, he claims, is the human appropriation of revelation, a cooling down of a living fire that is the meeting with God.[8] A religion that identifies the smoking embers with the roaring fire is headed for spiritual extinction. The living God, argues Buber, having spoken once, has not lapsed into eternal silence. As the living God, he speaks to our lives in the uniqueness of each moment. If so, Orthodoxy is a disastrous ossification of the spirit. Is there any truth in this charge?

9. INSECURITY

There is some truth in it.

Rabbinic Judaism is the Judaism of an age in which revelation has ceased. In the Bible, God speaks to man. In the rabbinic period (ca.

200 B.C. to A.D. 500) this is no longer so. Now Israel has the Torah, which was originally transmitted to man in revelation. This original revelation came in two forms: the written and oral Torah. In the rabbinic period the oral Torah comes to be written down. Interestingly enough, this writing down takes place at a time when God's speaking to man has ended. The revelation now lives not in direct address but in the existence of the written record of God's speech to man.

But because God no longer speaks directly to man, ascertaining the will of God in specific situations remains a problem. A person finds himself in a situation. He has several options and must choose one of them. Which shall he choose? To the believing Jew, the obvious answer would seem to be that he must do what God wills he should do in the specific situation. If God spoke to us in every individual situation and told us what he wanted us to do there would be no problem. But he does not and we must therefore find a second-best method for ascertaining his will.

This is where the law comes in. The law is a guide to action in the absence of specific commands in specific situations. Each situation, after all, is different. Ideally, God would issue specific commands for each situation. Second best is the law. The law constructs abstractions such as theft, murder, animals that chew their cud, etc. Having studied the law, we then turn to specific cases. In view of what this animal does with its food, is it an animal that chews its cud? Given this particular action by this particular person, is it an action that constitutes theft? There are no perfectly certain answers to these question. By using our reason, we do the best we can, deciding that this particular case sufficiently resembles previous cases of theft to be classified as theft, while another case does not resemble them sufficiently and is therefore not theft. Legal reasoning is therefore an attempt to fathom the will of God when he has not specifically expressed it in the case under consideration.

If we see the law in this light, then all reasoning with respect to the law of God must be conducted with fear and trembling and with the constant awareness that what we take as the divine will may not be it. Such an Orthodox Judaism would lack security. It would lack the confidence with which the Orthodox Jew turns to his rabbi for an authoritative ruling on the law, thinking that if the rabbi's ruling is "wrong" (in some sense of that word), then it is the rabbi's responsibility and not that of the person posing the problem. In so doing, we overlook the basic truth that if each person is responsible to God, then dependence on the ruling of another is no absolute defense. Since ultimately it is conformity or nonconformity with God's will that is decisive, the religious life becomes a life of insecurity lived under the sense of divine judgment.

But there is a way out of this insecurity. We can reject the view that in the final analysis we must attempt to guess God's will in the particular situation. God, we can argue, has revealed the law to man. Having done so, he has further stipulated that his will is to be interpreted by a particular group of persons, such as the rabbis. God then agrees that the law as he wills it will be the law as these persons interpret it. Under these circumstances, there need be no fear that the persons is question will come to a wrong conclusion, since, by divine decision, *any* conclusion the authoritative group comes to is guaranteed by God to be his will. And, indeed, there are rabbinic texts that support just such a view of things. Because the Torah has been given to man, no further interference from God is tolerable. A divine voice that intervenes in a rabbinic debate on a point of law is rejected as irrelevant because it is man and not God who decides the law.[9] It is safe to assume that most Orthodox Jews, knowingly or unknowingly, derive their security from some such scheme in which God has signed away his ultimate role as judge.

The security derived from this maneuver is a sham security. God has not delegated his powers. There is no person or persons who are beyond the judgment of God. If the rabbis cannot, by definition, make a wrong decision, then they also cannot make a right decision. If conformity with the will of God is not the proper criterion for evaluating a rabbinic decision, then there is no criterion at all for evaluating a rabbinic decision. And because rabbis can make wrong decisions, each individual is responsible for accepting or rejecting a rabbinic ruling. Each individual must ask himself what God's will is for his particular situation. In answering that question, the existing literature and living rabbis should be consulted. But after all the advice is in, the final judgment is that of the individual who must attempt to ascertain the will of God. No human advice, however learned, can take the place of individual decision based on the individual's understanding of the will of God.

There is therefore no logical way to be secure before God when God is silent and the Torah is the guide for conduct. The lack of inner turmoil that describes much of Orthodox existence probably results from a weakening of the sense of direct responsibility to God that is the basis of religious reality. There is a tendency for the law to become self- sufficient and for God the lawgiver to recede from the horizon.

10. THE CENTRALITY OF THE ETHICAL

In spite of everything that has happened, the ethical remains central in Judaism. It cannot be denied that the ethical has been by far the most popular route for abandoning Judaism. Wherever we turn in the nineteenth century, we find that as Jewish content erodes, so the emphasis on the ethical expands. The Ethical Culture of Felix Adler, while a uniquely American phenomenon, is also the logical outcome of the thrust of Reform Judaism. The Reformers, whose primary interest was to integrate their Judaism with German culture, understood that *the* element in Judaism that most readily lent itself to that integration was the ethical. Culminating in Kant, German culture had taken a peculiarly ethical turn, far more than other European cultures of the day. Thus, for example, French or Russian culture was not characterized by that obsession with honesty that is endemic to the German mind. The French mind is subtle and elegant, devoted to stylistic form but hardly to ethical seriousness. The absence of any concern with the ethical by Descartes exemplifies this cast of mind. The Russian spirit is far more concerned with sin and guilt than the French, but for the Russian it is the tragedy of violation of the ethical that is fascinating, not faithful obedience to the ethical as such. The military model in Germany, with its emphasis on obedience to duty and its distrust of pleasure as a legitimate motive for human conduct, culminated in the ethics of Kant. In this atmosphere, nineteenth-century liberal Judaism instinctively grasped the ethical content of Judaism as that aspect of the faith most congenial to the culture whose hospitality it desired. Ethical Judaism, to put it precisely, was housebroken Judaism.

The more authentic, ethnically rooted Judaism of eastern Europe never shared this focus on the ethical. With the revival of historic national Judaism in our time, the centrality of the ethical in Judaism diminished. And yet this cannot be done without doing even greater violence to the spirit of the tradition than that perpetrated by German-oriented Reform Judaism. The ethical is central in the deepest layers of Jewish consciousness. Anyone acquainted with ancient Near Eastern religion cannot help noticing, by contrast, the theme of mercy that attaches itself to the God of Israel. He has a deep and abiding concern for the suffering of the widow, orphan, and stranger, the weak and vulnerable who go unmentioned in the non-Jewish literature of the period. The overwhelming power of the God of Israel does not eclipse the voice of justice: Abraham dares argue against a divine decree of punishment when Abraham believes the innocent will suffer with the guilty (Gen. 18:16–33). This ethical strain is reinforced in postbiblical Judaism, so that it has often been remarked that rabbinic Judaism is an intensification of the ethical, since we can document in countless instances the rabbinic amelioration of the harsher aspects of biblical commandments, as, for instance, in respect to capital punishment, which is permitted in the Bible but practically disappears in rabbinic Judaism. The rabbinic intensification of the ethical—if that is what the *de facto* abolition of capital punishment amounts to—results from several factors, one of which is the increasing withdrawal from history that is the result of the end of Jewish sovereignty. The emphasis on the ethical can be interpreted as a preoccupation of the weak once state power has been transferred to the conqueror, who does not hesitate to oppress the weak. But whatever the reasons may be for the enlargement of the ethical in the rabbinic system, the process is continuous with the essential thrust of biblical thinking and its concern for justice and the protection of the weak. The ethical is therefore at the center of Judaism from its inception to the present.

11. A Nonautonomous Ethic

But it is not an autonomous ethic that is at the center of Judaism. It is not an ethic that is self-contained, separated from the divine command and standing on its own feet. It is not the ethics of the *Euthyphro* of Plato, in which Socrates poses the question, Do the gods love an act because it is pious (good?), or is it pious because the gods love it? Once this question is posed, the possibility of an autonomous realm of the ethical is born. If the gods love an act because it is pious, then it is not the divine act of commanding it that makes the act good, but the goodness of the act is a quality that inheres in it and the divine act of loving or commanding it is an effect of the preexisting cause, which is the quality of goodness that inheres in the act. And this quality of goodness would, theoretically, continue to inhere in the act even if, for whatever reason, the gods were not to love or command it. The fact that the gods love the act then becomes irrelevant, since its goodness does not derive from this fact. The divine command is then not the source of the obligatoriness of the act but the quality of goodness that inheres in it. The gods then love the act because of the quality of goodness that belongs to it, independently of whether the gods love it or not. Jewish ethics is not such an autonomous ethic. While such autonomous tendencies occasionally make themselves felt in Jewish ethics, such tendencies are secondary to its basic direction. At the center of Jewish ethics is the personal encounter with the God of Abraham, Isaac, and Jacob, who commands Israel, his chosen people.

To understand the issue that lurks behind the struggle between a God-centered ethics and an autonomous one, we must ask why the issue of autonomy is so particularly pressing in the ethical realm. After all, the problem of autonomy can be raised almost anywhere. Instead of asking whether a good act is good because God commands it or whether God commands it because it is good, we could ask whether two plus two equals four because God wills that this be so or whether God understands it to be so because it is so, independently of whether he wills it or understands it to be so. More abstractly, we can ask whether the structure of reason is a contingent creation of God, the result of his autonomous will, or whether reason, as the possibility of truth, has its independent being, to which God must acquiesce because it is not the product of his creation. Similarly, we can raise the analogous question in the realm of the aesthetic. Are those entities we find beautiful perceived by us as such because that is how God willed it or does God judge a beautiful thing to be so because it is so, independently of the opinion of God. Such questions have, of course, been raised and various options explored. The point is that they have never had the centrality that the question of autonomy has had in connection with the ethical. The God-centered position has seemed far more questionable in the ethical realm than anywhere else. To assert that nothing is inherently good or bad except that God commanding or forbidding it makes it so has seemed a particularly difficult view to accept. Is there nothing wrong with murdering my fellow man other than that God frowns on it? Were God not to frown on it, were he to command murder, would murder become good? Would the terror and suffering of my fellow man not be sufficient ground for condemning it as evil? Does only the will of God count and not the will of my fellow who wills to live and not to die at my hand? In injuring man, is it only the will of God that I violate? Is God the only one whose will ought not to be violated?

The need to push God out of the ethical realm stems from the recognition of the otherness of the other. The foundation of the ethical is this recognition. To believe that injuring the other is wrong only because God forbids it destroys the otherness of the other. If to sin against my fellow man is only to sin against God, then my fellow is nothing in his own right. Injuring him brings me up against God but not against the one I have injured. It is this that our ethical sensibility finds intolerable. If there is nothing about the being of my fellow man that stands against me and limits my freedom of action, then, it is felt, a divine command cannot place me in a position of obligation toward someone who does not morally exist in his own right. It is interesting to note the contrast in the language of the divine reproaches after Adam and Eve ate the fruit from the forbidden tree and after Cain's killing of Abel. In the former case (Gen. 3:9–11) we read:

> And the Lord God called unto the man, and said unto him, "Where art thou?" And he said, "I heard Thy voice in the garden, and I was afraid, because I was naked; and I hid myself." And he said, "Who told thee that thou wast naked? Hast thou eaten of the tree whereof I commanded thee that thou shouldest not eat?"

The transgression consists of a violation of the command of God who had forbidden Adam to eat the fruit of one of the trees in the garden. It is quite otherwise when Cain kills Abel. It must be noted that this crime is not preceded by a divine injunction prohibiting the killing of man. And when the crime has been committed, God does not charge Cain with violating his command. Instead, we read (Gen. 4:10): "And he said, 'What hast thou done? the voice of thy brother's blood crieth unto me from the ground.' " The indictment stems from the blood that has been shed. God is now the judge. It is not he who has been sinned against—at least not primarily—but the other, whose death does not preclude his pressing his case even in death, a case that is now carried by his spilled blood. Here is the root of the distinction between sins committed between man and God, which are forgiven on the Day of Atonement if there is true repentance, and sins between man and man, which are not forgiven on the Day of Atonement as long as the forgiveness of the fellow man sinned against is not obtained.

The realm of the ethical thus becomes possible because of the divine act of creation that brings into existence beings other than God whose reality limits my freedom and whose sphere of influence I must respect. The reality of others implies my reality as well. Kant was particularly concerned that the moral law not be imposed on man by an external force but that it be self-legislated, given to him by his own self and therefore autonomously obeyed. Just as the other cannot simply be an extension of God but must have his own autonomous rights, so must the self be the author of the law that is imposed—or rather, that it imposes on itself. While to some extent Kant would claim that this is also true of some of the fundamental principles of reason that are not given from the outside but imposed by the mind of the subject, nowhere does this become a matter of principle as with the ethical law. In Kant's view, the ethical law cannot exist except as self-legislated, autonomous rational law. Sartre has shown that even the enterprise of enslaving the other is meaningful only if the other is a free subjectivity,[10] so that in conquering it, we are subjugating a free being. And the same is true of the moral law. Moral obedience is possible only as free obedience. The virtue of those without choice is no virtue. A moral law that is external rather than self-imposed is destructive of the moral dimension because it is destructive of freedom. In order to make man a being for whom morality—and therefore sin—is a possibility, God had to create someone who is genuinely other than himself. If man is other than God, then he must appropriate the moral command, even if it is also the command of God, as his own command, freely chosen by him as an autonomous act of self-legislation.

We have stressed human freedom in the realm of the ethical and have maintained that it is this issue that prompts Plato's incisive question concerning the independence of piety (or the good) from the will of God and that it is also this issue that underlies Kant's stress of the self-legislating feature of the moral law. Yet, an essential ingredient is missing if we are to understand the matter. The issue is personhood. Morality is possible because there are other persons. Though I must view them through the filter of my own personality, they must emerge as persons in their own right. In my relationship to them, they are not simply extensions of myself but subjectivities of their own. The ethical always therefore relates to persons. For

Judaism, this has ramifications in two directions. God is always there, reminding me that the blood of my brother crieth unto me from the ground. And, in addition, the law that governs my obedience to God complicates the directness of the human relationship that is the foundation of the ethical.

12. THE ETHICAL AND LAW

It is not possible to be ethical without law. In the case of Kant, the ethical completely becomes law. But even if this is going too far, it is not possible to separate the ethical from law. What is the connection of the ethical with law? Why is there law in the Bible? If law is, as Buber thought, what is left when the fire of revelation cools into a rule of conduct, then why did the Bible not exclude law and focus on the burning fire at the moment of meeting?

Living revelation is something that happens to someone who can speak of it as "mine." The sense of mineness is the gift of God's creation of a self that becomes a "me." There is, as we must by now realize, an overwhelming act of divine renunciation in creating man, who then proceeds to view the world from his and not God's standpoint. If man has such "mineness," how much more must God have, who is the Absolute Subject, the eye that sees all and the ear that hears all. And yet, God permits another standpoint to coexist with his. While God remains the Lord of creation, so that he and his creatures are not coordinated in the framework that is being, and while God also remains the Lord of the good, so that he and his creatures are not jointly judged by the framework that is the good, God nevertheless permits himself to be integrated into a framework broader than he. The biblical narrative in which God is one of the characters is that framework. This narrative is not written from God's point of view. It is written from the point of view of someone for whom God is one of the characters in the narrative. The writer studies the interaction between God and the other characters in the drama. The logic of such dramatic writing tends toward some notion of fate to which even God would be subject. We see this process in Greek stories about the gods who become subject to the overarching, shaping influence of the story medium, which, by detaching itself from the particular point of view of any of the protagonists, tends toward a modicum of dramatic resolution and serenity, which, on the theoretical level, emerges as the notion of fate. As we have already seen, the biblical narrative never totally integrates God into a framework wider than himself. God always remains the over-whelming and mighty creator of heaven and earth and therefore the creator of all frameworks, to none of which he is subject. Never-theless, his inclusion in a narrative written from a viewpoint other than his own must not be overlooked.

We wish to understand the relation of the ethical to law. The origin of the ethical is the realization that there is another self than my own. Fundamentally, this first happens when I learn that there is a subjectivity other than my own. There is another being there who exists in his selfhood. For him I am object. I am thus outflanked. Whereas for me the whole of the universe extends from the center that is I, for him there is another center, and I am an object in his universe. At this point, two considerations arise that remain central to ethical existence. There is the meeting of two subjectivities, with all the complexities that this engenders. There is the Sartrian model according to which the meeting of subjectivities is a deadly struggle in which each attempts to reduce the other to the status of object lest the other rob one of one's own subjectivity. There is also, less pessimistically, the Buberian I-Thou relationship in which neither at-tempts to reduce the other to object but recognizes and confirms the subjectivity of the other. Without elaborating these two possibilities, we note only that in the situation of the meeting between one subjec-tivity and another, the standpoint of subjectivity is not outflanked. Each subjectivity comes face to face with another subjectivity, and whether his undertaking is to address the other and to be addressed by him or to conquer and enslave the other, no neutral domain into which both subjectivities can be fitted has been created.

Such a domain is law. The law imposes on both subjectivities the necessity of viewing themselves from the outside. The law is the same for all. The law speaks in terms of objectifying categories: it forces me to view myself as a leper or a thief, a firstborn son or the husband of a wife. Such categories are, of course, abstractions because I know myself in my subjectivity and transcendence and refuse to identify myself with any particular role that I have chosen to adopt or that has been thrust upon me by the course of events. The law cannot respect this truth. It must speak of lepers, husbands, thieves, and firstborn sons. In commanding and prohibiting this or that action, it creates categories of persons, which it regulates as in-stances of the categories formulated. In so doing, law alienates the self from itself and forces the self to view itself as others see it and not as it sees itself.

13. SELF-ALIENATION IN LAW

With respect to these two possibilities—the encounter with the other self who meets me and the integration of the self into objective categories that deprive the self of its natural primacy—we may ask, Which of these two modes preserves more decisively the reality of the other? In the direct encounter with another subjectivity, there is an immediacy of contact with the other. Each partner speaks out of his selfhood and the speaking is a speaking *to*, an addressing of a Thou in the situation of Buberian relationship. Neither side is then alone. Each side is confirmed in its subjectivity. This is, of course, less obvious when the relationship becomes less Buberian and more Sartrian. Instead of mutual confirmation, there is now the struggle of consciousness against consciousness, the attempt of each to fix its gaze upon the other and freeze it into thinglike immobility, thereby depriving it of its transcendent vitality and reducing it to thinghood. It might be argued that the subjectivity of the other is here revealed perhaps more sharply than elsewhere because the consciousness of the other strains to subdue the self's consciousness and thus impinges on it more sharply.

The legal relationship, unlike the direct relationship, is a mediated one. It is mediated by the alienation of the self from itself that the legal relationship presupposes. This insight is expressed by the well-known American proverb that anyone who is his own lawyer has a fool for a client. The litigant coincides with himself. He speaks out of the experience of his own subjectivity, but because he does so he does not view matters from the impersonal standpoint of the law. He knows what he knows passionately and subjectively (the two are synonomous) and is therefore unable to appropriate fully the objective, impersonal, and detached viewpoint of the law. It is difficult for man to climb out of his own skin and view his situation as others view it. Such an attempt is either strong evidence of great strength of character or of advanced dissociation from self. And yet, without this alienation from self, the ethical cannot arise.

What is the ethical? It has a number of components that must be kept in balance. First, is a sense for the other. I am not all there is. There are others who are as much subject to themselves as I am to

myself. This expresses itself in the recognition of a protected territory around the other from which I am excluded because it constitutes his sphere of influence. At this point there is no going out to
my fellow man but rather a withdrawing from him, a respecting of
his privacy, of his personal territory. Next is a drawing toward him
in love. The other must be experienced not only as strength but as
vulnerability. He needs my help because he is not self-sufficient. The
weakness of the other is the opposite of the power of his subjectivity.
Here I am no longer threatened by this power, and yet the other
does not turn into object—though there is always that danger in pity
—but instead into a nonthreatening, vulnerable subject with whom
I sense a solidarity in our common predicament. But in all of this,
there is a necessary element of alienation from the self that is prerequisite. If I am total subjectivity, then the fate of no other self but
my own can concern me. Total subjectivity is total self-absorption.
The other can become reality only if I can remove myself from the
absolute center of being and at least share it with the other.

This is the necessary alienation that is the ground of the ethical
and it is for this reason that the law and the ethical are intertwined
to the end of time. It is, of course, true that the ethical concerns itself
with my real fellow man rather than with categories of persons and
relationships that are created by abstractions and for which rules
seem fully appropriate. But the reality of my fellow man cannot arise
for me unless I have achieved some degree of distance from my own
self, which is the natural object of my concern. This self-alienation
constitutes entry into the legal realm, in which I must not view
myself as the exception but as an instance of the general law. Kant
understood this very well and it is for this reason he insisted on the
impermissibility of wanting to be an exception, thereby freeing
oneself from the claim of the categorical imperative, which applies
equally to all and therefore rules out private commandments addressed to a single individual or a single people as the carrier of a
historic covenant. The ethical law creates a community of equals
without a center. The law does not emanate from the will of any
given individual but from reason, whose essence is universality
rather than particularity. Every individual has a particular angle of
vision that constitutes the natural center of his universe. The ethical
demands that no attention be paid to this natural center. No individual may attach more importance to his perspective than to that
of anyone else. And this is true even of God.

14. God and Law

God is the natural ontological center. His viewpoint is the absolute viewpoint, which can mean either that it is the viewpoint that sees everything always from all possible points of view or that it is the most particular point of view, in comparison to which there are no other points of view. God is either the most absolute objectivity or the most absolute subjectivity. Perhaps these two absolutes merge into an identity when pursued to their extreme limit. But even if God is absolute subject and object, the creation of human beings introduces rival centers of subjectivity. In the first instance, these centers are rivals of each other: Cain's murder of Abel is an expression of this rivalry. Here subjectivity reveals itself as the possibility of violence. The subjectivity of the other can be extinguished and my center can thus be validated as against the other center. But this intersubjective rivalry is only a pretext. The deeper rivalry is not with the subjectivity that is equal to mine but with one that is superior to mine and that threatens to overwhelm mine. I turn on my fellow man because I can reach him, while I cannot reach God. Cain killed Abel not because of any injury that Abel had done him but because "the Lord had respect unto Abel and to his offering: but unto Cain and to his offering he had not respect. And Cain was very wroth, and his countenance fell" (Gen. 4:4–5). Cain's anger is at God who received Abel's offering of the "firstlings of his flock" but did not receive Cain's offering of the "fruit of the ground." Here is the first mention of sacrifice in the Bible. There is no explanation of why the thought of sacrifice occurs either to Cain or Abel. Instead, we are simply told that Abel was a keeper of sheep and Cain was a tiller of the ground and each brought something as a gift to God. What is the reason for the bringing of this gift? We are not told, but we can conjecture. It is an act of thankfulness. It is an act of appeasement. Perhaps it is both. Even if it is primarily an act of thankfulness, the element of terror cannot be far behind. One gift is accepted and the other is not. Can Cain, whose gift is not accepted, take this lightly? The clash between the divine and human subjectivities has already occurred with Adam, who would not obey the divine prohibition and became "as one of us, to know good and evil" (Gen. 3:22). The adversary relationship is thus established. Man is expelled from the Garden of Eden "to till the ground from whence he was taken" (Gen. 3:23). The very addition of the phrase "from whence he was taken" is significant. He is condemned to till the ground. But why is it necessary to mention, to man's shame, that this is the ground from which he was made? Not only is man not going to become "as one of us," an equal of God, but he is put to till the ground from which he was made. He is thus doubly reminded that he is not an equal of God but a creature made of earth, which he must now till by the sweat of his brow.

The primordial clash of subjectivities is thus the clash between God and man, and it is into this clash that law enters. There are thus two moments that must be kept in mind: the will of the lawgiver and the autonomy of the law. It must not be forgotten—though it often has been—that the biblical law is the will of God. As law, it is directed toward a class of actions. It forbids not this specific action contemplated by this specific person under these specific circumstances, but a class of actions that have something in common. The reality is the individual action, with all the specifics pertaining to it. Were the lawgiver in a position to enumerate specifically all the possible future acts he wishes to forbid, it would be clearly advantageous for him to do so. He would then be addressing himself to real situations. It would then not be necessary to wonder whether this or that particular action does or does not come under the forbidden heading. This is, of course, the basic difficulty with all law. No matter how precisely the forbidden act is defined, situations always arise in which it is difficult to know whether the act contemplated or committed fits into the definition or does not. In the case of the human lawgiver, an abstract definition is unavoidable because he cannot foresee the future and so cannot enumerate all the possible contingencies that may arise. Were he able to do so, he would not need any general definitions. He would point to one act and pronounce it good, another bad. But since he cannot envisage all possibilities, he is forced to restrict himself to general definitions and leave it to later interpreters to guess at his will, asking themselves what the will of the lawgiver would be in the specific situation that has arisen. By asking the question, "What is the law?" these interpreters are really asking themselves what would the will of the lawgiver be if he were here to express it, being cognizant of all the relevant circumstances. The interpreters have the abstract definitions before them and may also have specific cases in which the lawgiver expressed his will. By examining these cases and whatever definitions are available, the interpreter attempts to guess the will of the lawgiver, were he present to express it. In those cases where the lawgiver can appear to evaluate the decision of the lawgiver, an empirical verification of the interpreter's prediction concerning the will of the lawgiver may be feasible. It should be added that this process is quite conceivable without any abstract definitions at all. The interpreter might simply be presented with a number of cases and the decision of the lawgiver in each case. He may then be asked to guess what the decision of the lawgiver would be in some future situation that has both similarities to and differences from the previously known cases. Presented with such a puzzle, the interpreter might develop some definitions to guide him. But the Mishnah and British common law for the most part stay away from generalizations and stick to the case-law approach.

Biblical law is midway between case law and abstractly stated law. How exactly these two options are combined need not concern us here. Suffice it to say that the interpreter has an important role to play in the application of biblical law. When we read Exod. 22:5: "If fire break out, and catch in thorns, so that the shocks of corn, or the standing corn, or the field are consumed; he that kindled the fire shall surely make restitution," we ask, What sort of action constitutes kindling a fire? Suppose he had been carrying a fire that he had not kindled, is he as guilty as if he had kindled it himself? Suppose he had kindled it but put it out, or at least so he thought, only to discover that it was smoldering and had therefore burst into flame again? The interpreter who works with real cases is constantly faced with such problems. To a considerable extent, he is aided by talmudic law, which increases the number of cases as well as the definitions available to him. But no matter how many past cases there may be on record that, in various respects, resemble the case at hand, it is almost always true that the new case about to be decided has unique features and different interpreters may come to different conclusions about it. This is true of all legal systems and the Torah is no different in this respect.

15. What Is the Law?

But now we must be more specific. We ask, What is the law in this new case? The new case has some features in common with a number of cases in which the ruling was "permitted" and it has other features in common with a number of cases ruled "forbidden." Are the features it has in common with the former more significant than those it has in common with the latter or is the opposite the case? Here judgment comes into play, and that is why different conclusions can be drawn by different interpreters. But we must still ask, What is the meaning of the question, What is the law? There are a number of possibilities that must be examined.

When we ask, What is the law in a specific case, we may be asking, What is the intention of the lawgiver in this particular case? If so, then the best procedure would be to ask the lawgiver directly. Were we in a position to do so, there would be no problem. The law is defined as the will of the lawgiver (God, king, parliament, etc.) and the only relevant question concerns what that will is. Since, for one reason or another, we often cannot ask the lawgiver directly, we must guess on the basis of circumstantial evidence drawn from knowledge of his will in similar, but not identical, cases. After examining as many similar cases in which his will is known as possible, we can make a psychological surmise about what his will would be in this particular case. But it must be emphasized that any such conclusion is only a surmise because, in dealing with the will, a very small difference can make a very large difference. The will of the lawgiver may or may not be a rational will. It may simply be an exercise of will. The lawgiver himself may not know why he wills what he wills. The will of the lawgiver may, on the other hand, be rational. The lawgiver may will this or that not simply as an exercise in taste but as a means toward an end. He may will that his subjects abstain from this or that action because his goal is to prevent suffering or to secure public order or some other goal. Where the interpreter is aware of the end the lawgiver has in mind, he asks himself, when faced with a new case, whether permitting the proposed action would or would not further the goal sought. This itself needs to be divided into two questions: 1) Would the proposed action, in fact, further the goal sought? and, 2) Would the lawgiver evaluate the proposed action as furthering the goal he seeks? Since the law is defined as the will of the lawgiver, the second question would be the more decisive one in determining what the law is. In any case, where the will of the lawgiver is the law, the problem of the interpreter is to surmise the will of the lawgiver when it is unknown in a specific case.

The question, What is the law? can also be interpreted in less personal terms. The will of the lawgiver may not be the criterion but, instead, it may be the "meaning" of the law. What does the law forbid or permit? When the question is asked in these terms, a text is interpreted as having a meaning independent of the will of the law-giver. Having written the law, the text of the law stands on its own merits and means what it means, with the author having no privileged vantage point in interpreting it. The focus on the meaning of the legal text instead of the intention of the lawgiver is similar to the literary critic's insistence that a literary text must be read on its own terms and that external information not derived from the text itself cannot legitimately be used for interpretive purposes. The difficulty with this approach is a twofold one. First, it is not altogether clear that the meaning of any text can stand alone, divorced from the intention of the speaker. Words, after all, do not form themselves. They are put together by a speaker who wishes to communicate something to someone. We listen to or read the words to discover what the speaker or writer wishes to convey to us. While it is occasionally possible that the words before us mean something other than what was the speaker's intention, surely this cannot be the normative case but must be considered the exception. To insist that a text is independent of the meaning intended by the author is, it can be argued, to reify the text excessively. Secondly, whatever merits a method of text-centered interpretation may have, it encounters additional difficulties in the legal context. Here, as we have already seen, the problem is not so much to determine the meaning of the text itself as to apply it to unanticipated cases whose determination does not follow deductively from the meaning of the text. What kind of action, we have asked in connection with Exod. 22:5, constitutes kindling? Can we by analyzing the word *kindle* determine whether one who thought he has put out a fire when it was smoldering only to have it burst into flames again is to be held accountable for his mistake? This is not a question that can be answered by an analysis of the common usage definition of *kindle* but only by a knowledge of the purpose of the law and its underlying sense of justice. It is here that the problem of a divinely revealed law becomes acute.

Our problem remains: What is the meaning of the question, What is the law? when that question is applied to the law of God? The Torah is the word of God. The meaning of the Torah is the intention of the divine lawgiver, who is its author. It therefore follows that the only fully satisfactory way of determining what the law is in any specific case is to ask God. This is what Moses does when (Num. 27:1–11) the daughters of Zelophehad present their claim of inheritance. He does not make logical deductions from the law as he knew it. He does not use his judgment in discerning similarities and differences between analogous cases. He does not ask what the purpose of the law on inheritance is and then rule so as to advance the purpose he has discerned. He knows that he cannot discern God's purposes because God's thoughts are not his thoughts and God's ways are not his ways. This is the crux of the difficulty faced by the interpreter of divine law. It is otherwise in the case of human law. There, at least in principle, we can aspire to fathoming the goal of the lawgiver and we can therefore determine what interpretation will advance his purpose and what will hamper it. Once we understand his purpose we can make a reasonable guess as to what the lawgiver's will would be in the particular, novel case before us. All this is possible because we know or we think we know what purpose he wishes to achieve. But, generally speaking, we do not know this with God. He almost never tells us. He states his will. Sometimes, we think we can discern his purpose. This is particularly so in the moral realm when his command seems to coincide with the demands of the natural moral law. But God's commands are not restricted to this realm. The very distinction between moral and other commands is unknown in the Bible. There we find only divine commands expressing the will of God. Some of them strike a responsive cord in us, as if they merely confirmed what we would have thought anyway. And there are still other commandments that contradict our moral sense (e.g., the extermination of the Amalekites). And because this is so, we do not understand the "why" of even those commands we think we understand. There is only the sovereign will of Hashem, to which we are obedient because it is his will.

16. The Particular Situation

It therefore follows that there is only Hashem's will in this particular situation. The question that I must ask is, What is his will for me in this particular situation, under these circumstances, with these particular people involved? There is no law other than this will. Hashem did not create a law that commands in its own right. A law, as we have seen, is an abstraction that cannot consider individual cases. Only judges can consider individual cases. But the judges who interpret the divine law are particularly handicapped because they cannot fathom the purpose of the law. They therefore have to guess the will of the divine lawgiver in this particular case using the relatively abstractly stated law as their clue. They are not involved in an exercise in deductive logic nor in the invention of more or less probable hypotheses derived from known cases. They must ask Hashem to guide them to the discovery of his will. This is not purely pneumatic. Serious consideration must be given to precedents and the new case compared with the old. Nevertheless, there must also be a prayerful dialogue between the interpreter and Hashem in which the interpreter prays for divine guidance so that the wrong decision not be made, but the right one, the one that is Hashem's will, which is the ultimate test of the decision. The interpreter of the Torah is therefore not a thinking machine who unravels the implications of a text but a servant of Hashem who transmits the will of Hashem to those who inquire. He must therefore be in living dialogue with his lawgiver whom he serves. As a student of the Torah, he studies not an abstract legal code but commands set in concrete situations. Whatever prominence legal codes later assumed in Judaism, the Torah is not only a legal code. It is well known that it was when the Hebrew word *Torah* was translated into the Greek *nomos* that Torah became law. The correct translation of Torah is teaching. It is the story of God's encounter with Israel and of his will expressed in the context of that encounter. It is the personal interaction of Hashem with Israel as a people and with many individuals from among Israel and with some individuals from among the nations. The historic and narrative portions of the Bible are therefore not extraneous interruptions of a legal text but integral parts of the revelation recorded in the Torah. It is perhaps the legal portions of the Torah that require explanation, if anything does.

The truth of the matter is that Judaism has developed toward a self-understanding as law ever since the Biblical period. In rabbinic literature the halachic and the agadic are still interspersed but not as much as in the Bible. Most midrashim are compilations of nonlegal material, while the Mishnah is almost completely halachic. Later, the codes (especially that of Maimonides) emerge and gradually become normative. The codes are far more systematic than the Bible or even the Talmud. They tend to be more abstract, less case- and more principle-oriented than the Bible. But even before the emergence of the codes, there is a movement toward the autonomy of the law. Pivotal in this respect is the famous talmudic passage that tells of a dispute among the rabbis in which each side is convinced of the correctness of its interpretation.[11] As the dispute rages, each side calls for miraculous signs to confirm divine approval of its point of view. Finally, a heavenly voice is heard proclaiming the rightness of one of the positions. But, instead of this miracle bringing the debate to an abrupt and final close, the intervention of the heavenly voice is rejected because the Torah is no longer in heaven and, since it has been given to man, must be interpreted by human beings in accordance with the proper canons of interpretation. God, it seems, cannot intervene once the original revelation has taken place. This text has become the pillar of much contemporary thinking about the law in Jewish circles. It has cast a cloud of suspicion on all "religious" approaches to the law. It has served to vitiate all appeals to the spirit of the law as against its letter, though there are not a few texts that make precisely this distinction. In short, this text has helped to get God out of the law by establishing the law as an autonomous domain of human interpretation and application.

This is an incorrect interpretation of the text under discussion for a number of reasons. No one talmudic anecdote, no matter how arresting in content, may be read in isolation from the totality of voices that we must hear when we think about Judaism. In addition, the text can be read as an expression of skepticism that the heavenly voice (*Bat Kol*) was indeed the voice of God and not some illusion. There is further the question—to which we have already alluded— that if the will of God is not the governing criterion of the correctness of any given ruling, then what is? If it is the will of the interpreter, then the interpreter cannot be wrong, since, by definition, whatever he rules to be the law thereby becomes the law. From the point of view of the human situation this is inevitable. Any polity that has a law must create a person or persons who are the final court of appeal and from whose judgment no further appeal is possible. In the final analysis, such a body becomes a legislative one because there are no longer any standards by which its decisions can be called wrong. Are the interpreters of the Torah to be understood as autonomous legislators who need not fear error, since God has conferred on them the legislative function in which they are responsible to no one? It is understandable that political pragmatism would be sympathetic to such a human, autonomous legislature. It creates an unassailable organ of authority whose decisions are final because no dissenter can reject its rulings as contrary to the will of God, since, it is claimed, God has abdicated his will to that of the human authority. Where there are prophets who proclaim that the will of God was revealed to them, the potential for instability is immense. The appearance as well as the message of the prophet is unpredictable. Prophecy, unlike the monarchy and the priesthood, is not institutionalized. The essence of the law is stability and predictability. The law therefore depends on a constitutional framework that determines the settlements of disputes in a stable and predictable way. This leaves no room for divine intervention, which is necessarily noninstitutional and nonpredictable. But whatever the requirements of political stability may be, they cannot be purchased at the expense of the deactivation of Israel's covenant partner, the author of Israel's election and the creator of the universe. The tendency to push Hashem out of the law as well as the tendency to convert Torah to law must therefore, at least to a large extent, be read as a cooling of the fire of divine revelation into the ashes of human institutions. But it is not only that.

If the law has been given into the hands of the rabbis, then Hashem in effect says: My will is their will. Whatever they decide the law to be, that is the law as I want it to be. The advantage of this position is that it provides a theological sanction for an autonomous human legislative body. As a legislative body, the rabbis then have God's before-the-fact approval of their decisions in perpetuity. In effect, this abdicates the sovereignty of Hashem. Israel no longer lives under judgment. The logical corollary of this difficulty, as we have seen, is that the rabbis, in making their decisions, have no guidelines to follow. Since they have blanket approval of whatever course of action they decide to follow, there is no longer any particular reason for following one rather than another. The fear and trembling of displeasing Hashem, of forbidding what he wishes permitted or permitting what he wishes forbidden, vanishes and the domain of action shifts completely to the human realm, from which there is no further appeal. At this point a decisive shift has taken place in Jewish consciousness. The reality of Hashem diminishes. The law as interpreted by men becomes the dominant presence. It is now the Torah that is obeyed, not Hashem. While the Torah is understood as having been given by Hashem, as expressing his will, the Hashem who is behind the Torah becomes less and less distinct until the Jew's personal relationship with Hashem is completely eclipsed by obedience to Torah and not to its giver. In the New Testament, this is the charge Jesus levels at the Pharisees whom he considers men puffed up with their own learning who can no longer hear the word of God.

This is a fateful charge under which Judaism has labored for two millennia and that it has tended to reject with considerable passion. What can we say about this, in the context of our discussion?

17. THE LAW AND THE SILENCE OF GOD

In certain evangelical Christian circles, it is very common for individuals to say that God has sent them here or there, told them to do this or that, directed them to this or that destination. Those who have been born again in Christ place themselves at his disposal and henceforth it is he who directs their every step. What these sincere evangelical Christians do not understand is that their attitude undermines the authority of Scripture. If God speaks to every believer today as he did to Isaiah and Paul, then there is nothing preeminent about the biblical word, since every preacher who feels called transmits the word of God prophetically. If Scripture is unique, if it remains the word of God for all places and times, then it is so because the biblical writers transmit the word of God as no one subsequently does. The prophet who says "Thus sayeth the Lord" has been entrusted by God with his message as the rest of us have not. Only the prophets and, for Christians, the apostles speak with authority. They have been chosen and we have not. The church fathers, the medieval Scholastics, and the voices of the Reformation are also in the service of God. But not as the biblical authors were. The postbiblical voices speak from the authority of Scripture and not directly at the command of God. But if the Bible is unique, then prophecy or biblical authority must have stopped at some point. Judaism is very aware of the end of prophecy. At some point, men who said "Thus sayeth the Lord" ceased to appear. To the historian of religion, this is an interesting fact not easy to explain. For the believer, men who pronounced this formula ceased to appear because God ceased sending them. There is, therefore, a fundamental distinction to be drawn between the time of prophecy, when Hashem sends those who are able to say "Thus sayeth the Lord," and the time when that is no longer possible, when there is only the amassed record of the word of God as spoken by previous messengers but there is no longer the current speaking of Hashem to Israel through the prophets.

The rabbinic attitude reflects this fact. The rabbis know themselves not to be prophets. That time has passed. Hashem has withdrawn from his people. He has stopped speaking to it directly through his servants, the prophets. The rabbis know the difference between the prophets and those who teach the Torah in postprophetic times. The rejection of the *Bat Kol* is an expression of the realization that those times have passed and that Israel must now attempt to determine the will of Hashem by means of comparisons of earlier decisions, as in all legal reasoning. Clearly the procedures followed by Moses in adjudicating the claim of the daughters of Zelophehad—of asking God—is preferable,[12] and if the rabbis do not follow it, it is because it is a solution not available to them and not because reasoning from precedents is superior to hearing the command of the living God.

And now the Torah has been given to Israel. Israel is ruled by the Torah. The Torah is the presence of Hashem in Israel at a time when Hashem is silent, when he has withdrawn and left Israel to fend for itself. He has not, of course, fully withdrawn. There is a certain presence that remains. Nevertheless, it will not do to speak as if there were no silence. The author of these lines has not been commanded by Hashem to write this chapter and to say in it what he says. We cannot say that God has sent us to this city, at this time, to do this or that. This is the language of those who do not really understand what it is to be sent by God as Moses and Isaiah were sent. But neither can we speak of the total absence of God, as those theologians did who proclaimed (if not celebrated) the "death of God." The world and Israel have not been plunged into total darkness. In withdrawing, God has left life in our world, both physical and spiritual. There are no living prophets who proclaim the words of the living God here and now, speaking words that create new Scripture. But neither are the words of the old prophets stilled. They are words that, once spoken, continue to speak as long as there are men created in the image of God to hear them and as long as there are Jews faithful to the covenant of Abraham to read them. The presence of God in the world makes itself felt through his word in the Bible and through the people of Israel. The Bible and the people of Israel remain when he withdraws, and therefore he never withdraws fully and the world is never left completely barren of God.

The rabbis are sensitive to the withdrawal, which, even if not complete, is nevertheless real. They therefore do not refer to God lightly. The Mishnah does not often speak about God. It speaks about the human world. It enumerates the different kinds of seed used by the farmer, his utensils and tools as well as the different kinds of substances that may be used to kindle the Sabbath lights. The language of the Mishnah is one of the great resources of living Hebrew because it reflects the everyday world of the farmers and craftsmen of Samaria and Galilee, Jersualem and the coastal plain. God is not mentioned often but the life of the people and of the land is. The emphasis shifts away from Hashem. The Mishnah is, of course, the law. It is implicit that it is the law of God. It is therefore not an enumeration of the agriculture of Israel for its own sake. But it does largely, even as law, speak of the life of man and not of the deeds of God. God is not a character in the Mishnah, as he is in the Bible. In the rabbinic period, the direct speech of Hashem to Israel is an event of the past and it is now the Torah, both written and oral, that is the teacher of Israel.

The Talmud is the writing down of the oral law. The oral law was not meant to be put into writing. It was given orally to Moses as the commentary to the written Torah and was supposed to remain an oral commentary. But, with the passage of time, the oral law became garbled and knowledge of it diminished. It was then decided to write it down, at first in brief Mishnaic form and later more elaborately in the Gemara, which fills in the reasoning behind the rulings of the Mishnah. Nevertheless, in spite of the writing down of the oral law, it would be a grave mistake to erase the distinction between the written and oral law. Theologically speaking, the oral law can never be written down. The oral law is that part of the law carried in the Jewish people. The law does not only remain a normative domain that hovers over the people of Israel and judges this people. It does that, too, of course. But the Torah enters the being of the people of Israel. It is absorbed into their existence and they therefore become the carriers or the incarnation of the Torah. The oral law reflects this fact. And because this is so, we must once again examine the status of the people that carries the covenant.

The people is subject to the law. The law is the divine word as it makes its demands on the people. The law is heteronomous. It is not a creation of the people. It is not, as we have seen, a codification of the people's moral sensibilities. It comes to the people from Hashem as command. At times it seems to be in more or less agreement with the people's moral sensibilities, and at other times it comes as a cutting knife that penetrates human flesh. The people is faithful to all of the law, to that which "makes sense" and to that which does not. When it obeys what it does not understand, it experiences the otherness of Hashem, the distance between the thoughts of God and of man. That which is from Hashem comes from a realm beyond the understanding of man and will therefore display its origins. But while coming from Hashem it is also addressed to man and therefore, at least in part, is understandable to man and seen as a law of life, a law that, at least in large part, can be seen to be conducive to the individual's and society's welfare. In obeying the law, Israel is thus obedient to the divine command that is addressed to it.

But the law is addressed only to Israel. It is not a universal law, obedience to which is expected of all peoples. Apart from the Noachide commandments, the Torah is addressed only to Israel. In it, Hashem speaks to Israel. There is a well-known midrash that speaks of Hashem attempting to bestow the Torah on various nations,[13] all of whom reject it because its provisions, such as the prohibition of theft and murder, are found unacceptable. Only Israel accepts the Torah as soon as it is offered, without inquiring into its provisions. This midrash notwithstanding, the Torah cannot be conceived as addressed to any people other than Israel. Israel is not the accidental bearer of the Torah. The Torah grows out of Israel's election and Hashem's saving acts performed for his people. The Torah is Israel's obligation under the covenant, in the absence of which there would be no obligation toward the Torah. In fact, only the history of Israel is part of the Torah.

Though we have been speaking of Torah as law, we must remind ourselves of the limitations of this translation. Torah includes everything contained in the Torah, of which law is a part, but so are the stories of the saving acts of Hashem toward his people. The existence and history of the Jewish people therefore enters the fabric of Torah. The Torah is not a demand that exists apart from the being of Israel. Once the Jewish people is, the Torah has also come into being and once the Torah is, the Jewish people, to whom it applies, is made necessary. In the broadest sense, the Jewish people is the incarnation of Torah. If the Torah is demand, the Jewish people is the embodiment of that demand. A *talmid chacham* ("rabbinic scholar") is considered a living Torah. We merely extend this to the people of Israel, of whom the *talmid chacham* is but an outstanding member.

18. GOD, TORAH, AND ISRAEL

We are trying to explain the secularization of the halachah, its growing autonomy and the banishing of direct divine intervention from its decision-making process. We have spoken of the cessation of prophecy as a basic fact of Jewish existence. But we must now add another dimension to this explanation. We have insisted that Hashem has not given any group of human beings blanket authority to make the decisions they see fit with prior divine assurance that their decisions will please Hashem. This would be an act of divine abdication and would take Israel out of its life under divine judgment. At the same time, Israel is not a body foreign to the divine will and to Torah. God dwells in Israel. He dwells in the midst of its uncleanness.[14] He envelops Israel. Israel is Hashem's abode in the created world. Nothing that Israel does is therefore unrelated to Hashem. This does not mean, God forbid, that Israel is Hashem. Judaism does not accept Christian incarnation, with the people of Israel becoming the incarnation of God. To say that Hashem dwells in the Jewish people does not deify the Jewish people any more than to say that Hashem dwells in the Temple in Jerusalem is to deify the stones of the Temple. The stones do not remain unaffected. Anyone who has seen Jews kissing the stones of the Western Wall knows that stones can be holy without this constituting idolatry. And if stones become holy because Hashem dwells in them or near them, how much more is this true of the people of Israel. They are not stones. They are descendants of Abraham, whom God loved and with whom he entered into an everlasting covenant. They are the people who carry Hashem's presence into history and who are killed for his holy name. They are therefore a holy people. When the peoples of the world will come to recognize this, they will cling to the people of Israel as Jews today cling to the stones of the Temple of Jerusalem. Israel is not Hashem. But it is the dwelling place of Hashem.

This does not mean that Israel cannot sin. It does not mean that the individual or the nation as a whole cannot take a wrong turn. It is for this reason that we must reject any absolute view of *emunat chachamim*, faith that the rabbinic authorities teach the true word of God. Anyone who has ever known a true *gadol*, one of the great Torah leaders of the Jewish people, knows how tempting a doctrine of *emunat chachamim* can be. There is indeed good reason to depend on these individuals. They have become living vessels of the divine presence. In their presence we feel the encompassing love and wisdom of Hashem. They have destroyed their wills and substituted the will of their father in heaven. But they remain human beings and are therefore capable of sin.

There is no insight more significant for the thought of Saint Paul than the sinfulness of Israel. Paul looks at the Old Testament record and sees a faithful God and a sinning Israel. At every crucial turn, as God displays his mercy and love for Israel, Israel responds by disobedience and ingratitude. And this vision of a sinful Israel has penetrated deeply into the consciousness of Christianity. It has, of course, also penetrated deeply into the consciousness of Israel. We need not search long in rabbinic literature to convince ourselves that the rabbis attribute the various calamities of Jewish history to the sinfulness of Israel. The emphasis on the need for repentance, the return to Hashem, is pervasive in biblical and rabbinic thought. But in spite of this, the self-loathing of condemned sinners is not common among Jews. Basically, Jews feel good about themselves. While sin is a reality, the eternal election of Israel is a greater reality. However catastrophic the consequences of sin are—and they are frequently catastrophic—they do not bring about an ultimate change. They do not sever the bond between Hashem and Israel. They do not change the ultimate outcome of history, which moves toward the redemption of Israel and all of mankind. The bond between Hashem and Israel is eternal and cannot be severed by the deeds of Israel.

Were the divine demand (Torah) and the people of whom the demand is made (Israel) separate in their being, the condemnation of Israel as the transgressor of the divine law would have to be far more total than it is. The Kantian law condemns those who transgress the moral law. In a system in which law is supreme, the initial election of Abraham would have to have been a merited election resulting from an exemplary obedience to the divine demand. In spite of rabbinic elaborations, the Bible does not portray the election of Abraham as a merited one. Abraham's merits follow upon his election. The divine promise to make the seed of Abraham into a great nation is a divine decision not earned by any action on the part of Abraham. And just as the initial election is not earned by any act of Abraham, so the election cannot be undone by any act of Israel. Israel's election is a gift of Hashem and since Hashem is a faithful God, it will never be cancelled. We thus see the limit of human freedom. This limit consists of the inability of man to modify the fundamental program: the election and redemption of Israel and through Israel of mankind. What Israel—or, for that matter, the rest of mankind—does, can postpone the effective date of the fulfillment of the divine plan, but it cannot permanently alter it. The final outcome of Israel's history is not in Israel's but in Hashem's hands.

Hashem's indwelling in Israel is not the incarnation of Christianity, which results in a sinless Christ. Hashem's indwelling in Israel is "in the midst of their uncleanness." The sin of Israel is not dissipated by the divine indwelling. It is, in fact, heightened. To be the people through whom Hashem acts in history and yet not to be perfectly obedient, indeed to be very disobedient, is a terrible fact. It is a choice for which Israel pays dearly. But it is not a fact that drives the divine indwelling out. Hashem continues to dwell in and with this people "in the midst of their uncleanness." Their sin ceases to be the sin of that which is wholly other than Hashem, as if sin is a human possibility from which Hashem must remain ontologically separated. Hashem's identification with Israel, his indwelling in Israel is so intimate that Israel's sin does not leave Hashem untouched. The estrangement of Israel from Hashem when Israel sins is a divine self-estrangement. This is the reason that the estrangement cannot be permanent and final. Hashem returns to himself. He becomes one. When Israel is separated from Hashem, God's unity is impaired. The restoration of the divine unity, of the day when "God will be one and his name out,"[15] refers to the reconciliation of Hashem and Israel, the nonrealization of which flaws the divine unity. We must, however, reiterate that all this does not diminish the seriousness of sin. It is not an illusion dissipated by a Neoplatonic mysticism that substitutes divine "reality" for human "appearance," with sin restricted to the latter and excluded from the former. On the contrary, because the sin of Israel is very close to the being of God, it is a very serious assault on the presence of Hashem in the world through the people of Israel. The foundation of sin is thus always, directly or indirectly, the mutilation of Israel. Whether it is an external mutilation perpetrated by gentiles, who are thereby able to strike at the God of Israel, or whether it is a self-mutilation, as when Israel attempts to evict Hashem from his dwelling place in the world, the mutilation of Israel strikes at the being of Hashem, who has chosen to appear in the historical people of Israel. This is implicit in the divine promise to Abraham to multiply his seed as "the stars in the sky." An expansion of the number of Jews in the world, any improvement in their well-being is a strengthening of the divine presence in the world. Similarly, a diminution of their number and well-being represents a shrinking of Hashem's presence in the world. To be *Judenfrei* ("free of Jews") is to be abandoned by God. The emphasis in the promise to Abraham on his seed becoming as many as the stars in the heavens reflects the infinity of Hashem, which must be reflected—even if very imperfectly—by the multitude of the people of the covenant.

The ethical in Judaism is therefore never separated from the being of the people of Israel. Here we must speak cautiously because the truth can be easily distorted into an anti-Semitic caricature. Anti-Semites charge that Jews apply ethical standards to dealings with gentiles different from those applied to dealings with fellow Jews. Lending money with interest, for example, is permitted only when the borrowers are not Jewish. Jews, it is alleged, help only their own but not others. Many of these charges are simply based on malice and cannot be refuted rationally. The truth of the matter is that rabbinic Judaism demands a high standard of Jewish morality in dealing with gentiles, though this is often justified as being necessary in order to avoid desecration of the divine name, a concept based on the view that whatever generates disapproval of the conduct of Israel harms Hashem's reputation because the two are so closely intertwined. There is therefore an element of truth in the grievances of the anti-Semite. The Jew's ethical relationship with his fellow Jew is not identical with his ethical relationship with non-Jews. We must face this and attempt to understand it.

19. THE ETHICAL AND THE UNIVERSAL

To whom do we owe ethical obligations? To all human beings equally? Then why not to animals? If also to animals, then why not to plants? And why not to inanimate objects? If we owe ethical obligations equally to all human beings only, then do we owe such obligations equally to all human beings or is it permissible to prefer our own children? In fact, of course, we do prefer our own children, to whom we pay much more attention than to others. Is this simply a result of human weakness or is it morally justified to expend most of my resources on the welfare of my children and much less on the welfare of others? Kant specified rational beings as those deserving of moral consideration. For him the object of moral consideration reflected the nature of the moral law. Since the moral law is rooted in the lawfulness of reason, it becomes symmetrically attractive to select the rational being as the proper object of the rational moral law. But Kant's solution does not answer the question whether inflicting needless suffering on animals could constitute a transgression of the moral law. Nor does it justify morally the almost universal preoccupation with the welfare of one's closest relatives. In the devastating 1976 earthquake in Communist China, there was a report of an incident in which a father insisted on rescuing a local

Communist officer rather than his child, whose moans he heard but ignored in order to save the official, whose social value the father judged above that of his son. By the time he returned to the wreckage in which his son was buried, he found him dead. The Chinese Communist press pointed to this incident as an example of proper Communist behavior. It dramatizes the issue we are raising here. Do all rational beings, *qua* rational, have the same claims on my moral obligations or are there persons to whom I owe special consideration?

Judaism teaches that there are persons to whom I owe special consideration. And it is not simply a matter of kinship, though the special obligations due to my kinfolk must not be ignored. Ethical space is not geometric, centerless space. The ethical is rooted in the human presence in the world and human presence is always perspectival, centered. The space of the world radiates outward from a natural center that is I. I do not see myself, except by an extraordinary effort of the imagination, as one object among others. To do so requires my assuming a standpoint other than my own, since it is only from the point of view of this other standpoint that I am an object among others. Were I to attempt such a bifurcation of my self, I would embrace alienation as a philosophic first principle. A phenomenologically realistic ethics cannot therefore deal in geometric space. It must take into account the far and the near, the close and the remote. If obligation is not to be purely formal, as in Kant, it must be rooted in real relations with real persons, and these do not appear abstractly, lacking position in relation to my position, but very much placed in relation to me and the position I occupy. We therefore find a struggle in Greek tragedy between the obligations owed to the state, the more remote reality, and the family, the closer reality.[16] While Greek tragedy does not neatly resolve this struggle in favor of one or another of these domains, it must be realized that the state, while more universal than the family, is deeply rooted in the kinship of the people. The Greek state was not the modern rational state embracing tens and hundreds of millions of people. It was a deeply cohesive unit in which the phenomenological proximity of the family was extended but not totally erased.

In any case, the point is that even in the absence of the special status of Israel, reason does not force ethics into a mechanical egalitarianism. If such as egaliterianism is implicit in Kant, it is because Kant projects the noncentered space of Newton and the mechanics resulting from it into the ethical domain. Jewish ethics, on the other hand, preserves the distinction between the insider and the outsider. It is not a division that is ethically indefensible. We have had too much love of humanity and indifference and even hatred of the people around us. It is easy to love the abstraction that is humanity because it has none of the blemishes that real people have. When the author of 1 John, in order to emphasize the centrality of the love of fellow man, asks how it is possible to love God, whom we do not see, and not to love man, whom we do see,[17] he draws attention to the greater reality of what is near in contrast to what is more remote. The natural setting of man is not a universal humanity, shorn of the specificity of language, culture, and location, but a portion of humanity, even if that portion is not as small as his immediate family. In the case of Judaism, this setting is a nation that is an extended family. This point cannot be emphasized too strongly. Jews have a distinctly family feeling about each other, even if they have never met and even if they differ from each other culturally as in the case of western European Jews and Jews from Arab countries. The tie to the nation is therefore an extended family bond rooted in the Jewish understanding of the descent from Abraham as the definition of Jewish identity. It follows therefore that Jewish identity in terms of national cohesion is very strong. It is so strong that, for example, a sustained Jewish civil war in modern times in which Jews would kill each other on a large scale is inconceivable.

But there is more to the ethics of Jewish tribalism. Israel understands itself as "a priestly nation and a holy people." It is, as we have maintained, the nation through whom Hashem makes his presence felt in the world. It is the physical vessel of the divine indwelling. And Jewish ethics must never be separated from its theological basis. There is no Jewish ethics apart from Israel's historic mission of redemption. Jewish theology is historical. It deals with the mission of a people in the midst of human history. Pure ethics is nonhistorical. The ethics of Kant, which is an archetype of pure ethics, is ahistorical. It sets forth a teaching not bound to time and place but only to the universality of reason. The categorical imperative knows no temporal or geographic boundaries. It sits in judgment over the real deeds of real men and women in real history. The ethical grew in prominence in Judaism in the rabbinic period as Jewish sovereignty receded. National sovereignty is a prerequisite for appearing on the stage of history because history is the drama of the encounter of nations and not of individuals. The theological basis of Jewish ethics is thus rooted in the historical mission of Israel because there is no Jewish theology without history. And it is in the dimension of history that the limits of Jewish ethics are reached.

The archetype of this is the conquest of the land, commanded by Hashem and carried out by Joshua and his successors. It is a story that those who identify Judaism with a love of peace find deeply embarrassing. It is the outstanding example of a clash between the divine historic command and the ethical. And this clash is not perceived only by us, viewing events of the remote past. It was perceived by those involved in the events, since we are told frequently that Israel did not carry out the commandments of destruction, a failure for which it was often punished by Hashem. That the Jewish people has carried something of a bad conscience for occupying the land and expelling the prior inhabitants of the land is fairly evident. Rashi, as we have already said, quotes a midrashic text that inquires why the Torah begins with the narration of the creation of the world rather than with the first commandment.[18] The question implies that Israel needs to know the divine commandments but does not need to know who created the world. The text explains that the account dealing with the creation of the world was included in order to refute the nations of the world who might be inclined to accuse Israel of theft in the appropriation of the land owned initially by others. If the Jews are taunted along these lines, they can, by referring to the Genesis account, point out that since God created heaven and earth, he has the right to give it to whomever he sees fit and to deprive one nation of it and bestow it on another. That the account of the creation of heaven and earth has to be justified in terms of its usefulness in justifying the Jewish claim to the land of Israel shows how problematic this claim is in Jewish eyes. And it is problematic because Jewish consciousness, unlike that of other nations, never accepted war and violence as a matter of course. The requirement of the historical never stills the voice of the ethical in Jewish national history.

20. THE ETHICAL AND HISTORY

Nevertheless, the historical remains essential in Judaism. It may very well be that the ultimate factor that impelled Judaism to see the early Jewish Christians as outside of the covenant was the failure of the Jewish Christians to join in mourning the destruction of the Temple. For the rabbis, the end of Jewish sovereignty, even in the limited form in which it had been exercised in the period immediately preceding the destruction of the Temple, was an event of the greatest significance. In his preaching, Jesus seemed ready to write off the political arena as the domain of Caesar, while true Judaism was to be practiced by a private fellowship whose faith and ethics of love were to dominate, not the policy of a historic state, but the ethics of a voluntary association that had no intention of clashing with the authority of a foreign state and, in fact, had every intention of bowing to the foreign yoke imposed on Israel. Jewish spirituality never wrote off the state as of no interest to it. The Jewish prophets did not withdraw into private fellowships that despaired of reforming national life but, instead, they did not hesitate to take on the person of the king when they thought he acted improperly. The covenant, they believed, was not with individual Jews. It was with the people in the totality of its public life. The election of Israel excluded the possibility of foreign domination of the people, except as temporary punishment for Israel's misdeeds. In spite of Acts 1:6, where we learn that the first question posed to the risen Lord by the believing fellowship was, "Lord, wilt thou at this time restore again the kingdom of Israel?" a question that emphasizes the Jewish understanding of the political task associated with the messianic role, there is a marked lack of indignation over Rome's rule of Israel manifested in Jewish Christianity. Even if the notion of the ultimate political salvation of Israel did not completely vanish from Jewish Christianity, the immediate redemption of the individual was made possible by participation in the island of redemption in the unredeemed world that was the Church. The political hegenomy of Rome over Israel—almost total prior to *A.D.* 70 and total after that dating—was irrelevant to the fellowship because the Church's existence was in a dimension other than that in which Rome existed and ruled.

Such a maneuver is not open to Judaism. If Israel is not sovereign in the political realm, then the redemption has not yet occurred. Israel is meant to be ruled by Hashem, who is its only real king. Even the selection of a human king (e.g., Saul) is objectionable because it seems to contradict the exclusive right of Hashem to rule this people. How much more true is this when Israel is ruled by a foreign power! Anyone who does not perceive such a situation as temporary and subject to immediate correction does not fathom the inherent concern of Judaism with the historical as the domain in which human redemption must come to fruition. Therefore the conquest of the land is necessary. And therefore the potential for conflict with the ethical arises.

What can be done with this conflict? It can be argued that the state has a higher morality than the individual. We can speak of the historic destiny of peoples and start thinking in a Hegelian framework that does not so much amount to a rejection of the ethical as a loss of interest in it. Hegel, and later Marx, see the ethical conditioned by the historical and understandable only in terms of the function of an ethical system in the historic period of its appearance. Certainly, this frame of mind is not entirely foreign to the Bible. The Bible tells the story of nations with the individual appearing within the framework of national events. Yet the concern for justice is there in the midst of the historical. We think of the laws in the Pentateuch concerning parts of the harvest that must be left to the poor, of God's special love for the widow and the orphan, and of that style of compassion that has become so characteristically Jewish. This becomes especially prominent in the prophets, with their condemnation of the cultic sacrifices when accompanied by unjust conduct. Here a consciousness higher than the historical is reached. It is true that this is an inner-directed morality that applies mainly to the fellow Jew. But even this is not completely true: there are the passages about loving the stranger because we were strangers in the land of Egypt.[19] And even apart from that, one who loves and cares for the weak among his fellow Jews cannot long remain indifferent to the suffering of anyone human, created in the image of God. In this sense the universalizing tendency is irresistible, as we can learn from the history of rabbinic legislation which expands steadily to include non-Jews in its concerns. So while we must correct the ethical, ahistorical stress of so much of liberal Jewish theology of the past 100 years, we dare not swing to the opposite extreme and deny the centrality of the ethical concern in biblical and rabbinic Judaism.

Both in ancient times and in our time, the conflict is reflected in the relationship to the land. The land had to be conquered. The result has been that Jewish consciousness has vividly retained the memory of the land as having belonged to others before it came to belong to Israel. Other nations do not retain such memories. Their memory does not go back to a time when they did not occupy their land. In fact, the national identities of other nations are land-bound identities. The nation is defined by the territory it occupies. But Israel comes into national existence before it occupies the land. It becomes a nation on the basis of a promise delivered to it when it is a stranger in the land of others. This awareness of being a stranger is burned into Jewish consciousness. The God of Israel is not a God whose jurisdiction is defined by territorial boundaries. The peoples contemporary with Abraham were polytheists because their theological model was derived from political realities. In the political domain, every ruler presides over a piece of territory beyond whose borders his authority is null and void. It was therefore only natural that when a man leaves one territory and enters another, he ceases to be subject to the authority of one ruler and becomes subject to that of the other. This is as natural as it is for us to realize that when we cross from one state to another, we are no longer subject to the laws of the former state but to those of the territory we have just entered. The radical novelty of Hashem's teaching was that his jurisdiction extended everywhere. He was therefore not the God of only one territory but rather of a people who were subject to him wherever they were. They could therefore become a people before they entered their land and could continue to remain a people after they were banished from their land, a feat not imitated by any other people.

Nevertheless, the land figures very prominently in Jewish destiny. It could have been otherwise. As a God whose authority is not restricted to any particular land, Hashem could have chose a people permanently existing without a land perhaps as a sign that there is a God who rules not only over one territory but over the whole world. The normal and permanent condition of Israel would then have been homelessness. But Hashem did not do this. As soon as he commanded Abraham to leave his country and become a stranger in a land not his own (Gen. 12:1-2), he promised Abraham "I give this land to your descendants" (Gen. 12:7). At this point this is only a promise. The land Hashem has promised is still occupied by others. Abraham will not take possession of it, only his descendants. But the promise of the land is there from the beginning. It is as if Hashem also wishes to become a God of a land, but not as the other gods, whose authority is limited to the boundaries of their jurisdiction. The people of Hashem remains under the jurisdiction of its God no matter where this people resides at any given time. It therefore became a people many centuries before it finally obtains possession of its land. Nevertheless, Hashem is not unsympathetic to the bond to a land. He, too, wishes to have such a bond. The land that Israel obtains is the land on which the God of Israel dwells preeminently. He wishes to have an abode on this earth and not just in heaven. Had he wished to remain in heaven, he would not have had to create the earth, and even if he did create the earth, he did not have to become involved with its affairs as the God of Israel did. As one involved in human history, particularly in Jewish history, Hashem shares the land of Israel with the people of Israel. And even if his authority extends over all the earth, it permeates somewhat more sharply the land of Israel, which is holy because he dwells on it.

21. ETHICS, CULT, AND LAND

We thus find the ethical in Judaism supplemented by the cultic and the national. The election of Israel, as we have seen repeatedly, is a national election, and this implies a national domicile, which, because of the theological nature of Jewish existence, becomes also a divine domicile. The geographic dimension of Jewish election is tied to the cultic aspect of Judaism, which, in turn, is tied to the land. Sacrifice is not permitted outside of the land of Israel nor, indeed, outside of the city of Jerusalem. Sacrifice is spatial. It puts animals, which feed off the produce of the land, and the produce itself, to religious use. The sacrificial act is rooted in the agrarian economy. What is sacrificed is food and food is the gift of the earth. Sacrifice is inherently nonhistorical. While in Judaism some sacrifices, such as that of Passover, are tied to redemptive events in history, these are the exceptions. The basic cycle of sacrifices celebrates the alternation of day and night, while the festival sacrifices derive largely from the function of the festivals in celebrating the seasons in addition to the historic memories they preserve. Once the ties to the land was severed, the sacrificial cult had to end. If Judaism is seen as a composite of the ethical, national, and cultic, it must then be concluded that the cultic is the most dispensable portion of the composite because it has remained in suspension for a long time, while the ethical and the national have been kept alive. And while there is clearly much truth in this conclusion, it is not an observation whose significance must be exaggerated. Jewish history of the last century or so has proven that Jewish existence is national, and only the ethical incarnated in the Jewish people is Jewishly viable as ethics. The German Reform Jews who thought that Berlin was their Jerusalem because they were in Jerusalem whenever they obeyed the moral teachings of the prophets have been refuted by history. Berlin was not Jerusalem and the ethical in Berlin had no Jewish future; it quickly succumbed to the gods of the land on which Berlin was located. Jewish ethical existence cannot therefore be severed from the national and cultic dimensions of the covenant. These three ingredients must fructify and reinforce each other. Alone, each must die.

We have noted earlier that Jewish mistakes are holy. The reduction of Judaism to the ethical in modern times was a Jewish mistake because it substituted a very important part of the whole for the whole. It is tempting to say that it chose the most important part of the whole for the whole, and yet that would not be true. The most important part of the whole is the existence of the Jewish people as the earthly abode of Hashem. That is the bare minimum: that there exist a Jewish people among or in whom God dwells. It is vital that this people live ethically. When it does not, it is severely punished by Hashem. But sin does not drive Hashem out of the world completely. Only the destruction of the Jewish people does. Hitler understood that. He knew that it was insufficient to cancel the teachings of Jewish morality and to substitute for it the new moral order of the superman. It was not only Jewish values that needed to be eradicated but Jews had to be murdered. There are no Jewish values without Jews, and the most convincing intellectual refutation of Jewish values is worthless as long as the Jewish face is seen in the world. The Jew's being is a far more powerful act of teaching of Jewish values than anything else conceivable. And therefore, dreadful and horrible as Jewish sin is, it is not in the final analysis fatal. This is not said to minimize it in any sense. It is simply to understand the totality of the revelation in which teaching is fused with the existence of a people that becomes a physical embodiment of the teaching and whose land becomes a geographic epiphany and therefore the event that makes the ethical possible. The Jewish claim to the land can therefore not conflict with the ethical. The land belongs to the Jewish people because it was given by Hashem to Abraham and his descendants. That the competing claim to the land comes from a people that also considers itself seed of Abraham is not a historic accident. It confirms the person of Abraham as the source of right to this land and therefore represents a challenge to the proper lineage through which the election is transmitted. It illustrates once again that ethical issues in the context of Israel are always rooted in the covenant and election, the contact points through which Hashem's interest in the affairs of man are mediated.

Chapter 6

THE UNREALIZED

1. EXPECTING THE UNEXPECTED

All living is living into the future. The human being lives at the intersection of being and nonbeing. The past has been. Even if not fully understood or even fully known, the past is no longer possibility: its possibilities have been realized and thereby entered the realm of being. It is otherwise with the future. It has not yet happened. There is thus a decisive dimension of the "not" about the future as that which is not yet. Nevertheless, the being of the past and the nonbeing of the future cannot be absolutized. The past, for all its being, is also laced with nonbeing as that which is gone and is no longer. But for all these modalities of nonbeing that surround or even penetrate the past, it is still being that rules the past. And it is nonbeing that rules the future, though being is also intertwined with it. The future is not totally open. It is foreshadowed by the past. On the basis of the past, one can guess the future. And frequently the guesses turn out to be correct. But all such prediction remains guesswork. The future remains dark, even if it is not totally dark. The shadows that can be glimpsed in it are seen very imperfectly and can therefore be thoroughly misinterpreted. The darkness of the future predominates over its light.

If Jewish thought is, as we have said, a dark knowledge, then its orientation toward the future must be fundamental. It derives its darkness from its fixation on the future. If the main thrust of Jewish theology were derived from the past, then the self-understanding of

Israel would not be a dark knowledge. It would then understand itself in the illumination of its past being. It would then teach that the central event of its history has already taken place. But Judaism does not teach this. Unlike Christianity, Judaism does not believe that the central event of its history or of human history has taken place. This central event, the advent of the Messiah and the redemption of Israel and the world, has not yet taken place. It is still being awaited, and it is this waiting that characterizes the condition of humanity. To wait for someone is not to live toward a future that is totally empty, completely dark. He for whom we wait casts his presence over the landscape from which he is perceived as absent. We remember the absent one for whom we wait out of our recollection of the past when he was not absent. But since he is absent now, we wait for his appearance.

The tendency of religious communities is to celebrate the past, in which decisive salvational events took place that the community remembers and to which it clings. For this reason, religious communities in general and Judaism in particular have deep historic memories. A Judaism without its historic memory is inconceivable. The centrality in Judaism of remembering that God created the world in six days and rested on the seventh, that he elected Abraham and brought the children of Israel out of Egypt, and other such saving acts, need not be elaborated. The remembering of the giving of the Torah and its continuing normative authority for the house of Israel is fundamental. There is thus ample reason to place the emphasis in Judaism on the past, from which the tradition is derived. And yet, to do so would be to misunderstand the deepest truth about Judaism: that the truly critical, redemptive event is in the future and not in the past. However significant the events of the past have been, they are destined to pale when compared with *the* truly critical event that has not yet happened. It is this expectation that is at the center of Jewish faith.

The temptation is to view Judaism as a crystallized system that needs to be learned and obeyed but that is not part of the historic process. Empires and civilizations come and go, but the Torah is eternal, beyond time and change. The faithful Jew does not modify the Torah to make it conform to the spirit of his time; on the contrary, he judges the spirit of his time by whether, or to what extent, it conforms to the Torah. Here lies the secret of the survival of Jewish civilization with a degree of continuity that defies almost all historical rules. And yet, such a dehistoricization of Judaism is ultimately an escape from the living presence that addresses us when we feel ourselves truly addressed. The God of Israel is a living God and life is a projection into the uncertainties of the future.

"You are my slaves," says God to Israel according to the rabbis, "and not the slaves of slaves."[1] Obedience to God is therefore fully liberating and only obedience to God is fully liberating. The security that surrounds us is a sham security. The past is not determinative for the future. It is only to God that the individual is responsible, not to institutions or traditions or sages. The living God judges all these and we cannot hide behind books or holy persons, about whom God always asks, "Were you obligated to listen to me or to one of my servants?"[2] In spite of the tendency in some rabbinic passages to attribute to God an irrevocable delegation of his authority into human (i.e., rabbinic) hands, if such human authorities are not continually subject to God's judgment, then such human authorities are divinized and the word of God is silenced. Since to be human is to be responsible, the insecurity of freedom is inescapable.

To live freely is to live toward the future. That which is not yet, the deed not yet performed or the word not yet spoken, propels us toward the future. With regard to them, we are free precisely because they are not yet. And because freedom is frightening, human beings seek security in the shelter of the solid from which non-being is excluded. The person who lives in dialogue with the God of Israel knows that he has no security other than in that dialogue. He cannot therefore live with a Judaism of solidity. His Judaism must be a questioning and exploring one, a Judaism that expects the unexpected because it stands in relation to a living and not a dead God.

2. PROCESS PHILOSOPHY

The futurity of Judaism is not the futurity of process philosophy, be it in the spirit of Alfred North Whitehead or Teilhard de Chardin. Process philosophy of the twentieth century goes back to Heraclitus and his stress on flux. On metaphysical grounds, process philosophers introduce an ontology of an ongoing process in place of an ontology of being. The process of these philosophers is the process of nature.

But the futurity of Judaism is not a natural futurity. The future that Jews expect is a historic future. This future is not assured by the nature of things, as is the future of the process philosophers. The

Jewish future hinges on, and is derived from, the promise of God. It is not embedded in creation. When the prophet speaks of the messianic future in which the lion will lie down with the lamb (and in which both and not only one will rise) he is indeed foreseeing a transformation of nature, but this transformation is not an evolutionary but an apocalyptic one. It is a transformation that is discontinuous with nature as it has been. It envisages a break with the autonomy of nature brought about by God's intervention and not by the working itself out of the *telos* of nature.

The naturalism of process philosophies results in the integration of the ethical into a natural framework. In some cases, the natural is thus ethicized. For Chardin, the evolutionary process leads toward integration, of which the highest form is love. But there is something disingenuous here. The love that emerges from the biological is a species-preserving love. Nature is not interested in the individual, which it is ready to sacrifice for the species. Nature eliminates the unfit, an observation that played a critical role in Hitler's world view. The ethical—if we can use that term—that is the product of the evolutionary process is thus not the ethical of the command whose interest is not the species nor even the universalizability of the imperative, but the dignity of the unique individual, whose rights outweigh the *telos* of the evolutionary process.

Jewish futurity is therefore inseparable from the ethical.

3. The Present

Part of futurity is contemporaneity. To live into the future is to live in the present. The present is threatened both by the past and the future. Living either in the past or the future is to escape the reality of the present, compared to which both the past and the future are unreal. As between the two, the past is the greater threat to the present than the future simply because of the solidity of the past as compared with the relative unreality of the future. Nevertheless, undue concentration on the future is also destructive of the power of the present. He who foresees the future imposes on the future a solidity that deprives it of its futurity. That is why astrology is unacceptable to Judaism. The future cannot be "read" as the past is. It is the realm of possibility, not a veiled actuality.

Inauthentic religion is always characterized by a lack of contact with the present. The authentic Hasidic stories depict men of the spirit interacting with their contemporaries. They sleep in inns, converse with peasants, with learned and simple Jews, and with people in general. They are not closed to the present, to the persons who address them and whom they address. There is almost no trace of suspicion. Later, Hasidism withdraws into itself. It draws a defensive circle around itself because it has lost authentic conviction and is therefore suppressing its own doubts. Soon, Judaism is turned into a sect. Where previously Jews were separate but also participants in the economic, political, and intellectual currents of their times, in more recent times—perhaps since the beginning of this century—much of Orthodox Judaism has chosen the route of withdrawal. The legitimate concern with the separateness of the Jewish people comes to predominate. Almost all channels of contact with the world are severed and the most minute customs of the past are elevated to the rank of central, biblical commandments. The present is derogated, while the past is romantically glorified. At this point, Judaism has evolved into a sect.

The election of Israel and the command received by this people to remain a nation apart is not properly fulfilled by sectarian Judaism. History has been the judge in this matter. Those who withdrew into the wilderness of Judea in order to isolate themselves from the corrupt segment of Israel are no longer with us. The apocalyptic future they awaited did not and will not happen for them because they did not survive. Their severing of bonds with the rest of the house of Israel spelled disaster for them. God does not abandon the people of Israel, but he does abandon those who elect themselves an elect of the elect. One election is all that is possible.

It is therefore necessary, in the first instance, to remain a part of the contemporary people of Israel. Paul struggles with the question, Who are the real Israel? In many places in his writings, he seems to be saying that the real Israel is the spiritual Israel, which, for him, was defined by faith in Jesus. But more than the question of Jesus is involved here. However this "saving remnant" is defined, it is simply wrong ever to write off the vast majority of Jews as outside of the real Israel. The real Israel is not a hidden minority concealed among the masses of Jews. The legend of the thirty-six hidden righteous by whose merit the world persists deals with another dimension of the question. There is, within Israel, a hidden fellowship of the righteous by whose merit we survive. But these righteous are not the real Israel. They are the real saints among Israel. But Israel is the whole people, saints and sinners alike.

Contemporaneity is therefore contact with secular Israel. What does *contact* here mean? It does not mean a philosophy of pluralism, at least not in the sense that term is usually used. As the term *pluralism* is usually invoked in American Jewish circles, it means that there are various "legitimate" interpretations of Judaism, no one of which is entitled to exclusivity. God either does or does not want us to obey the dietary laws. If he does, then the Orthodox are right. If he does not want us to obey them or he is indifferent, then the Orthodox are wrong. The word *pluralism* cannot change the fact that not everybody can be right.

And yet, there is a sense in which pluralism is obligatory. In the logical sense a proposition is either true or its contradictory is true. But in the existential sense, things are quite different. If 79 percent of the population of Israel rides on the Sabbath, then I cannot pretend that the real Israel is that portion that does not ride on the Sabbath and that the rest cease to be of significance to Jewish history. Because all Jews are responsible for each other, because Israel is one, my identity as a Jew is influenced both by the Sabbath observers and the non-Sabbath observers. The identity of the composite Israel and therefore of each individual Jew is a composite of the kinds of Jews who identify themselves as Jews today, with all the ideological differences prevalent among contemporary Jews. On one level, of course, each Jew belongs to a particular interpretation of Jewishness that he prefers as the correct interpretation. But as long as he understands that the covenant is with the people as a whole, his particular Jewish identity will be seen as set in a people of many persuasions, some more and some less valid but all Jews in terms of their historic destiny.

But the situation we have described is not restricted to the intra-Jewish situation. It extends to all of humanity. There was a time when each family of humanity essentially dwelled apart. And this was partially true of Israel, whose apartness was a matter of the most serious religious obligation. In one respect, nothing has changed. The commandment to live apart remains binding. But the apartness is accompanied by a consciousness different from the earlier one. Today, all men are conscious of culture other than their own to a degree never known before. It is, of course, true that Jews have often lived alongside other cultures. Be it in the Arab world, in Spain, or in western Europe, Jewish culture has almost always flourished in symbiosis with another culture that acted as the host culture. Some of these host cultures were more congenial to the Jewish spirit, others less so. But the phenomenon of a Jewish culture embedded in a surrounding host culture is by no means unknown to Judaism.

But the current situation is different. Now it is no longer Judaism and *a* host culture. As long as that was the case, the dialogue was a monogamous one. It was *one* culture interacting with *a*nother. Now things are different. In our consciousness a whole family of cultures coexist. The communication revolution presents us with a multi-screen world (like the battery of monitors in the control room of a television studio) in which we can simultaneously view pictures transmitted by many cameras. The director determines which of these pictures is broadcast at any given moment. If, in his judgment, another picture at a given moment becomes more appropriate, he pushes a button and the audience stops receiving the first pictures and begins to receive the other. All this continues for the duration of the broadcast. While the audience receives only one picture at a time, the director sees all of them all of the time and selects one for broadcast.

All of us have become directors seated before the multiscreened monitor. The lives, values, and cultures of the most diverse peoples are revealed to us and coexist in our consciousness. The result is a certain relativization. Today, we live in a culture that we realize is one tradition among others. The deepest symbols of other traditions have become part of our imagination. In short, a certain global consciousness has dawned.

Judaism cannot ignore this development. In practice, this means that we can no longer ignore the gentiles. The separateness of Israel has never implied that the purpose of Israel's election is only Israel's redemption. The redemption leaves out no member of the human family. Jewish consciousness must become concerned about the religious life of other peoples. For Christians, this has traditionally taken the form of spreading the gospel and missionizing. Jews must learn to take seriously the religious experience of other peoples without viewing them as potential converts to Judaism.

To be a faithful Jew who is not closed to the religious life of others will not be easy. But it will be one of the challenges of the future.

4. RENEWAL

The future of Judaism must include Jewish renewal. Such renewal has occurred from time to time at critical junctures in Jewish history. In ancient time, the renewal in the time of Ezra comes to mind. In modern times, the appearance of Hasidism is a striking example of Jewish renewal at its authentic best. In all instances of Jewish renewal—and the examples cited are but two among many—the Jewish spirit has returned into itself and brought forth something entirely new that was also old. Much of the best Christian scholarship in more recent decades has come to realize that the "new covenant" at the foundation of Christianity is really a "renewed covenant," one that returns to "the" covenant, not to eclipse it by a new one, but to renew it, to draw new strength from it.

For renewal to be possible, there cannot be prevalent in Judaism an atmosphere that *a priori* rejects anything that is new. Such an atmosphere is the atmosphere of death. Death freezes and transforms life into the static and unchanging. In death, the only change that is possible is decay. In living religion, we are dealing with the spirit, which is the very essence of life. The deepest sign of the presence of God, the fundamental reason for the wonder that is evoked by all contact with the spirit, is the occurrence of the unexpected. Salvation comes from unexpected quarters, at unexpected times, and through unexpected agents. Help does not usually come where we seek it but from a direction from which we expect it least. The redeemer whom God sends is no brilliant orator but a stutterer who seems least fit to persuade the tyrant to let the people go. And God chooses these unlikely candidates so that it be clear to man that it is God and not the talent of his messenger that deserves praise. God cannot be boxed into any human schemes because all such human schemes are attempts to control God and he cannot be controlled. To live in the presence of God is therefore to live fully each day because God "renews each day the original creation."[3] The freshness of the world is there each morning, if only we permit ourselves to see it.

But the new of which the Psalmist speaks when he determines to "sing unto God a new song" is a newness of the spirit, not a novelty whose purpose is novelty for its own sake. It is for this reason that most of what has been new in Judaism of the last 150 years has not been authentic renewal. It has not been generated by spiritual persons but by socioeconomic conditions extraneous to the life of the spirit. It is generally conceded that the Reform movement in Judaism was not brought about by persons of spiritual authority such as Luther or Calvin but by the conditions of life of Western Jews, who found the Enlightenment opening doors to circles previously inaccessible. Only when more and more Jews had abandoned careful adherence to Jewish law did Reform Judaism arise to justify *de jure* what had long been the case *de facto*. These changes, which were then made *de jure*, were essentially secularizing moves designed to make Jewish life less discordant with the majority culture.

Authentic renewal always happens through the appearance of the *tsadik*, the saint who personifies in his very being the teaching of the tradition. Religious teaching is always teaching about life. It is therefore meaningless if it is not incorporated into existence. The preacher who proclaims "Do as I say and not as I do" removes himself from the domain of religious authority. Judaism is not a complex intellectual theory accessible only to scholars and men of great intellect. It is a demand made on each and every Jew. The Torah, it has been said, is easy to understand; it is only difficult to do.

The *tsadik* is therefore the person who is the pivot of Judaism. Throughout the ages, the community of Israel has recognized certain individuals as spiritual leaders. Such persons have generally been great scholars of rabbinic learning. Such scholarship has been a necessary but not a sufficient condition of leadership. Beyond the scholarship, the community made a judgment: that the person in question was a God-fearer. To put it simply, one felt God's presence in his presence. Such people eliminated their egos and lived to serve God and their fellow man. They loved those with whom they came into contact. They could do harm to no one. Those who came into their presence found themselves transformed, becoming what they had wanted to become and leaving behind them values that did not deserve their allegiance. In the presence of the *tsadik*, the Jew felt himself addressed in his inner self because he *knew* that for the *tsadik* he was a unique person and no one else. To enter into the presence of the *tsadik* was the closest approximation available to entering into the presence of God. If all this sounds very unreal, we must remember that in the nature of things, the only "proof" that can be offered is a meeting with a *tsadik*. It is true that exaggeration is always possible. The *tsadikim* we are talking about were human beings not immune to shortcomings. In some cases, a process of romanticization doubtless played a role, so that the picture we have of them is somewhat retouched. But there have been *tsadikim* in the world and there still are some, thank God.

But there are not as many as there used to be. The conditions of modernity militate against it. A true *tsadik* does not have a half a dozen different loyalties that compete for his attention. On our part, we are more critical; we no longer accept a person's self-presentation as necessarily final. We seek psychological insights which are based on images of man not derived from religious sources. However much the *tsadik* may attempt to exclude technological secularism from his repertoire, one way or another the religious relativism of our day diminishes his power of concentration and the purity of his tradition is compromised. The result is that left-wing Orthodoxy finds it almost impossible to produce an authentic *tsadik*. Its soil, and the soil of more liberal forms of Judaism, seems incapable of nourishing the kind of personality without which Judaism can neither be renewed nor even survive.

This is not a problem that can easily be solved. There is no curriculum that can be developed to produce saints. We can only lament their absence. The *tsadikim* of the past make their presence known today in the mode of absence. The community must know what is absent. Their absence cannot be permanent. God's covenant with Israel is irrevocable and those persons essential for the survival of his people will appear in God's good time. We can diminish the insincerity, the hardness of heart, the egoism, that permeates so much of Jewish life. We can honor those who deserve honor, such as the scholar and the God-fearer. And we must learn to look for and to recognize "great souls" when they appear, perhaps even in unexpected guises.

5. History

In our time, religion is caught in an uncomfortable dilemma. It is in danger of losing either its this-worldly relevance or its transcendental profundity.

From one direction, religion is constantly being pushed into greater concern with the real problems of this world. Hunger, disease, war, poverty, racism—these and many other problems clamor for recognition as religious problems. What good is a religion that ignores such abominations, that does not concentrate all its energy on their solution? In the light of the magnitude of injustice and suffering in the world, can religion concentrate on spiritual matters, on the inner life of man, on his soul rather than his body? By so doing, doesn't religion become an ally of the war-makers and the oppressors, diverting attention from the real problems that demand urgent attention?

These are pointed and powerful questions, and because of their validity religion engages itself in the affairs of the world. At first, it proceeds cautiously. It chooses two or three issues it considers "moral" and focuses on them. Gradually, religion learns that the issues are fairly intractable, not easily solved. Different "experts" proclaim different solutions. Because religion is eager to solve these problems and not just to talk about them, it throws in its lot with one of the expert points of view for their solution. In making this choice, religion makes certain factual determinations such as what the consequences of certain measures will be. As it gets more deeply enmeshed in the defense of the choice it has made, religion begins to sound less and less like religion and begins to sound more and more like one of the many voices in the ongoing political debate. Different adherents of the same religion then find themselves on opposing sides of the debate, not because they differ on the interpretation of their religion but because of economic, political, social, and psychological disagreements. Since these nonreligious differences often seem very deep, they are quickly confused with religious issues and religion finds itself the handmaiden of politics. The result is that one more political faction has been added and one more religion dissipated.

A variation of the scenario described above comes with even more tragic consequences. In this script, the moral passion of the religionist comes up against the intractability of the problem to be solved. Aflame with great moral zeal, the religionist vows to become effective. The revolutionist tells him that oppressors cannot be persuaded to yield their privileges by mere words. Power, it is said, comes out of the barrel of a gun, and since real social change can only be brought about by means of power, the religionist picks up the revolutionary's gun and learns to kill in order to liberate. The net result of either of the two scenarios under discussion is the absorption of religions into the ambivalent world of pragmatic judgments, in which all of us, to a greater or lesser degree, dirty our hands.

The alternative to all this, of course, is to keep religion in the sanctuary. The temptation to do so is great. In the sanctuary, divorced from the harsh realities of a sinful world, religion can preach its spiritual message without interference. It can cultivate art and music and other manifestations of high culture. But in so doing, it cuts itself off from the real suffering of man and runs the risk of learning to both sanction and profit from injustices that it ought to condemn them instead of learning to live with them.

How can this dilemma be overcome? In the Jewish situation, the problem we have described takes on a particular form. Judaism, to a large extent, has remained in the sanctuary because Jews had very few means to influence the non-Jewish world around them. Living as exiles in societies that Jews often did not perceive as their own, all available energy was invested in inner Jewish concerns. The Jewish communities in most countries were, of course, aware that Jews would be affected by events outside of the ghetto, but such events were understood as happening in the non-Jewish world, over which Jews had relatively little control.

With the Enlightenment, these attitudes began to change. Jewish participation in the affairs of the larger society became more possible, so that in time Jews became active in several political movements whose aim was the restructuring of society. But rarely did such Jewish participation take place as Jews. In fact, a new law began to operate: the more Jewish identification, the less involvement with questions of social improvement, while the loss of Jewish identity seemed almost to predispose toward greatly increased social participation.

Only since the establishment of the state of Israel have Jews reentered history. There now existed a state that was Jewish and this state had to function in the realm of history, as all states do. While a large majority of Israeli Jews are not Orthodox, Judaism found itself in a situation in Israel it had not known for nearly two thousand years. The techniques of scholarship and the frame of mind that were born in the Diaspora could not easily adjust themselves to coping with problems of statecraft that now faced the Jewish state. The retreat into pure spirituality, however, was no longer possible.

For almost two thousand years, Orthodox Jews have lived by the law. In practice this meant that when a Jew had a problem, he consulted a Torah authority who told him what to do. Very often, these problems were of a ritual nature, though the Torah itself does not distinguish between ritual and nonritual questions. It was assumed that the Torah authority consulted the code of law in which an identical analogue to the question posed could be found or, if there was no such identical analogue, a sufficient number of similar cases could be found that, together with a process of rational analysis, would yield the required solution.

We have already seen that by its nature law is best equipped to deal with a world of limited variety. Ideally, a world of consistent repetition would be most congenial of all for the law. If consistent repetition is not possible, then a world of limited variety can still be coped with. But a world of radical novelty is the most difficult of all because a mode of reasoning based on precedents would have almost no application at all.

The establishment of the state of Israel has brought about a crisis for Torah Judaism. This crisis expresses itself in many ways, from the notorious quarrels between the chief rabbis of the state to the secularism of a large segment of Israeli society. The root cause of the crisis, however, is the historic situation itself. As an illustration, we can take the problem of Judea and Samaria, territories that are biblically an integral part of the land of Israel and that came under Jewish control after the 1967 war. For some years there has been an ongoing debate about whether these territories must be kept at all cost or whether, for the sake of peace with Israel's neighbors, their return to Arab control can be contemplated.

There are those who have approached this problem from the halachic (legal) point of view. Rulings have been produced on both sides of the issue. Some argue on the basis of the sanctity of the land. Others emphasize that the saving of life in Judaism takes precedence over other considerations. Still others argue that such decisions must be left to military and political experts. The halachah, they claim, leaves the determination of certain technical issues to experts with special competence in the relevant disciplines. The Sabbath, for instance, may be violated when a sick person's life is in danger. But whether his life is actually in danger is left to physicians to determine. Similarly, whether the danger of war is increased or decreased by relinquishing control of a given territory is a military and political matter to be left to the experts. The truth is that all these approaches misunderstand the problem.

6. HISTORY AND LAW

Since the creation of Israel, Judaism has reentered history. Historic decisions cannot be approached on a primarily legal basis. Law prescribes conduct in essentially repeatable situations. History is a constant development of novel situations in which political decisions affecting the destiny of states have to be made. While Maimonides attempted to codify the laws that dealt with kings, the fact remains that we simply do not get the feeling in the historical books of the Bible that any conception of law was determinative. David, Solomon, and the other historical figures of the Bible meet us as political leaders deeply imbued with a sense of Israel's relation with God in a covenant of mutual obligations. There is a clear realization that the people and the king must obey God and that if they do not, the welfare of the nation will suffer. But this is not cast in a legal framework.

The critical decisions that face the Jewish people today must grow out of an interpretation of historical-theological considerations. Take messianism as an example. Maimonides included some demytho-logizing passages in his discussion of messianism.[4] The very tone of the passage is reflective of the reserve and caution that the halachist almost instinctively exhibits toward messianism. The messianic idea envisages a radical transformation of the status quo. There are some rabbinic opinions that this transformation will include abolition of most of Torah law.[5] Needless to say, such a suggestion is not easily worked into a halachic system that assumes that the Torah contains the expression of God's eternal law, whose status, according to at least one contemporary opinion, is *a priori* and no more subject to change than the most fundamental laws of logic. Because of the potential of the messianic idea to undermine Judaism's stable struc-tures, the halachah has dealt with it most cautiously, either opera-tively ignoring it or depriving it of its apocalyptic and cataclysmic dimensions. And yet, without heavy halachic underpinning, the messianic idea has remained central to Jewish consciousness. Time and again, messianic fever overwhelmed Jewish equanimity, and after terminating in failure the idea returned to its dormant state, only to reappear elsewhere with equal or greater power.

The Zionist idea at first appeared in a perfectly secular and prac-tical guise. Yet, perhaps from the very first, it was not difficult to detect messianic energies at work. However secularly disguised, a Jewish movement that spoke of the return of a dispersed Jewish peo-ple to its ancestral homeland, which would be turned into a moral paradigm for all humanity, could not for long be interpreted without reference to the messianic idea. And as the Zionist enterprise began to assume a less theoretical and more material form, the messianic aspect of the enterprise became more and more apparent. At this writing, the critical issue is Judea and Samaria, the territories that came under Israeli control in the 1967 war and that, in Arab opinion, must become the territory of a Palestinian state. Since these ter-ritories are an integral part of the covenanted land of Israel perpetually bestowed by God on the Jewish people, to the degree that the messianic-biblical idea is operative in one's understanding of contemporary Jewish history, the relinquishing of these territories is inconceivable, being contrary to the messianic thrust of recent Jewish history.

Because it was understood that strictly halachic categories are inadequate to deal with such problems, in certain more right-wing Orthodox circles the concept of *Daas Torah* was developed. Rendered into English as the "Torah view" or the "Torah attitude," the term reflects the realization that in many areas, a strictly legal ruling is not appropriate. Nevertheless, these areas cannot be left outside of the Torah domain. It is therefore possible for *Gedolei Torah*, the great men whose Torah learning is outstanding, to formulate policies that authentically reflect the Torah point of view and are therefore binding on the Jewish community. But the important point to understand is that the very development of the concept of *Daas Torah* extends the concept of Torah beyond the strictly legal realm. If that were not so, the policy determinations that are presented as *Daas Torah* would be presented as *Psak*, "legal determinations."

Because Judaism in our time has entered history, fundamental theological thinking is no longer a luxury. The issues that face us today—and the problem of Judea and Samaria is but one example—raise the most fundamental questions about the nature of Jewish identity and destiny. We can, of course, continue to grope in the dark, without making our presuppositions clear to ourselves. These presuppositions, the foundation of our religious-national existence, will never become fully clear to us. The knowledge that we will obtain will be a dark knowledge. But even that is better than remaining in total ignorance.

7. THE JEWISH PEOPLE

Can we still speak of the Jewish people?

Traditionally, the Jewish people was spoken of as *Knesses Israel*, the "Assembly of Israel." This was not just a collection of individuals. *Knesses Israel* was the dialogue partner of God. It was the Jewish people as one, entering into covenant, calling on God, being faithful and unfaithful, chosen and suffering. It embraced all Jews, present, past, and future. Each Jew was a Jew through membership in his community. At critical points in Jewish history, it was this community that made choices, selected options. It was this community that was addressed by the prophets, but it was also out of this community that the prophets were called. No prophet in Israel was conceivable without this community because it was this community that was elect.

At a seminar given by Martin Buber at Columbia University in the fifties, he said that there no longer existed such a *Knesses Israel*. Nowadays, he said, Jews were too fragmented. There no longer existed a common set of beliefs. There was too much disagreement about fundamentals. *Knesses Israel* had come to an end sometime around the Enlightenment, which undermined classical Jewish self-understanding. From then on, the concept of the Jewish people as one entity standing before God was problematic.

I remember being shocked when he said this. If there was no *Knesses Israel* anymore, then there was no Judaism and no individual Jews. Every Jew is a Jew only because of membership in the all-embracing people. It is the soil from which the Jew arises and into which he returns. At the end of his life, he is "gathered into his people," an expression the Bible frequently uses for the death of Jews. Dying is not a return to the "all" from which everything that comes into being arises, but a return to one's people where those who have gone before wait for those who are yet to come. How else could those who have come before remain so utterly vivid? Is Moses a historical figure who arose early in the history of the Jewish people or is he a sensed presence in the world of the believing Jew? Isn't Abraham very contemporary, so much so that he is often more contemporary than those around us? But if there no longer is a *Knesses Israel*, then these are all illusions. Then the bond that ties the Jewish people disappears and takes the people with it.

For a long time, I was very angry at Buber for his position. I saw it as symptomatic of his alienation from his people. And he was, of course, alienated. Deeply Jewish as he was, there was something distant about him. The real synagogue, with all its imperfections, was not his abode. He did not worship with other worshiping Jews. He stood aside, telling the tales of a somewhat idealized Hasidism whose early glories he depicted but whose current reality he ignored. In his soul, I said to myself, there no longer is a *Knesses Israel*, which means that he is no longer part of it.

Gradually, his basic thesis has become more understandable to me. We must not underestimate the rifts in the Jewish body politic. The secularism of many Jews is deep. Reform Jews are addressed by some of the commandments but not by others. And above all, there is confusion. Millions of Jews simply don't know what their Jewishness means. At certain critical junctures, signs of life appear. In some cases, this occurs when Israel is endangered. For others, it is at the point of intermarriage. For still others, even intermarriage is tolerable, but the Jewish alarm system is set off when Christian practices are introduced into the home. Still, the confusion is pervasive. And hundreds of thousands of Jews just drift away, never to be joined to the people again. The result is that non-Jews are even more confused. Is Judaism a religion? Can someone be a Jew and not believe in Judaism? Are the various kinds of Judaism (Orthodox, Conservative, Reform) different religions or are they branches of the same religion? Is Zionism part of Judaism and, anyway, how are they related? We cannot pretend that these are questions asked by the ignorant to which there are definite answers. We are all confused.

Is there, then, no longer a *Knesses Israel*, as Buber said? While I can understand why he said what he did, I still disagree with him. The Jewish people is still one. I say this without ignoring the deep rifts to which we have referred. Individuals always have and will continue to break away from the Jewish people. Some of these will be lost forever. But there still exists the metaphysical, mystical unity of the Jewish people. It always has and it always will.

Modern Israel could not have come into being without it. Out of people of the most diverse cultural and national traditions, Israel created one people. To be more accurate, it did not create such a people but found one in existence. In the early stages of the Zionist movement, European Jews had little acquaintance with non-European, Sephardic Jews. As the movement developed and especially with the advent of the state, it became very clear that non-European Jewry would constitute a large segment of the state's population. Yet the viability of a state made up of such diverse elements was never brought into question. There was a bond among Jews that was deeper than all the differences, which turned out to be far more superficial than would have been thought. And this same bond unites Israeli and non-Israeli Jews. There were those who asserted that with the creation of Israel, the Jews of the Diaspora and the citizens of Israel would quickly grow apart, since their life conditions were so different.[6] But this has not happened. In moments of crisis, Jews all over the world are one. The degree of concern for Israel shown by American Jews never ceases to amaze non-Jewish Americans. Do Americans of Irish, Italian, Hungarian, and other backgrounds show the kind of concern for their lands of origin that Jews show? Once again, the Jewish situation is unique.

However, all this cannot be taken for granted. There are powerful ideological forces working against unity. Among these, perhaps the most powerful is religious Orthodoxy. This paradox is both amazing and also understandable. Traditional Judaism is the core of Jewish identity. Given the centrality of unity in classical Jewish self-understanding, we would expect that Orthodox Jews would be the strongest possible influence for unity among Jews. But that is not the case, at least not altogether. Because Orthodox Jews see themselves as guardians of the authentic tradition, they do not find it easy to recognize other (e.g., Conservative and Reform) interpretations of Judaism as legitimate. Once these groups are seen as heretical, it becomes easy to read their adherents out of the faith altogether. One then refuses to associate with them or to serve on bodies on which they are represented. Particularly among the more right-wing segments of Orthodoxy, the tendency is to withdraw Jewish recognition from all non-Orthodox forms of Judaism and to reject association with them in any form. Orthodox Judaism, which should serve as the most unifying factor in contemporary Judaism, turns out to be a significantly divisive influence, whereas liberal forms of Judaism have a much easier time embracing the most diverse forms of Judaism as diverse but legitimate variations on a theme.

Once again, what is lacking in the Orthodox perspective is theological understanding. Orthodoxy is right in rejecting an easygoing attitude of toleration as irreconcilable with authentic Judaism. Judaism is not a debating society in which all views and practices are welcome as equally legitimate. Throughout its history, Judaism has rejected many views even while retaining some as acceptable. The acceptable range has consisted of a range of partly conflicting opinions. But while Judaism can embrace a range of conflicting opinions, it cannot accommodate all opinions. Some are beyond the pale and have been historically excluded. Again and again, Jewish history has shed sectarian views, which then tended to disappear.

This then is the truth in the right-wing Orthodox point of view. And yet, it is an incomplete view. Judaism is not an ideology that can insist on purity and exclude all impure versions. Judaism is the election of the Jewish people, which remains tied in an eternal covenant with God no matter what fallacious or partly fallacious views or sinful actions this or that segment of the people develops. In this respect, Christian identity is quite different. Being a Christian is a matter of faith. The Church is a spiritual community of those elected in faith. But in Israel, God made an irrevocable covenant with the offspring of Abraham, who constitute a natural family. In such a family, there are the good and the bad, the better and the worse, the more and the less faithful. They remain the people of election. They participate in its history. The nations of the world view this people as such a family. Those who hate Israel hate all Jews because they hate the body of Israel almost more than its soul. The unity of the Jewish people is therefore a family unity that does not disappear with ideological, even serious ideological, differences.

Jewish unity must therefore become a cardinal principle of Jewish life. Practically speaking, this will express itself in a number of ways. There must be no segments of Judaism that are not on speaking terms with each other. The importance of this can be easily overlooked. In view of the profound philosophical differences that separate various forms of Judaism, what is to be gained by the antagonists talking to each other? Since agreement is inconceivable, isn't such talking a waste of time at best and possibly a factor in exacerbating relations? To insist that all groups of Jews be on talking terms with each other is not to think that agreement is easily attainable or even attainable at all. There is a value in talking to each other in and by itself, apart from any "results" achieved. To talk with a fellow Jew is to be with him. To be with him is to look at him, to become aware of his mode of being in the world, of the reality of his being. No matter how profound our disagreements are—and sometimes they are very profound—taking seriously the fact that my fellow Jew exists and that he has the point of view that he has—however much I disagree with him—must have an effect on both sides. Let us realize that the alternative to speaking is violence. There is really no such thing as ignoring a fellow human being, much less a fellow Jew. Not to speak with my neighbors is a mode of relating to him, and even if this mode does not immediately express itself in violence, it points toward it because the alternative to speech is communication by deed, violent deed. And it is this in which the ultimate unity of the Jewish people, the existence of *Knesses Israel*, is put to the test.

The "*Altalena* incident" is a dramatic example of this.[7] During one of the U.N.-supervised truces that interrupted Israel's war of independence, the Irgun (a right-wing underground group) brought in a supply of arms on the *Altalena*, a ship that approached the beaches of Tel Aviv. The military forces under the control of the newly formed Ben Gurion government were afraid that the arms would be used in a "putsch" and opened fire on the *Altalena*. The potential for civil war was there. At this point, Menachem Begin, then head of the Irgun, gave orders not to return the fire. Violence among Jews was inconceivable to him. It apparently was not inconceivable to Ben Gurion.

If large-scale, organized violence between groups of Jews is possible, if war is possible among Jews, then the Jewish people is not one. I do not believe such violence is possible. Much to our horror, skirmishes, small-scale rock throwing, and individual crime among Jews are possible. But war is not. It is simply inconceivable. In spite of all the irritations and tensions that exist among Jews, were the possibility of war among Jews to arise, I am convinced that the bond that unites Jews would reassert itself and prevent such war. If this is so, then the messianic vision of the abolition of war is already realized in the community of Israel. But none of this can be taken for granted. It must be constantly cultivated and deepened. Consciousness of the unity must be raised from the implicit to the explicit. Without minimizing the serious differences among us, there must be a continuous effect made to counteract the forces of division, to explain the nature of Jewish election, above all, not to take with ultimate seriousness Jewish heresy. Jewish nonbelief is never as deep as it seems. Beneath the assimilated exterior of the furthest-removed Jews, there lurks the Jew of election. When and how this Jew will break forth is hard to predict. But the merit of the Fathers (*z'chut avot*) is there and it will overcome.

8. ISRAEL

There is no aspect of the Jewish future that will remain unaffected by the creation of Israel. That is not to say that the Diaspora will disappear. There was a classical Zionism that expected the disappearance of the Diaspora. From the point of view of this purist Zionism, no one can be a Zionist if he does not reside in Israel unless, perhaps, he is physically prevented from immigrating to Israel, as is the case with Soviet Jews. However consistent this may be from a purely logical point of view, it does not reflect reality. Most Jews do not now, and will not in the foreseeable future, reside in Israel. But this is only a physical truth. In the spiritual sense, more and more Jews will be in Israel even when they are not physically there. Israel is not a country in which Diaspora Jews merely take an interest. It is the house of Jews. Metaphysically speaking, those of us who are not there have left it temporarily. The Israeli *Yordim*, those who have left the country temporarily and find themselves staying overseas longer and longer, keep stressing that they are only away temporarily, that they will return as soon as they have obtained another academic degree, made a bit more money, etc. This attitude, in fact, has become a standing joke, especially when repeated year after year with the person in question remaining where he is. While there is obviously much self-deception at work here, there is also a theological truth at work. No Jew is ever permanently away from Israel. The exile is temporary. In our deepest unconscious, the land of Israel is our home from which we are temporarily parted.

When this is not the case, when a Jew comes to believe that he and his descendants are permanently resident in another country that is truly his home, something very serious in that person's Jewish identity has occurred. I am not inclined to read any Jew out of the house of Israel. And, as we have seen, a Jew's erroneous opinions need not be taken at face value. Nevertheless, we ought to be aware of what constitutes a real break in a person's Jewish identity. One such break, as we have seen, would happen were it to become possible for groups of Jews to perpetrate large-scale violence against other groups of Jews. Similarly, when a Jew no longer dreams of returning to his land but sees himself permanently resident in another country that he sees as his home, an essential element of Jewish identity has been lost. Judaism is simply inconceivable permanently separated from the land of Israel. Were that to happen, we would be witnessing a mutation, the appearance of something other than Judaism. The matter is analogous to the bond of Judaism to Hebrew. While Christianity can retain an authentic identity in spite of metamorphoses from Hebrew to Greek to Latin to German to English, etc., such a process is not possible in Judaism. Any Judaism that basically severs its bond with Hebrew becomes something other than Judaism. It is well known that the Reform movement greatly reduced the prominence of Hebrew in synagogue worship. When most Jews ceased to understand Hebrew, the rationalistic common sense of the early reformers dictated changing the service into a language, such as German, the people understood. But there is more to Judaism than common sense. Judaism simply cannot survive historically without Hebrew. The concepts expressed in the language are almost secondary. The holiness of Jewish election resides in Hebrew. Through it, *Knesses Israel* speaks and hears the word of God. Without it, the ideas contained in the revelation, the commands addressed to the people, cannot be heard. And in it, the secular lyrics of the latest Israeli song hit become part of Jewish experience. The result is that Reform Judaism has returned to Hebrew to a much greater extent than ever before. There is now no danger whatsoever of the disappearance of Hebrew from the Reform liturgy. The Jewish people has remained one.

The bond to the land of Israel is equally strong. Judaism is the religion of the land of Israel. It is a religion that is inconceivable without the land of Israel. The land is not simply a locale in which, it so happens, Judaism developed. It is an essential component of the faith because it is the location of God's preeminent dwelling, both past and present. In fact, the God of Israel is identified primarily in two ways: as the God of the Jewish people and as the God who dwells in Jerusalem. And because this is so, if the Jewish return to the land is to be taken seriously, then the cultic dimension of Judaism, which is so closely tied to the land of Israel, must gradually reappear in Jewish consciousness.

The cultic in Judaism revolves around the Temple worship. Temple worship, in turn, revolves around the sacrifices that were brought in the Temple in Jerusalem and so carefully prescribed in the Pentateuch, particularly in the book of Leviticus. At present, the sacrifices are but a memory for most Jews, for many Jews an embarrassing memory. Is this an aspect of Judaism that is permanently dead or is a future for it possible? It is a question that cannot be ignored.

Strangely enough, it is Christianity that has traditionally taunted Judaism for incompleteness because of its lack of sacrifice. These traditional Christian critics point to verses in the Hebrew Bible that connect forgiveness of sin with the offering of sacrifices. With the destruction of the Temple, the bringing of sacrifices by Jews ended. The Christian argument then is that since forgiveness of sin requires sacrifices and since there are no sacrifices in Judaism, the guilt of the sinner cannot be alleviated by Judaism. While, in one sense, Christianity also lacks sacrifices, it insists that the death of Jesus was the ultimate sacrifice, which ended all further sacrifice. Those who participate in the Eucharist partake in that ultimate sacrifice, which reoccurs (or is reenacted) whenever the Eucharist is performed.

Judaism has not taken kindly to this Christian criticism. The standard reply has stressed repentance as the mode of earning forgiveness for the Jew. There are, of course, good biblical supports for this. Again and again we are told, especially by the prophets, that just action and a humble heart are what God really wants and not fat bullocks.[8] To the modern mind, of course, repentance is a far more rational basis for God to forgive human sin than sacrifice. The net result is that sacrifice has faded from Jewish consciousness, for secular and liberal Jews in practice and in theory, and for Orthodox Jews in practice but not in theory. Orthodox Jews recite the prayers for the restoration of sacrifices, yet one wonders how real such a prospect is even for Orthodox Jews.

And yet the sanctity of Jersualem, of the Temple Mount and of the Western Wall, is a palpable fact. It is a basic fact of contemporary Jewish existence. Several years before Israel gained control of the Old City of Jerusalem, a French Jewish sociologist wrote a book in which he argued that the Jews of the Diaspora and those of Israel were two distinct peoples. For him, nothing illustrated this division more vividly than the attitude of the sabras (native Israelis) to the Western Wall. Speaking of the sabras, he wrote, "But if there is a holy place to which they are indifferent it is the Wailing Wall, the symbol of a past all trace of which, in their view, should be obliterated."[9] He said this because he was convinced that Israelis, unlike Diaspora Jews, had no interest in old walls from Temple times. They were contemporary, oriented toward solving problems of the day and not to dreaming about bygone times. Reality, of course, turned out quite different. Very soon after the appearance of the book, the Western Wall was made accessible to Jews. No bulldozers made their appearance. Instead, when access to the Wall became possible soon after the end of the fighting, an outpouring of Israelis took place unlike anything anyone had seen. That Orthodox Israelis rushed to the Wall was to be expected. But hundreds of thousands of secular Israelis came, touched by the same emotion that overcame the battle-hardened soldiers who cried when they liberated the Wall. The sanctity of this location is apparently quite clear to most Jews.

In concrete terms, the rebuilding of the Temple will, in time, become thinkable. This does not mean that the project will commence tomorrow. One of the necessary conditions for the resumption of sacrifice is the reappearance of prophecy in Israel. Only by means of prophecy will certain determinations be possible that are not possible at present. While most Jews have family traditions as to whether they are or are not members of the priestly class, these traditions are not fully reliable and only by prophecy will it be possible to make definitive determinations, a necessity if sacrifices are to be restored. But while the rebuilding of the Temple and the reestablishment of sacrifice is not an immediate prospect, it must become a thinkable idea. It is a thinkable idea because it is commanded in the word of God. It is inextricably interwoven with everything else in the Torah that Jews hold so dear. And it acts as a necessary corrective to the secularization of Judaism, which consists in its ethicization. There is a large portion of Judaism that does not deal with the moral law but with the pleasing of God as he commanded. And it is curious that the most striking manifestation of holiness is not connected with the ethical but with the cultic. It is this cultic holiness that will reappear in Judaism.

9. Art

There is an inherent relationship between cult and art. In a fundamental sense, cult is theater. In prayer, man addresses God. But the performance of the cultic act goes beyond the ethical and even the rational. In cult, the deed replaces the word. The deed is opaque, subject to interpretation but never reducible to its interpretations. Obedience to the divine command is the rationale of the cult but, very quickly, takes on a life of its own. Because the cult exists preeminently in the realm of action, it hallows the act, such as the slaughtering of animals, to the transcendental level. The cultic objects such as altars, animals to be slaughtered, basins, etc., transform the "idea" of the holy into holy objects existing in time and space. But because holiness is always, in one form or another, a manifestation of the presence of God, the holy space or time is the point of contact between God and the created universe.

Throughout history, art and cult have been intimately intertwined. Since cult demands some sort of performance, a sense of anticipation and climax, of timing and the flow of events, are crucial. But cult is not only related to theater, though that is probably its strongest bond. The architecture of the Temple and its contents demand a spatial thinking that stimulates the visual arts as nothing else does. It must be remembered that among the many artifacts past civilizations have left behind, those intended for ritual use are almost always the most elaborate and aesthetically the most significant. Finally, we need hardly mention the role that music has played in all worship. Singing and dancing entered modern Judaism through Hasidism, though even today there are significant segments of Judaism that refuse to take dance and music seriously from the religious point of view.

When compared with the other great religions of the world, Judaism has not made a great contribution to art and music. There is very little Jewish competition to the cantatas of Bach, Russian icon painting, or early Italian religious painting. It is not difficult to advance explanations for this fact, ranging from the biblical prohibition against graven images to the Jewish sense of insecurity, which made it far more advisable to be ready to move on very short notice than to build glorious houses of worship to compete with those built by the majority religion. Those arts, on the other hand, that are related to time rather than space, i.e., music and poetry, fared much better among Jews. The Hebrew Bible is, of course, one of the great literary documents of civilization. And music was always alive among Jews. While almost always borrowing from the musical tradition of the host culture, Jewish music—of which Hasidic music is a relatively recent example—succeeded in impressing on the foreign idiom a distinctly Jewish presence that reflected Jewish sensibilities. In literature, too, Jewish involvement is not insignificant, though, in modern times, the Jewishness of many Jewish writers is no longer central.

Yet in most Jewish circles today, art is hardly an agenda item. It is probably true that the more Jewishly involved a person is, the less likely he is to visit museums, read novels, or attend concerts. The two sensibilities seem almost to exclude each other. The number of Orthodox Jewish students interested in the sciences is considerable. The Association of Orthodox Jewish Scientists is an active organization with hundreds of members. The number of Orthodox students planning to work in music, poetry, acting, etc., is minuscule. The result is that the level of taste in the Jewish community—and not only in the Orthodox community—is very low. Families that could afford the best live in homes decorated in the most pedestrian taste, lacking all individuality and personal statement. And when an attempt is made to express some individuality, more often than not the result is merely weird rather than in good taste.

Why does all this matter? Or, to be more accurate, why does this matter from a Jewish point of view? It matters because we are here dealing in the profound sensibilities that determine the kinds of human beings we are. The phenomenon we are discussing expresses the fact that much of organized Judaism is currently attached to a bourgeois mentality that determines the style of its Judaism.

Since the French Revolution, European society has consisted of the bourgeois masses bitterly detested by a bohemian minority in furious rebellion against what it considers the soul-less life of the vast majority. Kierkegaard, Nietzsche, Heine, Thomas Mann, and Sartre are a few names who symbolize this struggle. As seen by them, the bourgeois are respectable citizens whose main goal is to conform to the rules of a mindless society. The typical philistine prizes security above all. He suppresses emotion and avoids risk, since caution is his watchword. The unconventional is his enemy. The artist whose devotion is to the free play of the imagination is perceived as a grave threat to the ordered universe of the bourgeois, who is profoundly frightened by the prospect of change, anything that threatens the status quo.

It is not difficult to see that there is an obvious affinity between Judaism and the bourgeois mentality. The emphasis in Judaism on the family, the law, and the community are not incompatible with the values of the bourgeois. We have seen that the rabbinic mind is, to a large extent, a bourgeois mind. In the rabbinic period, prophets are no longer heard. Inherent in prophecy is an element of the unpredictable and the noninstitutional, which the rabbis are not comfortable with. The Judaism shaped by them is predictable, orderly, and nonhistorical, in short, bourgeois and not bohemian.

The result has been that, to an increasing extent, Judaism has been losing its antibourgeois clientele. Our artists tend to leave the Jewish community. Some—and S. J. Agnon is the outstanding example—find it possible to draw on their heritage in their work. But there is very little Jewish art of quality. And this is a very dangerous development, not mainly because our synagogues and homes exhibit poor taste, but because a totally bourgeois Judaism will be a dead Judaism. The great souls of Judaism, as of any religion, are not cautious members of the middle class. They do not calculate their actions from the point of view of prudence. They do not hesitate to stick out, to be different, to risk everything on their mission. A bourgeois Judaism is dead because it is out of contact with the explosive ferment of the religious spirit. This spirit cannot be fully institutionalized. While religious institutions are unavoidable, if they are to remain *religious* institutions they must make provision for the dynamics of living religious experience, which is the antithesis of the bourgeois orientation.

The absence of the artistic in Judaism is therefore more than merely the prevalence of bad taste. Together with this bad taste goes an inauthenticity of its spiritual life. That Orthodox Judaism is more easily compatible with a career in nuclear physics, medicine, or law than with being a novelist, composer, or poet is an alarming development for Orthodox Judaism. It bespeaks an ossification in its spirituality of the most serious sort. Jewish culture, after all, is not advanced by physics or chemistry. But it is advanced by poetry and literature, music and painting. If believing Jews shy away from the humanities, it must be because they find it easier to be practicing Jews and physicists than to be practicing Jews and poets. Why?

It is not all that difficult to divide one's Judaism and one's physics. Physics is a very precise discipline with a clearly delineated subject matter. There is no inherent reason to globalize the method of physics into a method for the solution to all human problems. While there are those who have converted science into scientism by refusing to restrict scientific method to certain kinds of problems and, instead, turn it into a philosophy of life, practicing scientists are frequently very critical of this approach. They are fully aware that science is a "game" with certain rules rather than a key to human salvation. Deeply immersed in the details of their research, they find the attempt to apply the methods of their research to questions of morality and religion distinctly amateurish, possible only for someone who does not know much about the reality of scientific work. For this reason, Orthodox Jewish scientists can lead parallel lives in which their Jewish and scientific identities do not conflict with each other.

But this is far less possible for a poet. The imagination of the poet is a reflection of his spiritual life. Myth and metaphor are the currency both of religion and poetry. Poetry is one of the most powerful domains in which religious expression takes place. And the same is true of music, drama, painting, and dance. Not all artists are religious persons or have a religious interest. But even if they do not, and perhaps especially if they do not, art serves as a religion substitute. So one way or the other, the Judaism of a poet and his poetry cannot be kept apart too easily. And an inauthentic Judaism will be greatly magnified in the poetry, music, or painting of an inauthentic Jew.

For secular Jews, inauthenticity is an escape from Judaism, a looking away from it, a refusal to come to grips with it. It is an underlying shame at being Jewish, a dislike of Jews and therefore a dislike of oneself. For religious Jews, inauthenticity expresses itself in a different way. It is basically a crisis of belief. The Orthodox Jew lives and acts in a universe of discourse based on certain premises: that

God exists, that he chose the Jewish people, that he is aware of our actions, that he distributes rewards and punishments, that he hears us when we speak to him. However much the believing Jew acts in accordance with the tradition, he is aware that the above-mentioned premises are questionable. If he is a student of the Talmud, he prides himself on his excellent power of reason. He is, however, also aware that Torah rationality operates only within very sharply curtailed areas defined by the revelation on which Judaism is based. In most instances, our observant Jew is not prepared to investigate these questions. Yet however dimly he is aware of them and made uncomfortable by them, he senses that, in spite of all his observance, he does not have a personal relationship with God, whose very existence he somewhat doubts. Yet he cannot fully admit these matters to himself. The net result is tension in which belief and disbelief coexist and take their toll. The body expresses itself in its language and, after a while, the posture, the gait, the voice, and the whole body assume a certain rigidity that reflects the inner evasions. In short, he turns himself into an object, into the person seen by non-Orthodox Jews whose gaze is made determinative.

Once the Orthodox Jew sees himself in this light, there is a loss of spiritual self-confidence. Judaism can serve as the spiritual matrix of artistic creativity only as long as it is reasonably intact, as long as the Jew is not detached from, and ambivalent toward, his own Jewish identity. The absence of a Jewish literary, artistic, and musical culture is therefore a symptom of a serious spiritual crisis in Judaism. And it is not a crisis that can easily be solved programmatically. The process by which a culture generates serious art (a term that should be taken to include literature, music, etc.) is mysterious, rarely subject to institutional control. Nevertheless, the Jewish community can do more to stimulate Jewish art. Together with Torah study, it is the enterprise that deepens and develops Judaism. The natural sciences do not do this, nor do the social sciences. Particularly in the United States, several of the large Jewish organizations (the so-called defense agencies) in fact look to the social sciences for the intellectual underpinning of their programs. But the salvation of Judaism is not in the social sciences. While the social sciences have a certain value, e.g., measuring public opinion in various contexts, they cannot provide a basis for Jewish survival. Only authentic Judaism rooted in its past and looking to its future can do that.

As Jewish sophistication develops, the paucity of authentic Jewish art will be noticed and the significance of this fact appreciated. Its cure requires Jewish self-renewal, a need that is urgent on many other grounds as well.

10. FAMILY

Jewish existence is social existence. A person is a Jew because he belongs to the social organism that is the Jewish people. As social organisms go, the Jewish people is a particularly powerful one. For centuries, without the kind of power possessed by states, the Jewish people has retained the loyalty of millions of Jews for whom membership in this group was the single most important fact of their lives. Until recent times, the choice that faced the individual, to the extent that he had a choice, was which social organism was to obtain his loyalty. Very often there was no choice at all. Being born into a particular group settled the matter. In some cases the possibility of changing membership from one group to another arose. But what almost never arose was the possibility of no membership at all, of individual self-definition not derived primarily from group membership. This was simply not thinkable, whether with respect to national or religious identity. It was even more true, for example, of sexual identity. Men and women played well-defined roles derived simply from membership in the male or female sex. It was birth that determined the primary group attachments of the individual.

To a certain extent, that has changed in the Western world. The individual has in our times moved to the forefront. Social groups have not, of course, disappeared. But to an increasing degree they have moved into the background. The individual has come to look at himself: his needs, desires, attitudes, and choices. The emphasis on the autonomy of the individual has become so great that it has begun to dissolve even the most fundamental social organism, the family. More and more persons reject marriage simply because it creates a social organism that, at the very least, blurs the identity of the individual in favor of the family unit. The result has been the evolution of an ethic of the individual. Most of Western liberal thinking is deeply committed to the ethics of human rights, which it interprets with the emphasis on the rights of the individual against the power of the state.

Recently, some voices have begun to raise questions about these assumptions. When the individual becomes his own primary preoccupation, the result is narcissism. The self is simply not enough of a cause to satisfy human aspirations. We are social beings whose deepest fulfillment derives from service to the community. One of the Hasidic masters, it is told, asked God to show him heaven and hell. In hell he saw persons who could not bend their arms and, though surrounded by the greatest delicacies, were starving because their arms did not permit them to place the food in their mouths. In heaven, people had the same unbending arms, yet everyone was well fed because they all fed each other. The moral of the story is that if we devote ourselves only to our needs, we are left unsatisfied. But when we care for the needs of others, we are fulfilled.

Religious Jews and Christians cannot, therefore, join the "I" generation. There is a great deal of truth in the focus on the individual, particularly on the rights of the individual. It is the individual who is created in the image of God and who is sacred. But God has set human beings in communities. And among these, the community of Israel is central. It is the community elected by God for his service, to which he has joined his name so that he is known in all the world as the God of this community who is also the God of all humanity and of all creation. The Jew must, therefore, more than anyone else avoid narcissism. He must place himself in his community. He must live in it. Its tribulations must become his tribulations, its joys, his joys. Furthermore and possibly even more important, the community in which the Jew lives is not only the community of his contemporaries. It includes those Jews who have been and those who will be. Together, they include and constitute the *Knesses Israel* to which we have referred.

What does it mean to live in the consciousness of those who will follow us? Those who have preceded us have left us a legacy, a spiritual heritage that is substantial and concrete. But those who will follow us have not only left us nothing, they are not even real as yet. We cannot associate any name with them, nor a face. Yet, for the Jew, they are, or should be, as real as his ancestors and probably more important.

In the simplest, most elemental, and most important sense, the reality of those who will follow us demands that Jews not cooperate in weakening the family unit. Because of Jewish messianism, the birth of a Jewish child has always been a most significant event. Celibacy is unacceptable to Judaism because the central event of human history, the birth of the Redeemer, has not yet taken place. And celibacy is possible for Christianity because there is no future birth that remains essential. The Jewish family is thus the space in which the future membership of *Knesses Israel* is prepared. For Judaism, these future generations are not merely abstractions. In a capital case, according to the Mishnah,[10] witnesses who are to testify against the defendant are warned that if they are not telling the truth, the blood of the accused and that of his potential descendants who will not be born because of the death of the accused will be on the witnesses' head. To cut off a Jew is to cut off a line and thereby to become guilty of the murder of future generations. That is how real unborn Jews are to Jewish consciousness. The bond of the Jewish parent to his child reflects the faith that the Jews of future generations are already members of the house of Israel and that redemption will come to humanity through them. It is for this reason that childlessness or even having small families is such a serious matter for Jews. By so doing, the Jew refuses to replenish the seed of Abraham and thus contributes to thwarting God's redemptive plan.

Assimilation has seriously eroded a proper understanding of Jewish communal existence. Because the liberal stresses the individual, he sees all communities as voluntary associations into which and out of which the individual moves at will. But that is not true of a family and it is not true of the house of Israel, which is an extended family. Even if husbands and wives can divorce, the bond between parents and children cannot be severed. Membership in the people of Israel is such a family attachment. While the Church also sees itself as a community, it is as a community of believers that it understands itself. The bonds among Christians are therefore not family bonds. But Judaism's teaching is that it is the election of a human family—the seed of Abraham—that establishes a family of election through which salvation comes to humanity. Jewish consciousness must become aware of this. It is true that the essence of the matter is not the idea. The bond that unites Jews is not an idea and remains operative whether or not there is ideological agreement. Nevertheless, unless Jews understand why they are one (as long as they are Jews), the unity of the Jewish people will be endangered.

11. MESSIANIC JUDAISM

Authentic Judaism must be messianic Judaism.

Messianic Judaism is Judaism that takes seriously the belief that Jewish history, in spite of everything that has happened, is prelude to an extraordinary act of God by which history will come to its climax and the reconciliation between God and man, and man and man, realized. Messianism is therefore the Jewish principle of hope.

Hope in the human situation manifests itself in a number of ways, which can be understood as gradations on a continuum stretched between two positions. One of these is the sober, minimalist position and the other the apocalyptic, maximalist one. In the Jewish context, there is a strong strain of minimalist messianism in rabbinic thinking, best expressed in Maimonides' famous pronouncement designed to depict the messianic future in relatively sober tones.[11] The other, the apocalyptic position speaks of unprecedented upheavals that will transform the very basis of the natural and human orders. One of the issues at stake in the debate between the minimalist and maximalist versions of messianism is the continuation or modification of the Torah. For the minimalist, the Torah as we know it will remain in force in the messianic era. For the maximalist, everything, including the Torah, will change in messianic times.

Because rabbinic Judaism came into its own after the destruction of the second Temple, it fashioned a Judaism for the time of waiting. For this reason, it fashioned a sober Judaism in which the word of God through prophecy was no longer being heard. Without forgetting that there was a time when God spoke to his people and without giving up the idea that such a time will come again, rabbinic Judaism nevertheless structured a mode of life in which the reality of messianic expectation could easily wither, even while being daily reiterated. The rabbis were eager to avoid the opposite danger: frequent outbreaks of messianic enthusiasm revolving around false messiahs. Nevertheless, in spite of all precautions, the danger of false messiahs was not altogether avoided. The stress fell more and more on the minimalist messianic position as a preventive to the periodic messianic outbreaks, which caused great harm. In addition, the minimalist position was more congenial to the secular mind inclined to a naturalist interpretation of Jewish history.

And yet, messianic faith is very much alive among Jews. Jewish life could not have survived the Holocaust without it, nor could Israel have come into being. Such living messianism cannot be minimalist. It is really the contemporary situation that determines this. The difference between the world as we know it and the world as foreseen by the prophets is too great for a more or less normal evolution to account for the transition of the former into the latter.

The apocalyptic dimension of messianism stresses the extraordinary magnitude of the coming transformation, which is seen as cataclysmic, since nothing ordinary can put an end to the tired and broken world of history as we have known it.

Jewish messianism makes it possible for the Jew to hope when otherwise there would seem to be no hope. Beyond that, messianism is the principle of life in Judaism, preventing the past from gaining total hegemony over the present. Because there waits in the future a transformation of the human condition such as has never been known before, the past has only limited significance as a guide to the future. The saving acts of God will be unexpected, revising much of our previously held wisdom, bringing into being a new heaven and a new earth in which not only the body of Israel will be circumcised but also its heart.

The circumcised body of Israel is the dark, carnal presence through which the redemption makes its way in history. Salvation is of the Jews because the flesh of Israel is the abode of the divine presence in the world. It is the carnal anchor that God has sunk into the soil of creation.

NOTES

CHAPTER 1

1. Plato, *Meno*, 72; idem, *Euthyphro*, 6.
2. *Euthyphro*, 6.
3. Gen. 3:20-21.
4. Ibid., 1:26.
5. G. W. F. Hegel, *Phenomenology of Spirit*, trans. A. V. Miller (Oxford: Oxford University Press, 1977), pp. 111-19.
6. Gershom G. Scholem, *Major Trends in Jewish Mysticism*. (New York: Schocken, 1941), pp. 260-65.
7. St. Augustine, *The City of God*, book 22, chap. 21, in *Basic Writings of St. Augustine*, ed. Whitney J. Oates (New York: Random House, 1948), 2:642-43.
8. Exod. 3:14.
9. Martin Heidegger, *Being and Time*, trans. John Macquarrie and Edward Robinson (New York: Harper & Row, 1962), pp. 78-86.
10. Scholem, *Jewish Mysticism*, pp. 260-65.
11. Yoma 8:9.
12. Jer. 4:4, 9:26.
13. The basic commandment that all sacrifices must be brought in the one place where God "shall choose to cause his name to dwell there" is found in Deut. 12:11. Later, there is constant criticism of sacrifices brought in the "high places." cf. 2 Kings 18:22, 23:4-20. Sacrifices on the "high places" were often to idols but sometimes to the God of Israel. See 2 Chron. 33:17.

14. Isa. 3:16.
15. Aristotle, *Nicomachean Ethics* 1094–96.
16. Sören Kierkegaard, *Concluding Unscientific Postscript*, trans. David F. Swenson (Princeton: Princeton University Press, 1941), p. 174, writes: "The objective truth as such, is by no means adequate to determine that whoever utters it is sane; on the contrary, it may even betray the fact that he is mad, although what he says may be entirely true, and especially objectively true." Kierkegaard tells the story of an escaped lunatic who, in order to convince people he is sane, keeps saying "the earth is round." Though what he says is true, the fact that he says it to people who are not in need of this knowledge marks him as insane.
17. Tosefta Hagigah 2:3.
18. Bava Mezia 59b.

CHAPTER 2

1. René Descartes, "Discourse on Method," in *Descartes Selections*, ed. Ralph M. Eaton (New York: Scribner, 1927), p. 21.
2. See "On the Jewish Question," in *Writings of the Young Marx on Philosophy and Society*, ed. Loyd D. Easton and Kurt H. Guddat (New York: Doubleday, 1967), pp. 216–48. For anti-Semitic passages in Marx's letters, see *The Letters of Karl Marx*, ed. Saul K. Padover (Englewood Cliffs, N.J.: Prentice-Hall, 1979), pp. 306–7, 435.
3. In capitalism, Marx complains, "everything becomes saleable and buyable." See Karl Marx, *Capital: A Critique of Political Economy* (New York: Modern Library, 1906), p. 148. In the same section, he frequently uses the example of a Bible that is exchanged for twenty yards of linen (pp. 123, 129, 131, etc.).
4. See Ernest Jones, *The Life and Work of Sigmund Freud* (New York: Basic Books, 1955), 2:364–66.
5. Especially Gnostic religions. See Hans Jones, *The Gnostic Religion: The Message of the Alien God and the Beginnings of Christianity* (Boston: Beacon Press, 1958).
6. See Luke 12:53 ("They will be divided, father against son and son against father") and 14:26 ("If any one comes to me and does not hate his own father and mother and wife and children and brothers and sisters, yes, and even his own life, he cannot be my disciple"). Such ideas do not seem to have Jewish origins.
7. Lowrie quotes Hanna Mourier, who writes that "Kierkegaard's motive in this breach was the conception he had of his religious task; he did not dare to bind himself to anything upon earth lest it might check him in his calling; he must offer the best thing he possessed in order to work as God required him." See Walter Lowrie, *Kierkegaard* (Gloucester, Mass.: Peter Smith, 1970), 1:95.

8. Simone Weil, *Gravity and Grace* (New York: Putnam, 1952), pp. 216–22.
9. St. Augustine, *City of God*, book 8, chap. 1, 2:100–101.
10. Ibid., 2:94–96.
11. Karl Barth, *Church Dogmatics* (Edinburgh: T. Clark, 1936), vol. 1, part 1, p. 1.

CHAPTER 3

1. See Martin Heidegger, *What Is Called Thinking?* trans. J. Glenn Gray (New York: Harper Torchbooks, 1972).
2. Hegel applies this analysis to such concrete and yet abstract words as *this, here, now,* and *I.* The application to *you* is a natural extension. See G. W. F. Hegel, *Phenomenology of Spirit*, trans. A. V. Miller (Oxford: Oxford University Press, 1977), pp. 58–66.
3. Ludwig Wittgenstein, *Tractatus Logico-Philosophicus* (London: Routledge and Kegan Paul, 1922), p. 189.
4. Martin Buber, *I and Thou*, trans. Walter Kaufmann (New York: Scribner, 1970), p. 123.
5. Ibid., pp. 160–61.
6. Exod. 15:11.
7. Scholem, *Jewish Mysticism*, pp. 63–67.
8. Exod. 33:20.
9. 1 Kings 8:27.
10. Gen. 12:1.
11. Yoma 8:9.
12. Hegel, *Phenomenology of Spirit*, pp. 111–19.
13. The use Sartre makes of Hegel's master-slave ideas is to be found in his *Being and Nothingness*, trans. Hazel E. Barnes (New York: Philosophical Library, 1956), p. 370.
14. Buber, *I and Thou*, p. 123.
15. Jer. 2:2.
16. B. Avodah Zarah, 3a; B. Kiddushin, 31a.

CHAPTER 4

1. Wittgenstein, *Tractatus Logico-Philosophicus*, p. 187.
2. Exod. 3:14.
3. Immanuel Kant, *Critique of Pure Reason*, tr. Norman Kemp Smith (New York: St. Martin, 1958), p. 505.
4. Kathleen Freeman, *Ancilla to the Pre-Socratic Philosophers* (Oxford: Basil Blackwell, 1952), fragments 2, 6, 7, 8, pp. 42–45.
5. Kierkegaard speaks of "existential pathos," which is an expression of human subjectivity. See *Concluding Unscientific Postscript*, pp. 347ff.
6. Heidegger, *Being and Time*, p. 32.

7. Plato, *Phaedo*, 100–105.
8. Parmenides teaches that being "has no coming-into-being and no destruction, for it is whole of limb, without motion, and without end." Freeman, *Pre-Socratic Philosophers*, fragments 7, 8, p. 43.
9. Martin Heidegger, *Platons Lehre von der Wahrheit* (Bern: Francke, 1947), p. 42.
10. Heidegger, *Being and Time*, pp. 256ff.
11. Ibid., pp. 131ff. See also *Platons Lehre von der Wahrheit*, p. 99.
12. Karl Barth, *Anselm: Fides Quaerens Intellectum* (Richmond, VA.: John Knox, 1960).
13. Gen. Rabbah 1:5.
14. Heidegger, *Being and Time*, p. 30.
15. Paul Tillich, *The Courage to Be* (New Haven: Yale University Press, 1952).
16. Gen. 4:2.
17. Sartre discusses the absent Pierre in *Being and Nothingness*, p. 9ff.
18. Martin Heidegger, *Die Selbstbehanptung der deutschen Universität* (Breslau: Korn, 1933).
19. Many of these accounts are collected in Guido Schneeberger, *Nachlese zu Heidegger: Dokumente zu seinem Leben und Denken* (Bern, 1962).
20. Martin Heidegger, *Unterwegs zur Sprache* (Pfullingen: Neske, 1959), p. 269. On May 31, 1976 the German magazine *Der Spiegel* published an interview with Heidegger dealing with his relations to Nazism. It appeared in English translation in *Heidegger: The Man and the Thinker*, ed. Thomas Sheehan (Chicago: Precedent, 1981), pp. 45–67. In the same volume, see also "Heidegger and the Nazis" by Karl A. Moehling, pp. 31–43.
21. Paul Tillich, *Systematic Theology* (Chicago: University of Chicago Press, 1951), 1:235ff.
22. Exod. 3:14.
23. Spinoza, *Ethics*, part 1, definition 6.
24. Paul Tillich, *Dynamics of Faith* (New York: Harper, 1957), pp. 51–52.

CHAPTER 5

1. Rashi comments on Exod. 24:10 ("they saw the God of Israel") that they were deserving of death for so doing. See *The Pentateuch and Rashi's Commentary*, tran. Abraham, Isaiah and Benjamin Sharfman (Brooklyn, S.S. & R, 1949), v.2., p. 284.
2. Exod. 24:7.
3. Deut. 6:8.
4. Deut. 31:3–6.
5. 1 Sam. 15:1–30.

6. Quoted by Maurice S. Friedman, *Martin Buber: The Life of Dialogue* (New York: Harper & Row, 1955), p. 262.
7. Martin Buber, *Two Types of Faith* (New York: Harper & Brothers, 1961).
8. Martin Buber, *The Eclipse of God* (New York: Harper & Brothers, 1952), p. 173.
9. Baba Meziah 59b.
10. See Sartre's discussion of sadism in *Being and Nothingness*, pp. 379–415.
11. Baba Meziah 59b.
12. Numb. 27:1–11.
13. *Mekilta*, ed. J. Z. Lauterbach (Philadelphia: Jewish Publication Society, 1933–5), 2:234.
14. Lev. 16:16.
15. Zech. 14:9.
16. See the *Antigone* of Sophocles.
17. 1 John 4:20.
18. Rashi on Gen. 1:1.
19. Exod. 22:20.

CHAPTER 6

1. B. Kiddushin, 22 b.
2. B. Kiddushin, 42 b.
3. From the rabbinic prayer recited before the Sh'ma.
4. Melachim, XII, 1.
5. Some relevant texts are B. Shabbat 141 b and B. Niddah 61 b.
6. This is the thesis of Georges Friedmann, *The End of the Jewish People?* (New York: Doubleday, 1967).
7. For Begin's account see Menachem Begin, *The Revolt*, (Los Angeles: Nash, 1948), pp. 154-65. Another account can be found in Frank Gervasi, *The Life and Times of Menachem Begin* (New York: Putnam, 1979), pp. 245-61.
8. Examples are Hos. 6:6, Isa. 1:10-16, and Jer. 7:21ff.
9. Friedmann, *End of the Jewish People?* p. 120.
10. B. Sanhedrin, 37a.
11. Melachim, XII, 1.

INDEX